Itinerant Teaching

Tricks of the Trade for Teachers of Students with Visual Impairments

SECOND EDITION

Jean E. Olmstead

AFB PRESS

American Foundation for the Blind

Printed in the United States of America

Library of Congress Cataloging-in-Publication Data

Olmstead, Jean E., 1943-
Itinerant teaching : tricks of the trade for teachers of students with visual impairments / Jean E. Olmstead.
p. cm.
Includes bibliographical references and index.
ISBN 978-0-89128-878-7 (pbk. : alk. paper)—ISBN 0-89128-879-1 (ASCII disk)
1. Children with visual disabilities—Education—United States. 2. Teachers of the blind—Training of—United States. 3. Visiting teachers—Training of—United States. I. Title.

HV1631.O46 2005
371.91'1'0973—dc22

2004024661

The American Foundation for the Blind—the organization to which Helen Keller devoted more than 40 years of her life—is a national nonprofit whose mission is to eliminate the inequities faced by the ten million Americans who are blind or visually impaired.

It is the policy of the American Foundation for the Blind to use in the first printing of its books acid-free paper that meets the ANSI Z39.48 Standard. The infinity symbol that appears above indicates that the paper in this printing meets that standard.

Dedication

This book is dedicated to itinerant teachers,
Who spend a lot of time behind the windshields of their cars,
Who carry bulky, delicate materials in and out of schools, often in inclement weather,
Who can turn the dingiest hole in the wall into a cheery classroom,
Who have the special opportunity to work with students on a one-to-one basis for periods of two to three years at a time,
Who can switch from working with a preschooler to working with a gifted high school senior and provide meaningful lessons to both,
Who answer patiently every time someone in the faculty room assumes they are substitute teachers and asks, "Who are you today?"
Who are organized, dedicated, and self-motivated,
Who are safe drivers and good map readers,
Who recognize that having a sense of humor is a survival skill,
Who realize that they have assumed their roles because they are helpers and that they are most successful when their students help themselves,
Who are patient but know when to be impatient, and
Who rise to the challenge of being itinerant when neighborhood schools are the appropriate placement for their students with visual impairments.

Contents

Acknowledgments

Although writing a book is essentially a solitary experience, a writer is influenced by experiences and information gleaned from both formal and informal situations. Much of the information and strategies and most of the forms in this book evolved as a group effort by itinerant teachers in the Visually Impaired Program in the West Contra Costa County Unified School District in Richmond, California. I acknowledge the most recent itinerant teachers—Faith Dunham-Sims, Natalie Knott, Sue Loy, and Karen Yamamoto—for their dedication and creativity. Our secretary-transcribers, Ann Kelt and Theresa Yeomans, are recognized here for their efforts in keeping the program running smoothly.

Other itinerant teachers, too numerous to name, have not only contributed to the ideas in this book but have also given me support, feedback, and affirmation during the development of both editions. I thank you wholeheartedly for your support and advice. Not only have important sections been added to this revised edition, but also additional forms have been provided at the requests of many teachers. The success of the first edition of *Itinerant Teaching* was far greater than could have been imagined, and feedback and support from you readers have encouraged and heartened me through the process of producing this edition.

In addition to personal friends and my daughter, Adrienne, I feel I must sing the praises of Natalie Hilzen, Director/Editor in Chief of AFB Press, who guided me through the production of both editions. Her breadth of knowledge about the many facets of issues concerning people with visual impairments, as well as her ability to guide a writer through the publishing process, are impressive. Ms. Hilzen has the facility for coaching a recalcitrant writer as needed and the wisdom of knowing when to be patient with a writer's foibles. Her editing skills are remarkable, and she always keeps in mind the targeted audience—in this case, a new itinerant teacher in the boonies of the Midwest with no peers within a 500-mile radius. For this edition, Ellen Bilofsky, AFB Press Managing Editor, also ably guided me through the editing and production. I thank both of these ladies for their assistance, perseverance, and patience, and for appreciating my desire to acknowledge their skills here.

—J.E.O.

Foreword

When I was an itinerant teacher, admittedly, many years ago, I dreamed about having a book like *Itinerant Teaching.* Years later, in 1991, when I was associate executive director of the American Foundation for the Blind (AFB), I was shown our new publication by Jean Olmstead. I immediately thought, "Why wasn't this book around when I started out!?" *Itinerant Teaching*—or, more precisely, Jean Olmstead, speaking through its pages—was the experienced pro I needed to talk to but didn't have at the time. The original edition of this great resource for teachers of children who are blind or visually impaired was published some 14 years ago. Much has changed for teachers since it first appeared. However, we are fortunate that Jean Olmstead, then and now, undertook the hard work and applied the gritty determination needed to offer support to teachers who are itinerant and to give them their due.

When Jean Olmstead wrote *Itinerant Teaching*, she broke new ground. Educational services for students with visual impairments had undergone many changes since the 1950s, when children with visual impairments were educated primarily in residential schools. With the passage of the Education for All Handicapped Children Act in 1975 and the move toward mainstreaming, these changes seemed to accelerate. Children who were visually impaired were expected to remain in the regular classroom as much as possible. Scattered geographically and present in small numbers in local school districts, they were visited on site by teachers who often needed to travel long distances to provide individualized services to a highly diverse group of children. The challenges of doing so were of course experienced by the dedicated teachers who undertook this complex work but were not documented or analyzed as part of an important national discourse. Jean Olmstead changed all that by writing *Itinerant Teaching*, by making countless national presentations on the topic, and by helping to found Division 16 of the Association for Education and Rehabilitation of the Blind and Visually Impaired, which was dedicated to itinerant teaching.

The topics covered in Jean's book reflect both the changing role of the itinerant teacher and the changing models of the itinerant teacher and the teacher consultant. In the past, students deemed most appropriately served under the itinerant model were those with relatively few special education needs that could be met in general education classrooms. Although these students needed some instruction provided directly by a teacher of students with visual impairments or an orientation and mobility instructor, in general they required intermittent and limited support from the teacher of visually impaired students. Many students were served indirectly through the teacher consultant model, in which teachers visited and consulted with general education personnel but infrequently dealt with students directly. These students were much on their own, and this delivery model allowed for large caseloads. What has happened to these models? Over the last several decades they have in fact merged, with teachers confronting the larger caseloads of the indirect teacher consultant model while striving to meet the needs of students who require many more specialized services and direct instruction and support.

Today, the role of the itinerant teacher continues to expand, not only as a direct result of the merging of previous service delivery models and the movement toward inclusion, but also because of factors such as the critical shortage of teachers, the frequency of multiple disabilities among visually impaired children, and the recognition of the importance of the expanded core curriculum. The increasing size of teachers' caseloads has raised serious and widespread concerns about whether teachers can indeed do all the work required of them and that they want to do. New topics in this second edition of *Itinerant Teaching* reflect the new realities of the itinerant teacher's changing role. Readers will find suggestions on addressing larger caseloads, the expanded core curriculum, work with paraeducators, and stress management, as well as new chapters on multiple impairments, assistive technology, services for infants and their families, and orientation and mobility.

I believe that both new and experienced itinerant teachers alike will find this expanded edition of *Itinerant Teaching: Tricks of the Trade for Teachers of Students with Visual Impairments* to be a welcome edition to their professional library as they enter the new millennium. Jean Olmstead and her contributors are the experienced pros we all need to talk to sometimes.

Susan Jay Spungin, Ed.D.
Vice President
International Programs and Special Projects
American Foundation for the Blind

Introduction

In the past, itinerant teachers, armed with information about visual conditions, assessment, curriculum, and adaptations for students with visual impairments, often had to develop organizing schemes, strategies, and techniques to be effective and efficient while serving students at several sites. Few structural guidelines existed on how to deliver high-quality educational services to a diverse group of students who might be scattered all over a state. The goal of the first edition of this book was not to reiterate information available in college courses and teaching texts; rather, it was to provide nitty-gritty, practical suggestions that a teacher could use to be an effective educator while living an itinerant life.

Partly as a result of the original publication of this book, more attention has been given to the special role of itinerant teacher and the demands involved, and colleges and universities have addressed these issues more formally. In light of the many changes that have occurred over the intervening years since this book first appeared in 1991, however, the itinerant teacher's need for organizing principles and supportive strategies has not diminished.

Changes in legislative requirements, demographic trends, and beliefs about what constitutes best or promising practices have caused both new and experienced itinerant teachers to learn about working with a wider range of student populations (including those in age from birth to 3 and those with multiple impairments), incorporate the expanded core curriculum into their students' programs, become proficient in using ever-changing technology, work with paraeducators, and stay abreast of regulatory mandates. As I contemplated these changes, I realized that although I could address these issues, other professionals had more expertise in certain areas that could be shared to the benefit of the readers of this book. As a result the following people have graciously agreed to share the wealth of their experience in the areas indicated:

James Carreon, assistive technology
Lori Cassels, working with paraprofessionals
Frances Mary D'Andrea, music education and miscellaneous gems
Faith Dunham-Sims, orientation and mobility, stress management, and organization
Jane N. Erin, working with students with multiple impairments

Cinda Wert Rapp, providing services to infants and their families
Jane Stewart Redmon, the rural perspective, updating her original chapter
Mary Alice Ross, adaptive physical education

In addition, to new chapters and sections contributed by these experts, readers will find this new edition of *Itinerant Teaching* to be revised and updated in many ways. A chapter containing tricks of the trade collected from teachers throughout the United States who attended presentations on itinerant teaching has been added to this edition. Elizabeth Jennewine Watson reworked the cover illustration, and Pat Davis created the sketch that ends the book. Theresa Postello and Jerry Kuns contributed to the appendixes. I extend wholehearted thanks to these contributors; without their assistance this edition would not be as thorough and useful a resource. During this age of changes in the field, wise teachers realize that they cannot realistically be experts in every area and that consulting with those who have more experience in an area is not only sensible but prudent.

As in the first edition of *Itinerant Teaching*, I have suggested strategies for working with students with visual impairments that are effective in the geographic area where I taught. Although legislation dictates many facets of our job, for many reasons all school districts do not use the same criteria such as terminology, timelines, guidelines, and forms. Be aware that practices different from those addressed in this book may be prevalent where you work. Utilize the ideas presented that are in accordance with the guidelines and protocols of your school district.

In the following pages, I use the term *visually impaired* to cover the entire range of visual functioning from mild visual impairment to total blindness. As before, I have included sample letters and forms in several sections to demonstrate how they can make our jobs easier. The forms appear filled in, as we have used them (all the names of people and places are fictitious; resemblance to actual persons and schools is unintentional and coincidental). Adapt and use those that will be helpful to you; enlarge those you wish for people who use large print. Blank copies of many of the forms appear in Appendix E if you wish to use them as they are.

I hope that new itinerant teachers find my suggestions to be pertinent and valuable but not overwhelming. Take your time to settle in to the job, and utilize the strategies that seem to fit your situation as you develop your own style and techniques. For those who are more experienced, I hope you find some helpful hints and—more important—validation for the good job you have been doing.

CHAPTER

The History and Philosophy of Itinerant Teaching

Education of visually impaired students in the United States has changed greatly since the first residential schools for blind children were opened in the 1830s. Early in the 20th century, local school districts established special classes for visually impaired pupils, enabling some children to live at home. Later, local districts instituted resource room programs: some of the students were enrolled in general education classes and went to the resource room for special assistance. Natural outgrowths of community-based educational programs were the itinerant programs begun in California in 1938 and in New Jersey in 1943.

General education students who receive itinerant services live at home and attend their neighborhood schools, where their educational needs are typically met by classroom teachers in cooperation with a traveling (itinerant) teacher who is certified to teach visually impaired students. For many students this placement maximizes learning and provides a peer group at similar cognitive and academic levels for interaction. The schools in which the students are enrolled can be said to "own" the education of these students. The general education teachers to whom the students are assigned have the primary responsibility for educating them in the core curriculum. The itinerant teacher travels from school to school, providing special materials, consultation with school personnel, and individualized instruction in disability specific skills that encompass what is known as the expanded core curriculum. This includes compensatory academic skills, including communication modes; social interaction skills; recreation and leisure skills; use of assistive technology; independent living skills; career education; visual efficiency skills; and orientation and mobility (O&M). Visually im-

Each child needs to have the option of different placements—itinerant programs, resource rooms, special classes, and residential or special day schools—as his or her needs change.

Courtesy of National Braille Press

paired students who are enrolled in other special education classes need to receive similar support from a teacher of visually impaired students.

Placement in an itinerant program is most appropriate for general education students who can benefit from extensive participation in regular class activities, will use adapted materials and special equipment and techniques, and can function as members of a general education class when the conditions for fulfilling their special needs may be less than ideal. Because, for example, not every worksheet will be adapted for them and not every peer will be understanding and accepting of their needs, these visually impaired students need to be able to adjust to and cope with a variety of conditions and reactions.

Despite the limitations of placement in general education classes, visually impaired students who are served by itinerant teachers may benefit from the extra support and opportunities for social and other development inherent in attending schools with their siblings and longstanding neighborhood friends. Because they live at home and may not need to engage in long daily bus rides, they may participate more readily in after-school and other community programs and avoid interruptions in their relationships with their families. Their parents may find it easier to participate in school activities because the school is nearby and familiar to them. In short, these visually impaired students interact in the kind of environment in which they will later live and work.

In recent years, the education of students with multiple impairments has changed drastically, from isolated sites to special classes and full inclusion at regular schools. As these students have moved into the mainstream of their local schools, they have increasingly begun receiving services from itinerant teachers of students with visual impairments. Indeed, for some itinerant teachers, students with multiple impairments form the numerical preponderance of the teachers' caseloads. More about serving these students can be found in Chapter 6.

Itinerant programs, resource rooms, special classes, and residential or special schools all have their places in the continuum of services for visually impaired students. Each has its advantages and its disadvantages. Each needs to be available to every student according to his or her needs and abilities, as determined by the individualized education program (IEP) created for the student in accordance with the Individuals with Disabilities Education Act (IDEA). Careful, continuing, systematic assessment provides information that allows the team working on a student's IEP to make a judicious decision about which program will be the most appropriate placement for him or her. The placement should maximize learning and provide a peer group for interaction that is at a similar cognitive and academic level. If the peer group is operating at a higher level than the student with visual impairments too much time and effort may be spent with remedial work at the expense of other important lessons, such as the expanded core curriculum.

No child should be restricted to one particular program. Each needs to have the option of alternative placement as his or her needs change. Some students in resource rooms, special classes, or special schools may move to itinerant programs as they acquire the skills necessary for greater independence. Some students in itinerant programs may benefit from spending a year or two, or even a summer, in one of the other settings to receive the more concentrated instruction and support that are difficult to provide on an itinerant basis. This flow among different programs is essential to providing services that will fulfill the potential of each student.

CHAPTER

The Itinerant Teacher: Being Effective

When new classroom teachers arrive at their first assignment, they are usually assigned a room and a mailbox, a group of students who are relatively homogeneous at least according to age, a set of textbooks and teachers' manuals, classroom equipment and supplies, and a bell schedule. I do not imply that the first year or so of teaching is easy, but new classroom teachers often may have a fair amount of structure to support their work and help them improve their competence.

In contrast, new itinerant teachers usually have to establish their own structure. Sometimes the only information they receive is a list of students, who may range in ability from multiply impaired to gifted, vary in age from birth to 21, and be located at several sites that may or may not be in close geographic proximity. New itinerant teachers gather information from school records and observations. They consult with classroom teachers and school administrators to set up a schedule in which the best times to work with students in their classrooms or in separate rooms, as needed, are coordinated with the times that appropriate rooms are available for their use; move materials and equipment into each school; and determine which needs of the students they will address if the needs are not already delineated in current IEPs. They will be expected to assess referrals by conducting functional vision assessments and to assess the visual functioning of the visually impaired students in their program at mandated intervals, currently every three years.

To be effective, itinerant teachers do the following:

- Utilize or develop school or community resources to help with important areas of learning, such as living skills, recreational and leisure activities, and motor development, that may be difficult to address because of the limited time they can spend at each site.

- Serve as liaisons among the students, parents, school personnel, and medical, community, and professional resources.
- Establish rapport and take a cooperative, flexible, yet assertive approach because the relationships they foster are vital to the successful inclusion of their students.
- Are observant and use their ingenuity, creativity, and intuition to facilitate their students' learning and integration.
- Strive to develop a keen understanding of people and are able to communicate with people of a wide range of ages, abilities, and backgrounds.
- Keep abreast of resources, new technology, and trends in the educational field by attending conferences and receiving information from organizations and businesses that serve visually impaired people.
- Are effective advocates for their students and encourage students to advocate for themselves.
- Maintain a realistic perspective about what they can accomplish.
- Do their best to anticipate problems before they arise.
- Work well both on an individual basis and as members of a team.
- Maintain a sense of focus and priorities, and recognize the importance of good organization skills.

TEACHERS' ROLE AND RESPONSIBILITIES

Teachers of students with visual impairments need to be clear about their role, which is to work on disability-specific skills that make information and instruction meaningful and accessible for visually impaired students. Given today's large caseloads, they do not have the time to teach a subject another teacher could address. If students have learning difficulties in addition to their visual impairment, careful assessment may lead to placement in special programs or classes or to time spent with other specialists. The students enrolled in these and other special education programs are still eligible for services related to their visual impairment.

The itinerant teacher's role in general is to work on vision-related or disability-specific skills, that is, on skills related to the expanded core curriculum. (For more on this topic, readers can consult *Foundations of Education*; Koenig & Holbrook, 2000.) Teachers of students with visual impairments may spend a great amount of time on history with a student who reads in braille, but they are not history teachers. History teachers teach history, and itinerant teachers provide the braille instruction necessary for students to participate in the history class. (It is therefore essential that the itinerant teacher has advance notice about classwork to be able to preteach the braille needed. When that's not possible, the teacher should be in the class with the student to interpret new braille symbols. If the student has to leave the class to work with the itinerant teacher, he or she will lose valuable class time with the history teacher and the class.) However, an important point to note is that although instruction may usually be designed by the regular classroom teacher and made accessible by the teacher of students with visual impairments, this teacher must also be prepared to design and deliver original instruction in unique skills that are specific to the needs of individual students. For students who read braille, then, the itinerant teacher is the primary instructor of reading and math, especially in the early stages of instruction. This is because reading and math are being taught through the medium of braille; separating the concepts from the code when learning to read, write, and compute should not be considered.

Overall, despite time pressures and the myriad details that need to be organized and kept track of as part of an itinerant teacher's life, a primary focus of the teacher needs to be determining the appropriate accommodations a student needs in order to learn, participate in school activities, and succeed in work and life. At the basis of this effort are specialized assessments, which need to be conducted by the teacher. Functional vision assessments, learning media assess-

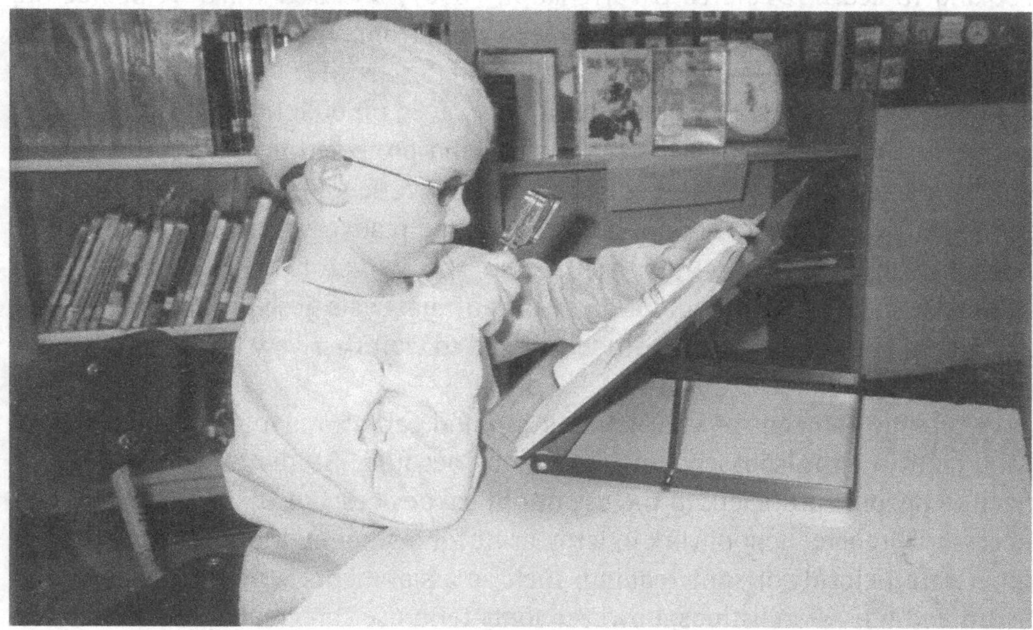

The best reading medium for a student is determined by his or her individual needs. This student uses a magnifier to gain access to the same books at the same time as his classmates.

Jean E. Olmstead

ments, and assistive technology assessments (discussed in Chapters 3 and 9) are crucial activities that need to be conducted with regularity. Part of the teacher's role is to observe the student's performance to make certain that the conclusions drawn from previous assessments are still relevant to that student's current needs and abilities. Many sources of information exist on how to perform these critical activities (see, for example, *Looking to Learn* [D'Andrea & Farrenkopf, 2000]; *Learning Media Assessment of Students with Visual Impairments* [Koenig & Holbrook, 1995]; and *Foundations of Education,* Volume II [Koenig & Holbrook, 2000]).

These assessments identify the primary and subsidiary ways in which a student obtains information from the environment. This, in turn, helps the teacher to identify the student's primary learning and communicating media, whether print, braille, auditory input, or a combination of these. The media can change over time; some students who are able to read print may be more efficient readers if they work in braille.

An important responsibility of the teacher is not just to determine the student's most effective learning medium but also to support his or her work in that medium. For this reason, obtaining instructional materials in appropriate formats is a crucial part of the job. Throughout this book, therefore, references are made to the need to order braille materials as far ahead as possible to obtain them on time for students, and the need to obtain and enlarge materials, if appropriate, in time for a student to use them with the rest of his or her class. It is equally important to support the use of low vision devices by students for whom they have been prescribed. People who use optical devices need to receive training in their appropriate use and also need to practice using them. (Activities to help students become comfortable with and skillful in the use of such devices can be found in *Looking to Learn* [D'Andrea & Farrenkopf, 2000].) It is also worth remembering that using low vision devices can liberate a child from reliance on large print. Optical devices provide immediate access to materials of all kinds, including independent access to classroom materials displayed on bulletin boards and charts, written on the blackboard or white board, and projected on a screen. Students will have less access to large print when they leave school, and most printed materials outside of school are not adjusted for the reader with low vision. In addition, the use of devices can also lessen the work of teachers who would otherwise have to enlarge great quantities of materials, just as it diminishes the number of situations in which students need to wait passively for materials to be enlarged for them.

Keeping the needs of your student in mind can also involve a balancing act that takes on-the-spot circumstances into account. Students with low vision need to become proficient in the use of optical devices, but these aids should not necessarily replace schoolwork in large print for a student. Monoculars and magnifiers are helpful for spot reading, such as assignments written on the chalkboard and television listings; however, long-term use can create postural tension

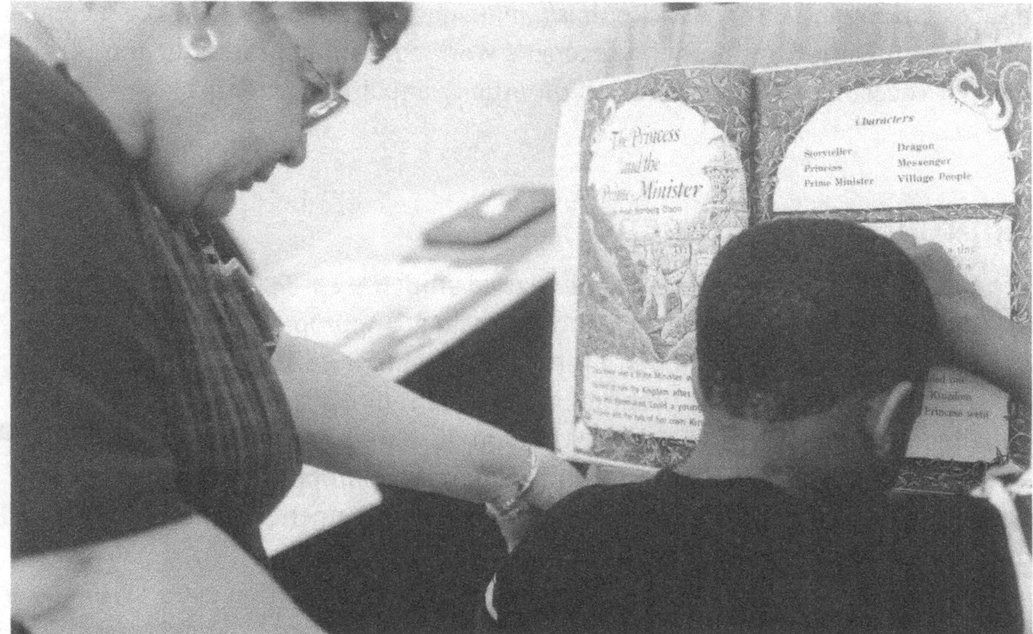

For many children, having materials in large print while gradually learning to use optical devices is a helpful transition.

Chad Batka/American Foundation for the Blind

as well as lengthen the time needed to perform a task. Electronic devices are helpful, but only at times when isolating the student from his or her peers does not deprive the student of interaction with classmates. When kindergarten students are sprawled on the floor leafing through books, their peer with low vision should be—deserves to be—in the midst of them, not at a video magnifier tucked away in some corner of the classroom.

In many cases, school-aged children should have as many materials in large print as possible while gradually learning to use optical devices that have been prescribed for them. Now as never before, more material is available for adults in accessible media: in large print, in audio options, and via electronic means. In addition adults have greater choice over how much reading they incorporate into their lives. Students do not have that option; they are required to spend a great deal of each day performing visual tasks. As long as they are expected to read within the parameters of the school day and in the evening for homework as well, it may be important to provide large-print materials for them, even if adapting the materials may not always be convenient for the teacher. Of course, the decision about what materials and equipment will be provided to students is ultimately the responsibility of the IEP team.

BASIC ASSUMPTIONS

For visually impaired students to be effectively served in an itinerant program, at least four basic factors should be true. Therefore, in presenting the material in this book I have made the following assumptions: (1) the students are in appropriate placements, (2) the teacher has a manageable caseload, (3) working conditions, such as the length of the teacher's work day, are appropriate, and (4) the teacher is certified in the education of visually impaired students.

Appropriate Placement

The first assumption is that visually impaired students enrolled in general education classes and served in the itinerant program are appropriately placed. To meet the needs of individual students, a range of placement options needs to be available, including an itinerant program, a resource room, a special class for visually impaired students, and a special or residential school. The IEP team, with input from all its members, decides which placement is appropriate for a student at a particular time. The student may move from one placement to another as his or her needs and abilities change.

For visually impaired students enrolled in general education classes, itinerant placement is indicated when they can function independently at an appropriate academic level, utilize special equipment and adaptive techniques, and display adequate skills in activities of daily living and socialization when the itinerant teacher is not at the site. Therefore, if a student is exhibiting age-appropriate behavior and measurable, continued academic progress, itinerant placement is suitable even though the student may require relatively extensive intervention from the itinerant teacher.

Manageable Caseloads

The second assumption is that the itinerant teachers in a program have realistic, manageable caseloads. Administrators and teachers alike need to recognize that caseloads can fluctuate widely. The number of students an itinerant teacher can serve effectively depends on the students' needs and the transition time generated by the caseload, as well as the number of referrals to the program for visually impaired students. The time the teacher spends with each student is based on student need, not the convenience of the school system or the teacher's schedule. When the students need less intervention and are closely grouped geographically, a particular teacher may be able to provide services to 14 students successfully. However, if the students need extensive support (including more direct instruction, large amounts of adapted materials, and more consultation and observation), 5 students may be all that the same teacher can serve adequately. Sometimes, albeit rarely, an itinerant teacher's caseload may consist of one student who is reading in braille and operating at a high academic level. The concentrated instruction that this allows may enable the student to develop the skills necessary to enter college directly rather than having to attend additional programs or search for other avenues to learn skills the itinerant teacher did not have adequate time to address. The support system in the program can also affect the itinerant teachers' caseload. The presence of O&M instructors, transcribers, paraeducators (often referred to as aides in schools), and up-to-date equipment may allow the teachers to serve more students.

The caseload profile shown in Figure 2.1 is an example of a form that could be used to organize and analyze information about your caseload. Because the size of a teacher's caseload has such a significant impact on his or her ability to deliver effective services, caseload size can become a topic of concern. Approaches to establishing caseloads of teachers within a district are discussed in more detail in Chapter 3. Division 16 of the Association for Education and Rehabilitation of the Blind and Visually Impaired (AER) on Itinerant Personnel has information available (see www.aerbvi.org) that can be used to analyze individual teachers' caseloads and serve as a basis for discussion with the supervisor or district office.

Appropriate Working Conditions

Working conditions are seldom delineated for itinerant personnel in teachers' union contracts with school districts. All classroom teachers usually have a clearly defined teaching day that includes such items as a conference/preparation period and a lunch break. Itinerant teachers' days need to be defined comparably so that they can provide comprehensive services to their students within the designated working day.

The caseloads of itinerant teachers should allow them, within the daily total of teaching minutes negotiated for classroom teachers, to provide direct services (work one-on-one with students) or monitoring services, or both, as specified on students' IEPs (see "The Importance of Monitoring Services"). In addition, teachers should have time available in their schedules to assess referrals; assess their students' visual functioning on a regular, legally specified basis; and make the transition between sites. The minutes stipulated on the IEP for direct services, monitoring, or a combination of direct and monitoring services should reflect the total time needed for observations, consultations, and adaptation of materials for each student.

Furthermore, itinerant teachers should have a conference/preparation period equal to that of classroom teachers in the school district. During this period, the itinerant teachers should be able to work in their offices where materials and records are stored so they can more easily prepare for lessons, collect needed materials and equipment, complete paperwork and write reports, make and receive telephone calls, plan in-service programs, and order materials. In addition, a lunch break free of other duties at an appropriate time and at a stationary site (not in the car or otherwise en route) should be scheduled.

FIGURE 2.1

Caseload Profile for Visual Impairment Program Staff

Teacher J. Olmstead
Date 11/15/05
Number of schools served 4
Working day 8:25-3:30

Available weekly minutes 2125
Minus preparation/conference minutes 250
Minus lunchtime minutes 200
Remainder available 1675

Total minutes per week per IEPs 1127.5
Total minutes transition time per week 400
Total committed minutes per week 1527.5

Student Name	*School/Grade*	*Direct Service Minutes*	*Monitoring/ Consultation Minutes*	*Vision Status (Acuity) and Other Disabilities*	*Total Weekly Minutes per IEP*	*Comments*	*Braille (Yes/ No)*	*O&M (Yes/ No)*
1. E. Biggs	Sheldon / 2	120 daily	daily 75	20/450 O.U.	975		yes	yes
2. J. Montez	Sheldon / 5	0	45/quarter	20/100 20/150 multiply impaired	5	Needs FVA	no	no
3. V. Chou	MDHS / 11	30/week	10/week	20/70 O.U.	40		no	no
4. B. Denning	SHJ / 7	0	90/semester	20/100 O.U.	5		no	no
5. C. Robbin	SJH / 11	0	45/semester	20/350 20/100 multiply impaired	2.5		no	no
6. B. Dickens	Lake / 5	2 x 30/week	40/week	20/150 O.U.	100	Needs technology assessment	no	yes
7.								
8.								
9.								
10.								

The Importance of Monitoring Services

Monitoring services (also called consulting services) include adapting classroom materials for students' use, either directly or in conjunction with a transcriber; discussing the materials that are appropriate for a student with the classroom teacher; observing the students periodically and reviewing their progress; and consulting with and providing information to classroom teachers, other school staff, family members, eye care specialists, and community resources.

Monitoring services are equally as crucial as the direct services you provide, because monitoring services directly affect your students' successful participation in the educational process. It is essential that the time needed to provide adapted materials, observe students, and confer with pertinent people involved with the students be protected within the IEP process; when there is not adequate time to perform these duties, students are not receiving appropriate services according to their disability-specific needs.

In some school districts, policy dictates that monitoring minutes cannot be specified in addition to direct service minutes. In that case, it is vital that the number of direct IEP minutes reflects the total time needed to provide comprehensive services, including the activities listed here as part of monitoring or consulting.

Teachers whose sponsoring agencies, such as county offices of education, may not stipulate working conditions for classroom teachers should work under comparable conditions.

Some teachers' contracts state that no teacher can be required to work beyond the normal school day on a regular basis. Most teachers recognize that they will at least occasionally perform work duties after school hours. However, if an itinerant teacher is consistently spending six hours per week working outside the prescribed working day, his or her working conditions are being violated, and additional support, such as another teacher, a paraprofessional or aide, or a transcriber should be hired. If your teachers' contract contains a clause relating to this issue, the appropriate bargaining agency will support you in getting additional help if administrators balk at your request.

For many years, travel time has been acknowledged as an important part of the itinerant teacher's workday. Given the complexities of the teacher's role, a more appropriate term to use is "transition time," which more accurately encompasses the activities a teacher has to perform between the end of a lesson at one site and the beginning of one at another school. The tasks inherent in transition time are performed in addition to activities delineated by IEP monitoring minutes, such as adapting materials, consulting about the students' activities, or observing students.

The following transition activities may be performed during the time from the end of one lesson at one site and the beginning of one at another site. (Items marked by asterisks may not be performed at every site.)

Components of Transition Time

The teacher:

- has the student assist in putting away materials and equipment.
- walks the student back to his or her classroom.*
- returns to the workroom.*
- completes a record of the work done and jots down pertinent information for the next lesson.
- gathers materials to take to the car.
- uses a cell phone or locates a telephone on site to return or make important calls.*
- walks to and checks mailbox.
- makes additional telephone calls as necessary.*
- has an impromptu conference regarding a referral or important issues.*
- checks school records regarding referrals or information about students.*
- checks the main calendar in secondary school offices.*
- returns workroom key.*
- signs out.
- says goodbye to office staff.
- carries materials to car.
- drives to next site.
- finds parking place.
- gathers materials for next lesson and takes them into the school.
- says hello to office staff.
- checks mailbox.
- uses a cell phone or locates a telephone on site to make or return important phone calls.*
- obtains key to workroom.*
- walks to workroom for next lesson.
- has an impromptu conference regarding a referral or important issues on the way.*
- refreshes memory for upcoming lesson.

- walks to classroom to get student.*
- walks back to workroom.*
- has student assist in setting up needed materials and equipment.

Certified Teachers

The fourth assumption is that the teachers who are itinerant in a program are certified in the education of visually impaired students. In addition to utilizing good teaching techniques, the itinerant teachers have a thorough understanding of the social, psychological, and medical implications of visual impairment and the impact of visual impairment on each student's learning style ability and interaction with his or her school, family, and community. They are also knowledgeable about appropriate interventions that will enhance an individual student's participation in the educational process.

UNMET ASSUMPTIONS

All too often one or more of these basic factors are not in place, in which case the services the students receive are in all likelihood ineffective. If a student is not appropriately placed in the itinerant program, the teacher needs to gather information in a precise manner and present it to the parents or guardians and school administrators to help them understand which needs of the student are not being met. Alternative placement that would provide the additional services necessary should be considered carefully. If the IEP team does not approve the alternative placement or other obstacles are present, the team may consider other options, such as having the student stay in school longer than the traditional 13 years to allow the student extra time to acquire the necessary skills.

Also, itinerant teachers need to monitor their caseloads carefully; they can too easily become unmanageable. When this occurs, the teacher has a legal and ethical right to refuse to accept additional students, while lobbying for the hiring of another teacher, a transcriber, a paraeducator or program aide, or an O&M instructor as needed. Taking a firm stance can be a very uneasy experience, but appropriate services are vitally important so that the students can receive the educational program to which they are entitled. Completing the Caseload Profile presented in Figure 2.1 earlier in this chapter can document the fact that the time needed to provide appropriate services to your students exceeds the total number of work hours. If you present it to your supervisor, make sure that the total number of minutes accurately reflects the time needed to address your students' disability-specific needs. Educating parents or guardians and the students themselves can enable them all to support the campaign. Sometimes administrators respond more readily to parental concerns than to those of the teachers. Because caseload size and personnel shortage have a profound impact on the quality of education that children receive, this topic has recently received increased attention. Principles of how to analyze appropriate caseload size as a way of providing documentation to administrators and advocate for more time, services, and staff for students are a focus of concern for Division 16 of AER.

In these days of teacher shortages, an itinerant teacher may have only an emergency credential when he or she is providing services. Often the teacher will be working while taking the classes needed to become fully certified. No doubt teachers in this circumstance have a very hectic life; they are teaching without full knowledge of what the job entails and completing their own classwork at the same time. It is vital that they find credentialed mentors in their programs or in the community who can provide assistance and answer questions as they arise.

As a credentialed teacher of visually impaired students, especially when there is only one teacher in a program, you may feel that you have to know everything. This can lead to feelings of inadequacy as well as overload. It is impossible to know everything—but it is possible to know whom to ask for assistance and support. Even teachers with many years of experience talk over puzzling situations with their peers and call on experts at the local, state, and national levels for information and support. Participating in professional conferences, workshops, and electronic discussion lists also provides opportunities for brainstorming and gathering information.

In the hurried complexity of traveling from site to site, effective itinerant teachers need to keep in mind this goal: to encourage, educate, and allow each student to be an independent, competent, contributing member of society and an advocate on his or her own behalf. They should remember to discourage passivity by never doing anything for students that students can do themselves. The teachers' sense of success and accomplishment comes from knowing that students are able and willing to take responsibility, commensurate with their developmental levels, to meet their own special needs.

REFERENCES

D'Andrea, F. M., & Farrenkopf, C. (Eds.). (2000). *Looking to learn: Promoting literacy for students with low vision.* New York: AFB Press.

Koenig, A. J., & Holbrook, M. C. (Eds.). (1995). *Learning media assessment of students with visual impairments: A resource guide for teachers* (2nd ed.). Austin, TX: Texas School for the Blind and Visually Impaired.

Koenig, A. J., & Holbrook, M. C. (Eds.). (2000). *Foundations of education* (2nd ed.). Volume II: *Instructional strategies for teaching children and youths with visual impairments.* New York: AFB Press.

CHAPTER 3

A Typical Year

In addition to providing individualized instruction, an itinerant teacher can expect to be involved in certain basic, structural processes and activities during the school year. The following sections outline these basic activities and offer suggestions for establishing caseloads, providing textbooks, setting up a schedule, providing in-service programs, creating IEPs, devising transition IEPs, assessing referrals, conducting mandated assessments, arranging for standardized tests, performing other special activities, and completing end-of-year activities. The activities are described in roughly the same chronological order that they present themselves to a teacher's attention during the school year, but this order will vary somewhat in each individual's experience. In particular, setting up caseloads and ordering textbooks are best taken care of in the spring before the new school year that begins in the fall. "Through the Year: An Itinerant Checklist" presents a rough outline of the tasks performed at the end of the school year to prepare for the fall term and those that must be carried out at the beginning of the school year.

Many of the activities described in this chapter include details such as procedures, deadlines, and forms to be used, to comply with national, state, and local school district regulations. In this chapter I've tried to avoid stating those particulars since many seem to vary from state to state and from district to district. Follow the time frames and use the forms as directed in your district.

Your colleagues in your program for students with visual impairments will no doubt be helpful in providing information about the procedures and guidelines used in the district as well as in the program. If you are the only itinerant teacher of visually impaired students, however, your immediate supervisor will be the

Through the Year: An Itinerant Checklist

Various tasks are typically performed at the end and the beginning of each school year. The listing that follows begins with the end of the year because many tasks are done at that time in preparation for the start of the next year. It's likely that most, but not all, of these tasks will be ones you perform. The time frames are flexible.

End of the School Year

Last six weeks of school

- ❑ Get lists of texts to be used the following year and follow through with your ordering procedures (see Figure 3.1).
- ❑ Begin returning to your office or other storage location any materials and equipment that won't be needed through the end of the school year.
- ❑ Begin sorting through papers and file or dispose of them.

Last three weeks

- ❑ Establish caseloads for the following year.
- ❑ Share student files and information with your peers to whom your students will transfer next year.
- ❑ Prepare for and keep track of final examinations and special schedules, especially in secondary schools.
- ❑ Orient those students who will be going to a different school to the new sites.

Last week of school

- ❑ Clearly label large pieces of equipment that will stay at a school site over the summer for continued use in the fall. Notify a site administrator in writing as to where and how the equipment will be stored.
- ❑ Return all other equipment and materials to be checked in and stored in your office or storage place where it can be easily located.
- ❑ Return all keys, texts, and other items checked out at school sites.
- ❑ Edit or write information-sharing letters for your students' teachers to be delivered a few days before school starts (see Figure 3.5).
- ❑ Clean out your car trunk so that it will accommodate your vacation equipment and supplies.

Beginning of the School Year

Two weeks before school starts

- ❑ Check secondary school sites for your students' schedules. When you have all of them, organize the schedules as needed.
- ❑ Braille and enlarge students' schedules as needed.
- ❑ Request a mailbox at each site as needed.

One week before school starts

- ❑ Distribute informative letters to classroom teachers' mailboxes (Figures 3.5, 3.6, 3.7).
- ❑ Meet with elementary teachers and others as needed.
- ❑ Confirm that the texts ordered in the spring are the ones that will be used (Figure 3.8).
- ❑ Consult with and begin training paraeducators.
- ❑ Start delivering books and equipment to schools and to students' homes when applicable, using the Materials on Loan Form (see Figure 10.1) to record the items.
- ❑ Check IEPs to determine direct service time for each student; use a blank schedule form (Figure 3.4) and self-stick notes or your PDA to start planning a schedule.
- ❑ At sites where you will not be working with students in their classrooms, consult with administrators about rooms to work in. Borrow or check out necessary keys.
- ❑ Orient students to new sites; with some secondary students, practice the routes they will need to take. Some students may appreciate learning the layout of each of their classrooms; you may be able to borrow a school's master key to look in each classroom.
- ❑ Remember to be calm and breathe deeply!

First few weeks of school

- ❑ Check each of the schools to which you are assigned to determine that the students are actually in attendance at those sites.
- ❑ Spend time in classrooms with students with more extensive need for your intervention.
- ❑ Confer with and observe students and teachers to trouble-shoot and correct inappropriate situations before they become habitual.
- ❑ Work closely with classroom teachers and paraeducators.
- ❑ Set up in-service workshops and meetings with teachers and other staff members as appropriate.
- ❑ Establish and begin your schedule as soon as possible.
- ❑ Gather materials for your car trunk: boxes, forms, equipment, and materials you will be using at several sites.
- ❑ Contact your students' parents or guardians. Introduce yourself if needed and give them your work phone number and e-mail address. Discuss your schedule with their children. Let them know that you'll be contacting them as needed and that you're available to consult with them throughout the school year.

source of that information, embellished, perhaps, by other itinerant personnel, such as speech therapists. Additional information may well be presented at district meetings for new teachers. Many districts provide ongoing training for special education teachers regarding compliance with IDEA and other regulations as needed. Don't feel shy about asking for information and clarification; it's much better to complete a task correctly the first time than to do it wrong and have to correct it.

ESTABLISHING CASELOADS

In a district with only one itinerant teacher, the caseload is predetermined. In larger programs, students should be assigned to teachers in May or June of the previous year to expedite the provision of services in the fall.

If the program administrator is involved in the process of assigning caseloads, the teachers can provide important information regarding their students' needs. (See Chapter 2 for additional discussion of caseloads.) Some of the factors that should be presented, preferably in written form for each student, include the following: the number of minutes for direct contact or monitoring needed each week, including the amount of time needed to obtain or prepare materials; the length of time the student has worked with a particular itinerant teacher; and the site to which the student is assigned. Another important factor is the amount of time required to do the following: consult with school personnel, observe students, assess referrals, conduct functional vision assessments, assess learning media, make the transition between sites, and have conference-preparation and lunch periods. Because administrators may not be aware of all the demands of an itinerant position, involving the teachers in the process of establishing caseloads may result in more cohesive, effective services to students. The teacher of students with visual impairments needs to alert the program supervisor if the needs of students are not being met because of the size of the caseload; it is up to the school system to add staff as needed.

In some instances (and in my view, preferably) the itinerant teachers in a program can be responsible as a group for establishing their caseloads for the coming year. One strategy for doing so entails each teacher completing information on a card for each school he or she is currently serving. On each card should be the school name and the names of the students at that site with the number of minutes specified in their IEPs for direct and monitoring services for each student. The card should also include the total number of minutes of service required at that site. In most instances it's advisable to have two sets of cards clearly marked: one for sites with students who receive services from itinerant teachers of visually impaired students and one set for students who receive O&M instruction.

Each teacher brings the cards to a meeting where they are placed in the middle of the table. One by one, teachers pick a card, indicating an interest in serving the students at that site. When all the cards have been taken, each teacher adds up the total minutes on his or her cards to ensure that each has a reasonably equitable number of IEP minutes.

During this process, there is considerable discussion, more often than not. A teacher might choose a card and another teacher may give cogent reasons why he or she should serve that site or that student instead. For example, if a student is making a transition to a new school, the second teacher, who has already served this student for three years, may feel that support from someone familiar with the student's abilities and needs will ease the transition.

Establishing caseloads as a group may be a somewhat lengthy process and cards may be traded more than once. However, teachers' cooperation and flexibility in working together can lead to more balanced and diverse caseloads (what I call an eclectic approach to caseload assignment) as well as caseloads determined in the students' best interests and according to their needs.

Three different approaches can be used in assigning students to itinerant teachers:

Approaches to Assigning Caseloads

- *Geographic approach.* In the geographic approach, the area served is organized into as many parts as there are itinerant teachers, in such a way that each teacher has an equivalent caseload. This approach works best in a large geographic area. It reduces the individual itinerant teachers' travel time, which allows for more contact time in each school. However, using this approach may make it difficult to achieve caseloads balanced in terms of age levels, types or degrees of visual impairment, and individual needs.
- *Needs-specific approach.* In the needs-specific approach, itinerant teachers may specialize in working with elementary school students, secondary school students, or students with multiple impairments enrolled in special classes. This approach reduces the number of materials with which the teachers need to be familiar. However, there are disadvantages to this approach, particularly for older students. Each secondary school student will have more teachers with whom the itinerant teacher will need to consult (five or six per student as opposed to the usual one per elementary school student), and secondary school students are more difficult to schedule for contact time with their itinerant teachers because of their more rigid class schedules.
- *Eclectic approach.* In the eclectic approach, students are assigned to teachers according to severity of their visual impairment, service time as delineated on the IEP, heterogeneity of grade level, and class assignment. Each teacher has some secondary school students, some elementary school students, and some students in special classes, as well as some familiar students and some new students, some students who require considerable attention, and some students who need only monitoring. Using this approach is possible in areas in which the distance necessary to travel is not an inhibiting factor.

Whenever possible, it is advisable to assign only one itinerant teacher to each site where there are students. Doing so reduces confusion in the schools and is a more effective use of the itinerant teacher's time. An exception may occur when the services of an O&M specialist are also required at a site.

Becoming familiar with a student's visual, academic, and social functioning takes some time on an itinerant basis, so a teacher should be assigned to a student for more than one year. However, working with the same teacher on a one-to-one basis for several years can foster a student's undue dependence on the teacher. In a district with more than one itinerant teacher, students' progress may be enhanced by rotating the itinerant teachers every three years or so. It is helpful to the students, parents, and school personnel if more than one teacher reiterates important suggestions. It is also likely that a new teacher's fresh approach may increase a student's progress. However, it is wise to avoid transferring a student from one itinerant teacher to another when the student is making another type of transition, such as moving from an elementary school to a junior high or middle school.

PROVIDING TEXTBOOKS

Making sure that students have their textbooks and other materials in the appropriate media is a crucial responsibility of every teacher of students who are visually impaired. The concomitant responsibilities, of course, are making sure that the appropriate media for each student have been determined, that their appropriateness is assessed continually, and that students know how to use these materials. This may involve teaching reading and writing in braille or the use of low vision devices, tape-recorded materials, or e-books.

Ordering Books

If you are a new itinerant teacher for visually impaired students for whom textbooks have not been ordered, determine from their IEPs which students need adapted materials and in what formats and contact the students' classroom teachers to get lists of the textbooks being used. It is advisable to complete this task as quickly as possible because books may not be delivered until two to six weeks after they have been ordered. In some states, it can take months. If a book needs to be brailled, delivery may take even longer.

Whenever possible, order textbooks during the spring before any given school year. As early as possible, but at least two months before the end of school, begin gathering lists of books your students will be using for the following year. Books can then be ordered in June in the appropriate medium or electronic format or brailled, enlarged, or taped over the summer and be available for use in September. Be sure to get complete information about each book (full title and edition, author, publisher, latest copyright date listed, and international standard book number [ISBN]) to expedite ordering. Be sure to check the edition numbers and copyright dates to ensure that the specified edition is the one being used for the next academic year. If a student needs braille books—especially high school textbooks in mathematics, science, or other technical subjects—pay special attention to ordering early. It takes time to transcribe these books if they do not already exist in braille editions.

To obtain lists of textbooks at elementary schools, confer with each principal to determine which teacher or teachers will provide the information about the texts being used. Secondary schools are more of a challenge because not every teacher uses the same texts. After you obtain the list of courses for the next year for each student, check with the school's textbook clerk or other designated individual for information about the textbooks. If the clerk is not available or is not certain about a textbook for a particular class, you may find it necessary to ask an administrator to have your student assigned to a particular teacher and then to contact the teacher to determine which books will be used.

Different states handle the ordering of textbooks in different ways. Check with your local school district for the procedures you need to follow. The sample book order form shown in Figure 3.1 may serve as a guide to the information you should obtain. Be sure to give teachers or clerks enough time to complete the forms, but provide clear deadlines and instructions on how they should return the forms to you.

When you have the information you need, check all the sources that may be able to provide the texts. Your state instructional materials center, web sites, and electronic mailing lists may be good sources; some texts may even be downloaded for students' use. In addition, companies and agencies that provide texts in braille, large print, on tape, or in electronic formats are listed in the *AFB Directory of Services for Blind and Visually Impaired Persons in the United States and Canada* (2005); a few such sources also appear in Appendix A to this book. You may also be able to obtain adapted books from state or local agencies or nonprofit groups. If you are unfamiliar with such agencies or groups, your colleagues in the program for students with visual impairments are good sources of information. The organizations listed in Appendix B are useful sources of information as well.

Purchasing textbooks is often expensive. Make decisions judiciously about purchasing or borrowing books or ordering them on tape or other media. For example, if you have the option of borrowing any adapted texts, do so if the braille is transcribed accurately or if the print size is appropriate for a given student's use. Borrowing a textbook is particularly wise if it is likely to be used only once in your district. When considering whether to order large-print texts, check whether an evaluation has been conducted to see if use of a low vision device with print book is preferable for that student. Before ordering textbooks on tape, be sure that your students have the necessary listening skills to benefit from

FIGURE 3.1

Book Order for September 2005

Please return this form to Jean Olmstead by 5/25/05 so books for your student who is visually impaired can be obtained for the start of school.

Please put this form in my mailbox or send it to me at Central School via e-mail or school mail.

Thanks.
Sincerely,

Jean Olmstead
Jean Olmstead
Itinerant teacher of students with visual impairments
320-4500
jeo@xxx.edu

Student Charles Santos

Teacher of Visually Impaired Students J. Olmstead

School Wright Grade 6

Large Print ✓ Braille ______

Title *Real Math, Grade 6, 3rd ed.* Level/Edition *Green* ISBN *0-12345-123-X*
Author *Willoughby et al.* Publisher *Open Court* Copyright date *1998*

Office Use Only

Source	*Date Ordered*	*Date Received*
In V.I. Program Office		

Title *Our World Today* Level/Edition ______ ISBN *0-12345-124-X*
Author *Bacon* Publisher *Allyn & Bacon* Copyright date *1999*

Office Use Only

Source	*Date Ordered*	*Date Received*
Available from the State		

Title *Reading Literature* Level/Edition *Grade 6-Gold* ISBN *0-12345-136-X*
Author *Chaparro et al.* Publisher *McDougal, Littell* Copyright date *2000*

Office Use Only

Source	*Date Ordered*	*Date Received*
American Printing House		

using taped materials. If necessary, teach a lesson on the use of the tape player, four-track tapes, tone indexing, and so forth. Various electronic formats, including compact discs (CDs), e-books, and Web-Braille are increasingly available from such organizations as Recording for the Blind and Dyslexic and the National Library Service for the Blind and Physically Handicapped (see Appendix A). If, as a last resort, you need to enlarge books on a copier for a student, be sure to refer to the student's functional vision and learning media assessments so that you clearly understand the student's visual needs and produce a print size appropriate for his or her use.

Using the Books

In the fall, before delivering the books to the schools, double-check with students' teachers to make sure that the texts you have ordered match those that will be used in their classes. It may not be feasible to check with the teachers in all districts, particularly in rural areas, but doing so can ensure that your students receive the books they need and reduce the amount of materials you load into and out of your car.

Students need to be able to use their texts as independently as possible. Therefore, make certain that page numbers in braille and large-print texts correspond with those of the smaller-print texts, and check for texts such as elementary mathematics books and social science textbooks in which color plays an important role. For students for whom such color will be meaningful, you may choose either to order those large-print texts in color (a relatively expensive choice at this time) or to color in important areas in enlarged books so the students have access to the same information as their classmates. You could also obtain a copy of the smaller-print book and scan pages with important information in color. If this is your choice, your scanner will need to have color capability. The pages can be enlarged and printed out (on a printer that will produce color as well as accommodate 11-×-17-inch paper). The enlarged pages can be added to the enlarged texts.

The original print size of texts, worksheets, and other materials can vary widely. If you enlarge all materials by the same proportion for students who need large print (for example, by 130 percent), some print may be too small or too large for effective reading. It is essential to conduct a print media assessment every year to determine the correct print size required by each student who reads in print. You may find it helpful to obtain three measures: the optimal size and the largest and smallest sizes the student can use effectively. Keep records of those sizes by the copier or computer you use most, and also keep them with you in case you need to enlarge materials at another site. Make sure your transcriber (if you have one), program assistant, classroom teachers, and parents or guardians are also aware of the print sizes appropriate for individual students' efficient reading.

3 measures

Students need to be able to use their texts as independently as possible.

Courtesy of National Braille Press

Work with the classroom teachers and the students, particularly in elementary schools, to organize the volumes in the classroom so that students can easily find the volumes they need. In addition, take time to teach the students how to use books published in several volumes. Students may require a special arrangement of desks or tables or both to have enough room to use their special books and equipment. Make sure the seating is arranged so that the students are an integral part of the class and are placed where they can use their vision, low vision devices, and other nonoptical aids optimally.

A student may have 30 to 40 books to be used at school. If you enlarge or braille and bind many volumes, the spines and covers may all look the same. Two procedures can facilitate a student's finding a specific volume more quickly:

Labeling Textbooks

- *Label books consistently.* Choose a format you like, and use it for every volume. For example, if you use the wording in the sample label in Figure 3.2, your students will find that the title is always listed first; the information on the volume second; and page numbers third on both the spines and covers of volumes.

- *Color-code labels on large-print books, using templates and marking pens.* Always use a particular color and symbol for each subject. For example, if mathematics books have red circles, students can locate the volumes with that symbol before reading for specific information. Figure 3.3 is a sample of a color-coding system that can be used to designate the subjects of students' books.

FIGURE 3.2

Sample Book Label

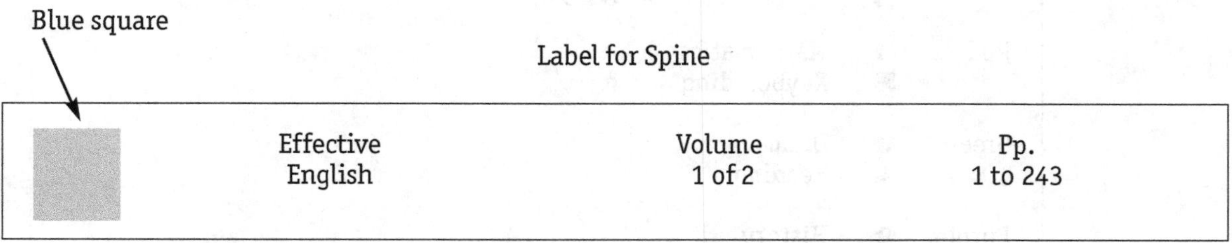

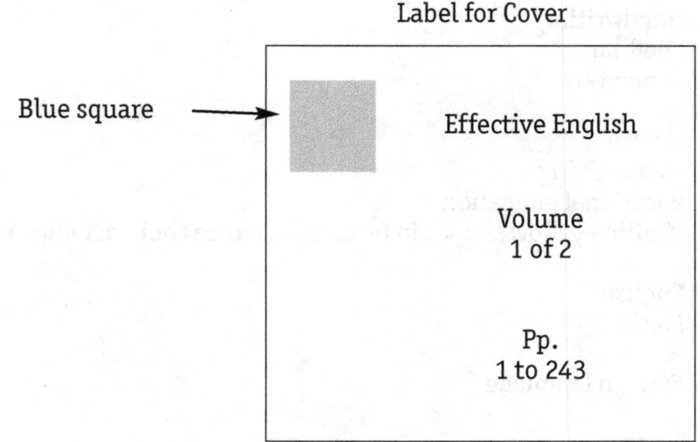

If a student uses many texts on tape, color-coding the tapes by subject area can help the student find the ones he or she needs. You could use the sample system suggested here or let the student set up another system.

SETTING UP A SCHEDULE

Many itinerant teachers are responsible for establishing their own schedules. The process is complex and time-consuming and should be done with care; you generally have to live with your schedule for 10 months.

Time for the following components should be included on your schedule:

Components of a Schedule

- Direct services or monitoring services, or both, for students as specified in their IEPs. The minutes specified for monitoring should include adequate time for adaptation of materials for students' use; conferring with the transcriber or program assistant; observations; and conferences with school staff members, families or guardians, eye care specialists, and community resources.

FIGURE 3.3

Sample Color-Coding System for Students' Books

Red:	●	Mathematics
	■	Keyboarding
Green:	●	Drama
	▲	Reading
Purple:	●	History
Orange:	●	Handwriting
	■	Spelling
	▲	Computers
Yellow:	●	Health
	■	Family living
	▲	Vocational education (Outline yellow shapes in black to enhance their visibility.)
Blue:	■	English
	▲	Music
Brown:	■	Foreign language
Black:	▲	Science

- Assessments when appropriate in areas of visual functioning, appropriate learning media, attainment of core curriculum skills, use of technological devices, O&M skills, and other assessments as needed.
- Assessment of newly referred students.
- Transition time between sites.
- Conference preparation periods.
- Lunch breaks.
- Meetings with other itinerant teachers in your program.

Your goal is to establish your schedule as soon as possible in the fall to provide regular services as soon as possible. Also, because itinerant teachers have to compete for work space with other personnel (nurses, speech therapists, psychologists, and others), establishing your schedule as early as possible may facilitate your assignment to appropriate working spaces. Schools in some districts have been getting more crowded for a number of reasons, and competition for work space can be fierce.

To begin thinking about your schedule, you must have an approximate idea of how much time each of your students requires: for example, a half hour twice a week or an hour five times a week. To find this out, check the students' IEPs, which will specify the number of contact or monitoring minutes, or both, needed. Itinerant teachers with no input from other teachers of visually impaired students will need time to assess their students' needs. Through a review of information on each student's visual functioning and academic progress and observations of students, a new itinerant teacher will gain insight into the students' needs.

Making Preliminary Preparations

If you and your colleagues will be having regular meetings, determine the day and time so each of you can avoid scheduling students during that time period. Schedules for secondary school counselors and their students are usually available at schools two weeks before the school year begins. Start gathering information on students' schedules at that time, because after school begins the counselors and other staff are inundated with schedule changes and new enrollees.

The benefits of gathering the information early include the following:

Benefits of Gathering Scheduling Information Early

- You can be sure that your students are assigned to appropriate courses. A helpful counselor will also facilitate your students' assignment to classroom teachers whose classes are structured to promote the students' participation.
- With the counselor's assistance, you can manipulate students' schedules to counteract eye fatigue and strain. You may alternate classes that involve many visual tasks with those that emphasize less precise visual learning or, for students who experience eye fatigue in the afternoon, schedule classes with more visual tasks in the morning.
- You can check all your students' schedules for appropriate times when they are to work with you. If three students at three different schools have periods when they are available to work with you at the same time, changing their schedules will facilitate your scheduling. Also, if you have two students at one school, you can schedule their instructional time back to back, so that you can see them one after the other and hence avoid using your time inefficiently. If a student's schedule needs to be changed, it is easier for all concerned if the change is made before school begins. When a school has special programs such as block scheduling (different schedules for different days or weeks, such as alternating Block A with Block B), your schedule will no doubt need tweaking. You may have to create two schedules—one for week A and the other for week B.

- If you plan to have a regular class with a student—that is, to see the student every day—you can schedule that time as a formal class. Seeing a student for a period every day is beneficial for those students who need more support; it's certainly wiser to see the student at the same time every day than to pull him or her out of five classes every week. A school administrator can help you devise a title for the course and show you how to report attendance and grades. Another option is to attempt to get the class adopted and listed among the school district's course offerings. Federal law mandates that the course's name not contain any references to special education; possible titles include Technology Skills or Vocational Skills. After you've chosen an appropriate name, you can petition the school board, with your supervisor's permission or assistance, or both, to adopt the course at both junior and senior high school levels. The course title and number will then be in the district's computer system, and it will be easier to schedule students for that class in subsequent years.
- You can prepare handouts for the classroom teachers in which you discuss your students' needs, ask for information, and put them in the teachers' mailboxes before school begins. Samples are provided in the section Providing In-Service Programs in this chapter. The teachers will then have advance notice that a visually impaired student will be in their class, and they can give you helpful information before they are inundated with students and myriad organizational chores.
- You may be able to request access to your work space for certain periods before school begins. Being able to set up at the beginning of the year gives you a head start in providing services to the students at that site.

Scheduling Students

Look at your students' needs as you begin to think about your schedule. If you have an elementary school student who requires daily contact of an hour or more, consult with the student's classroom teacher about appropriate times to see the student. Otherwise, it is usually advisable to schedule secondary school students before you schedule your elementary school students, since secondary school schedules are usually more rigid because of the structure of individual class periods. Next, find out the times when elementary school and special-class students (such as those in classes for students with multiple impairments) will be available. Keep notes on when each student can be seen on which days, and juggle the times on your schedule as they seem to fit best for both the students and the most effective use of your time. (This is the kind of process for which self-stick notes and, for some people, personal digital assistants [PDAs] were invented.) For example, give students who tend to experience eye fatigue in the afternoon a slot in your schedule later in the day, when you can exert some control over the visual tasks to be performed. For example, when a student is experiencing eye fatigue after a long day of visual tasks, you may choose to read assignments to him or her. Since most school holidays are on Mondays and Fridays, it is wise to avoid those days for scheduling students you see once a week.

Scheduling students before or after school or during lunch, when possible, allows them to participate fully in their regular classes. If this requires you to come to work earlier or leaving later than your normal work day, you should be able to take compensatory time off by either coming in later or leaving earlier on other days. Another possibility is to be reimbursed on a per diem basis for the extra time. However, such a schedule is, of course, difficult to arrange for every student, so arrangements have to be made to see various students during the regular school day. Depending on the students' IEP goals, you may provide support for the academic program in the classroom or pull the student aside in the room for shorter one-on-one instruction. If more intense individual instruction necessitates pulling the student out of class, arrange for the most effective time with the classroom teacher. Also, have a clear arrangement with each teacher involved about whether the students will be responsible for the time they miss in class and, if so, how they should make that time up.

Try to see students during times when making up the work they miss is not a major problem. The content of the class missed and the teacher's flexibility will affect your decision. A physical education teacher may be willing to excuse a secondary school student from class, but only once per week; therefore, you may need to arrange to see the student during another nonacademic period, such as home economics or art, if you are to see the student twice a week. Be diplomatic with other teachers during negotiations about scheduling, and understand the importance of each class; at the same time, be assertive enough to schedule students as often as is necessary to provide effective services.

While you are conferring with teachers, keep in touch with school administrators to make sure rooms are available at the times you can see your students. You may need to make several adjustments before you can arrange a schedule workable for all participants.

Also, during this scheduling process, check with your students' teachers to make sure they are using the texts you have ordered, deliver books and equipment to the schools and students' homes, and adapt worksheets. This can be a trying time with so much to accomplish; be calm and flexible, and cooperate with everyone for the benefit of your students. Do not be surprised or upset if the process takes at least three weeks. You may be encouraged by knowing that establishing a schedule becomes at least somewhat easier the more you do it.

When your schedule is firmly set, confirm the times when the student will be pulled out of other classes to meet with you, with the teachers involved. Usually, the wisest use of time is for secondary school students to report directly to you, rather than checking in with their regular teachers first. Set up a way to handle the reporting of attendance. You can ask the regular teacher not to mark a student absent on the days you see him or her, and arrange to be responsible for informing the teacher and the attendance office when the student is not present. If the teacher inadvertently marks the student absent when the student is with you, it should be easy to clear those absences with the teacher and the school's attendance clerk.

Finally, you can ask the counselors of your secondary school students to avoid making changes in the students' schedules later in the school year that would affect your scheduled time with the students. With the counselors' permission, you can leave a note on their copies of the students' schedules reminding the counselors to call you if a change in schedule is being considered.

Scheduling Other Components

After you have set up times to work with your students, there should be adequate time left in your schedule for the duties performed during the monitoring minutes specified on the students' IEPs as well as additional duties (see the sample schedule in Figure 3.4 for an idea of how all these components fit in a schedule). Monitoring duties include the following:

Monitoring Components

- *Adaptation of materials.* Providing adapted materials for students on a daily basis is an essential part of your job. Schedule time to consult with your transcriber (assuming you have one) or program assistant to braille, tape, or enlarge the materials necessary to facilitate students' participation in class activities. Even if someone else, such as a transcriber, adapts most of the materials, you will no doubt need some time for proofreading or for last-minute work that needs to be adapted immediately.
- *Observations and consultation.* In effective programs for visually impaired students, itinerant teachers have adequate time to observe students at different times during the year and to consult regularly with their classroom teachers, IEP team members, other school staff, parents or guardians, eye care specialists, and appropriate community resources. The observations and exchange of information enable you and the teachers, families, and resources to assist students based on their needs and capabilities.

Various additional duties might include these:

Additional Duties

- *Assessment for referrals.* Duties of an itinerant teacher often include performing functional vision assessments for referrals to the program for visually impaired students. Adequate time for this assessment should also be included in your schedule. You may assess referrals during time designated for monitoring and consultation on your schedule, or at times when other students are absent.
- *Assessments.* You will be conducting assessments of your students according to mandated time frames in areas of visual functioning, appropriate

FIGURE 3.4

Schedule Jean Olmstead, effective 10/1/05

Time	*Monday*	*Tuesday*	*Wednesday*	*Thursday*	*Friday*	*Notes*
8:00	Davis George Gonzalez	Referrals, teacher conference or student observation	Spenser Conferences and materials preparation	Davis George Gonzalez	Westerly Mary Lee	Davis George Gonzalez Spenser Ellen Jackson John Martinez Linda Smith Paul Wong Southport Kathy Doe Westerly Mary Lee Grant Joan Grady David Jones Michael O'Brien
8:30	Travel	Travel	Travel	Travel	Travel	
9:00	Office Preparation period	Grant Joan Grady David Jones Michael O'Brien	Southport Kathy Doe	Southport Kathy Doe	Grant Joan Grady David Jones Michael O'Brien	
9:30						
10:00	Travel		Travel	Travel		
10:30	Spenser Paul Wong		Referrals, teacher conference, or student observation	Spenser Paul Wong Ellen Jackson	Travel	
11:00						
11:30	Lunch Teacher conference, materials preparation				Office Lunch	
12:00		Lunch Teacher conference	Travel	Lunch		
12:30	Travel		Davis George Gonzalez	John Martinez	Preparation period	
1:00	Southport Kathy Doe	Travel	Lunch Teacher conference		Travel	
1:30	Travel Referrals, teacher conference, or student observation	Westerly Mary Lee	Travel Office Preparation period	Travel Office Preparation period	Referrals, teacher conference, or student observation	
2:00	Travel	Travel	Travel		Travel	
2:30	Spenser Linda Smith ↓	Office Preparation period	Spenser Linda Smith ↓	Visually impaired program meeting ↓	Spenser Linda Smith ↓	
3:00						
3:30						

Note: Dotted lines separate different activities at the same site.

learning media, attainment of core curriculum skills, use of technological devices, O&M skills, and other areas as needed. It's crucial to allocate adequate time to perform them effectively.

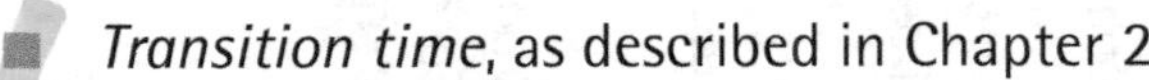

- *Transition time*, as described in Chapter 2.
- *Conference preparation periods.* Each itinerant teacher should have a daily conference preparation period scheduled at the office where the materials and records for visually impaired students are stored. During this period, you can prepare for your lessons with students, gather or prepare the materials to be used in the lessons, and perform other tasks, such as writing reports, ordering materials, completing paperwork, planning in-service activities, and receiving and making telephone calls. Because your access to the office is probably limited, you will find it helpful to schedule at least one preparation period at the end of the day so that you can stay as late as you need to catch up with work.
- *Lunch breaks.* You should be able to schedule a lunch break at an appropriate time of the day. You will often find that you have the best rapport and relationships with classroom teachers in schools where you eat lunch. Scheduling lunch at different schools during the week will broaden your base of communication. The best use of time is to schedule a student before or after the lunch period, if possible, on the days you eat lunch at the site. Also, if many materials need to be adapted, it's wise to schedule your lunch once or twice a week at the site where your transcriber works (most convenient if this is also your office site) so that you can consult about the adapted materials.

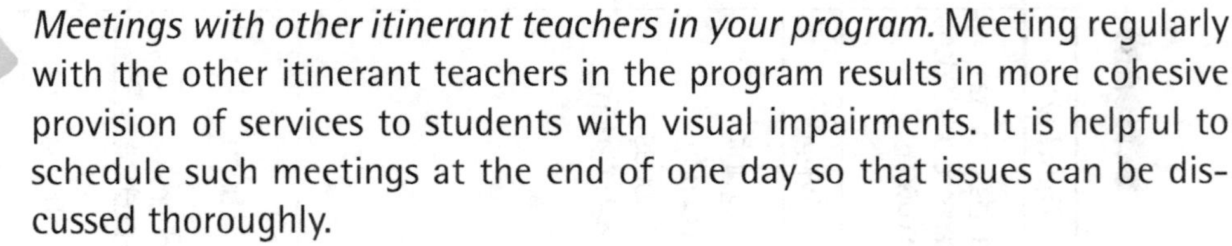

- *Meetings with other itinerant teachers in your program.* Meeting regularly with the other itinerant teachers in the program results in more cohesive provision of services to students with visual impairments. It is helpful to schedule such meetings at the end of one day so that issues can be discussed thoroughly.

SHARING INFORMATION

In addition to scheduling and organizing time and equipment, working cooperatively with key school personnel is a critical concern of the itinerant teacher. Teachers in general education classrooms who have students with visual impairments in their classes need practical information so they can have realistic expectations of the students' participation and help to make effective adaptations. Providing information and suggestions for classroom teachers and other staff members who have daily contact with the students (such as secretaries, custodians, cafeteria workers, yard supervisors, and bus drivers), as well as family members or guardians, is one of the more important roles of the itinerant teacher. It directly affects whether the students' educational needs are met effectively and expedites the participation of students with visual impairments in school activities. Continuing collaboration with educational personnel is discussed in more detail in Chapter 4.

It is particularly important, however, to make contact at the start of every year with all the people involved in your student's educational program to provide information about the student's special needs, especially to personnel who may not have worked with the student before. You can do this both in formal in-service programs and in informal meetings with school personnel, both of which settings are equally important and valuable.

General Considerations

Tailor your provision of information to the individual teacher's experience. Working with a new teacher may involve more time observing in the classroom and consulting about adaptive techniques. A veteran teacher who has already worked with a student with visual impairments may no doubt need less consultation.

On-site meetings with groups of classroom teachers should be arranged with a site administrator who will either ask the teachers to the meeting or ask you to invite them. At sites where only one classroom teacher is involved with the visually impaired student, confer with that teacher to schedule a time when you can meet to discuss the student's capabilities, special needs, and mutual concerns. The supervisor of the program for students with visual impairments should be involved in arrangements for general information sharing or in-service programs to which teachers from different sites are invited.

Plan your in-service activities thoroughly. Coining short phrases helps teachers to remember key issues. The expression "The helping hand strikes again" succinctly categorizes overprotection or doing too much for students. The booklet *When You Have a Visually Impaired Student in Your Classroom* (2002) is a helpful resource to distribute at in-service workshops (see also Hudson, 1997; Holbrook et al., 2000).

Many teachers have never met a person with a visual impairment; fewer still have had such a student in their classes. Be prepared to respond to questions and concerns and to deal with a wide range of attitudes. Sometimes it is effective to invite the previous year's regular classroom teachers to in-service discussions and have them share their experiences with students' new teachers.

You may find it advisable to negotiate with your supervisor about reimbursing teachers' attendance at formal, lengthy in-service programs and establishing a budget code for reimbursement. Even nominal payment can help to alleviate feelings of being overburdened. A more lengthy in-service program for a classroom teacher may be indicated when the student's impairment entails adaptation of most of the curricular materials and activities. In this circumstance, it is a good idea to use the district's or program's money to pay for a half-day substitute for the teacher so that intervention techniques can be thoroughly discussed.

Another option is to use the schools' staff enrichment days for in-service workshops. Many districts now require a certain number of hours to be completed by teachers each year. Negotiate with the site administrators to use this time with your students' teachers. Emphasize the importance of the in-service activities and explain the nuances involved in having students with visual impairments in regular classes. The booklet *Seeing Eye to Eye* (Lewis & Allman, 2000) is designed specifically to present these issues to administrators. When the general education classroom teachers understand these complexities, they, the students with visual impairments, and other students in the class will have more effective and productive relationships.

Participation of Students

When students are involved in an in-service activity, they become doers rather than what might be termed done-to-ers. They also gain experience and confidence in talking about the implications of their visual impairments. Teachers may be more responsive and empathic if the students are present. Also, they will sometimes ask questions only the students can answer. These factors need to be weighed against the possibility that a student's presence may inhibit a candid discussion of some teachers' concerns. It is advisable to be alert to this possibility and to check back with teachers in private about any questions they may have.

The students' ages and levels of functioning will influence the extent of their participation. For example, some 5-year-olds could be involved as consultants in planning, demonstrate equipment or techniques, and name three games they like to play. Older elementary school students can be more involved in planning and presenting information about their visual functioning.

Junior high school students can prepare for an in-service program by writing or typing a report that includes the following: an explanation of their visual condition, corrected acuity and its functional significance, school activities for which they need no assistance, activities and tasks that require remediation, how classroom teachers can help them, and what the teacher of visually impaired students does for them. By the time they are in high school, when students have been involved in the process for a number of years, they can assume the major role in presenting in-service programs and writing letters to teachers about their needs. Although students' participation is mentioned sparingly in the following descriptions of in-service activities, your students will benefit from being included in every aspect as much as possible.

Meeting with Teachers Whose Students Work with Braille

Although a meeting early in the year with the classroom teachers of any student with visual impairments is important, meeting at the earliest opportunity with the teachers of students who work with braille is crucial. It is helpful to meet with classroom teachers in the spring before the upcoming school term or before school starts in the fall. For teachers at the secondary school level, try to arrange one meeting with all the teachers. Before the meeting, you may wish to distribute some letters similar to the samples presented in Figures 3.5 and 3.6, in which you describe the preferred reading and writing formats of the student and provide other preliminary information. You need to make certain that the texts you ordered in braille or on tape correspond to the ones that will be used in class. Make arrangements for classroom seating that allow the student to be an integral member of the class and to have enough desk space for effective use of materials. Other areas for discussion include the following:

Topics to Discuss with Teachers

- An explanation of the student's visual condition.
- A description of the student's visual acuity and the impact of the student's visual condition on his or her visual functioning (light sensitivity, color recognition, among others).
- The use of special equipment (computer, braillewriter, electronic notetaker, slate and stylus, tape recorder, and so forth).
- The use of braille or taped texts. Provide a braille book to demonstrate how braille texts correspond to regular text—word for word and page for page—and how pictures, graphs, maps, and other visual elements are handled.
- The use of worksheets in braille or on tape.
- The process the student will use to complete assigned work: for example, brailled work will be interlined; or the student will type, tape, or do assignments on a computer.
- The role of a paraeducator, if one is provided.
- Arrangements for occasions when materials have not been adapted: for example, a paraeducator or peer reads the material to the student.
- Expectations about the student's work: for instance, some lessons may be modified, but generally the student should be expected to perform the same tasks as students who are not visually impaired and should be graded according to the quality of his or her work.
- Expectations about social behavior: for instance, behavior should be appropriate for the setting; eye contact should be encouraged.

FIGURE 3.5

August 30, 2005

Kathy Polanski, who uses braille to read and write, is enrolled in your 4th period math class.
I have been planning extensively to facilitate her participation in your class.

I look forward to meeting you and her other teachers on Tuesday, September 2, at 1:30 p.m. in Room 202 as previously planned. Please put the following items in my mailbox or e-mail them to me before then, or bring them to the meeting:

1. A list of the texts you will be using this year with the following information: title and edition, author, publisher, copyright date, and ISBN number.
2. Any handouts you have already prepared for her class. Please write on each your name and the approximate date you expect to use it in class. If the handouts are stored in your computer, we'll discuss the procedure for e-mailing them to me or a transcriber.
3. Any work you have planned to put on the board.
4. A list of anything else you can think of that Kathy will need for your class.

I will answer any questions you may have at the meeting and look forward to working with you this year.

Sincerely,

Jean Olmstead

Jean Olmstead
Itinerant teacher of students with visual impairments
320-4500
jeo@xxx.edu

- Extra time that the student may need to complete the work in braille.
- The need to verbalize and explain activities and board work in more detail.
- The role of the teacher of students with visual impairment and how you will be working on an itinerant schedule.
- The role of the O&M specialist, who may demonstrate and discuss travel techniques.
- Arrangements for getting materials or worksheets in braille or on tape.
- Arrangements for the times when it is appropriate for the itinerant teacher to work with the student.
- Information about how to contact you.

You will present a lot of information for teachers to absorb, especially if they have never taught a visually impaired student. You may find it helpful to provide

FIGURE 3.6

September 2, 2005

Re: Kathy Polanski

We have already discussed how to e-mail worksheets to my office. Any other work to be brailled for Kathy should be put in my mailbox with your name and the date you will use it in class. Please give it to me at least two days before you plan to use it. Assigning a responsible classmate to assist Kathy with work that is not brailled would be helpful.

Until Kathy becomes more proficient with computer skills, she will braille her work and give it to you. Put it in my mailbox, and I will interline (i.e., write out line for line) exactly what she has brailled and return it to you for grading.

Please contact me if problems arise. I will work with Kathy during the third period daily and can assist her as she needs help.

Helpful hints

1. There's little need to change your vocabulary. The use of words such as "look," "see," and "watch" is appropriate.
2. Verbalize, verbalize, verbalize. This is important because Kathy cannot see everything your sighted students can. Some teachers find it helpful to pretend they are doing a radio program. Please ask me any questions you have about how to describe objects and provide information.
3. Please be considerate as well as practical with Kathy's seating arrangements. Her orientation and mobility specialist will contact you regarding her seat assignments.
4. Standards for appropriate behavior are just as important for Kathy as for any other student.

Thanks for your cooperation. I'm available during lunch on Thursdays and after school on Mondays and Wednesdays for conferences. Leave a note in my mailbox or e-mail me if you need to talk with me.

Sincerely,

Jean Olmstead

Jean Olmstead
Itinerant teacher of students with visual impairments
320-4500
jeo@xxx.edu

some of the information in written form (see Figure 3.6). It is more important, however, to be available throughout the school year for consultation, answering questions, and providing reinforcement, either informally in the faculty room or formally in scheduled meetings (see Chapter 4 for more information on working with other school personnel). Making your availability known informally and formally is advisable too.

You may find it valuable to conduct an in-service program for the entire faculty, especially if a school has never before had a student who reads in braille. You can present more general information and demonstrate some equipment, adapted materials, and techniques. Showing a film, such as *What Do You Do When You See a Blind Person?* (2000) can also be effective.

School personnel and administrators also need information about working with a blind or visually impaired person. Give fact or tip sheets and helpful suggestions to administrators, counselors, secretaries, clerks, yard supervisors, custodians, cafeteria workers, and bus drivers. These can include pertinent information about students' visual functioning, special needs, and levels of independence.

Meeting with Teachers Whose Students Read Print

For students in secondary school who read print, you may choose to put a letter similar to the sample in Figure 3.7 in teachers' mailboxes before school starts so the teachers will know that they will have a visually impaired student in their classes. Copies of the letter should be distributed also to principals, vice principals, nurses, counselors, and other staff members who will be involved with the student. If some time will elapse between your distribution of the letter and your meeting the staff, you can attach a copy of your photograph to the letter to make it easier for teachers to recognize and find you.

Having the teachers complete a questionnaire similar to the one in Figure 3.8, which should accompany the letter you send, can give you necessary information. Be clear about when their responses should be in your mailbox. A second letter, similar to the one in Figure 3.9, can be given to pertinent personnel when you have established your schedule at the school.

Letters and e-mail messages are helpful but do not take the place of face-to-face meetings. In the case of a secondary school student, confer with the school administrator to schedule a group meeting at the beginning of the year with all your students' teachers. The administrator may suggest that you meet individually with each teacher during a conference period; however, a brief meeting after school is a more efficient use of your time. Also, meeting in a group may stimulate discussion of common concerns.

At the meeting, emphasize the fact that the classroom teachers are responsible for the visually impaired student just as they are responsible for other students in the class. Your role is to provide materials, instruction, and suggestions for techniques that will facilitate the visually impaired student's learning and participation in class activities. Discuss the student's visual condition and its implications, the student's strengths, what intervention techniques will enhance the student's participation in class, and what services you will provide. If a paraeducator will be working with the student, she or he should also attend the

FIGURE 3.7

August 28, 2005

Dear Mrs. Jones,

Paul Heinz, who is enrolled in your 1st period English class, is visually impaired. He has albinism and his eyes and skin are particularly sensitive to light. Paul needs the following accommodations:

- Preferential seating. He should not have to face bright lights or windows. A front row seat is best for him in most situations.
- Black-on-white copies of handouts. His reading speed and accuracy will increase if you give him worksheets with high contrast.
- Large-print texts. Some large-print books have been ordered for Paul's use. To help me deliver the texts, please complete the attached sheet.

I will be working with you and Paul this year to provide appropriate materials and adaptations to facilitate his participation in class activities. I will contact you again soon. If you have questions in the interim, you can put a note in my mailbox, send an e-mail, or call my office.

Sincerely,

Jean Olmstead

Jean Olmstead
Itinerant teacher of students with visual impairments
320-4500
jeo@xxx.edu

meeting and the teachers should receive clear information about the paraeducator's role (information about this topic is discussed in Chapter 4). If the teachers have already received written information from you, reiterate your schedule at the school, procedures for contacting you, and procedures for acquiring materials in large print if the student uses these. Offer to teach them how to enlarge worksheets using copiers on site; teaching them the skill and providing paper in the appropriate size may ensure that last-minute worksheets will be adapted to the appropriate size. Emphasize the fact that the student with a visual impairment should be graded according to the standards of the regular students, unless modifications of assignments are delineated in the student's IEP. Ask the teachers to inform you about any problems that seem to be related to the student's visual impairment.

For elementary school students, individual conferences may be arranged with each teacher, emphasizing the same information. In some school districts, teach-

FIGURE 3.8

To Mrs. Jones

Please complete this questionnaire and put it in my mailbox by 4th period, Sept. 7.

Thank you,

Jean Olmstead

Jean Olmstead
Itinerant teacher of students with visual impairments

1. Texts to be used in class:

Title and Edition	Author	Publisher	Copyright Date	ISBN No.	Dates Used
English Grammar Comp.	Warriner & Griffith	Harcourt	1998	0-12345-678-X	1st Sem.
Focus on Lit & Viewpoints	McFarland et al.	Houghton Mifflin	1999		2nd Sem.
Animal Farm	Orwell				

2. I use ☐ no ☑ some ☐ many worksheets.
3. ☑ Yes ☐ No My worksheets sometimes involve print smaller than the size used here.
4. ☑ Yes ☐ No I use the chalkboards, whiteboards, overhead projector, films, or PowerPoint presentations at least three times a week.
5. ☑ Yes ☐ No I would like to learn how to enlarge worksheets using the office copier.
6. The best time to confer with me is

   Day of week Tuesday

   Time/period Third

   Location Room 101

FIGURE 3.9

September 30, 2005

To teachers of the following visually impaired students:

George Harmon   Ann Sawyer   Rosie Chen   Kevin Rodriguez

I now have a schedule at Belmont:

Monday:	Period 3 Kevin Period 7 Ann
Wednesday:	Period 7 Ann
Thursday:	Period 3 Kevin Period 4 George Period 5 Rosie
Friday:	Period 7 Ann

I plan to be available for conferences regarding these students' participation in your class during lunch on Mondays or after school. Please contact me if your student experiences visual or academic difficulties in your class.

I have placed large-print copies of the *New World Dictionary* and *Roget's Thesaurus* in the library here. Please leave a note for me if your student will need to use an encyclopedia for research. I have a large-print copy that I could also put in the library.

Each of these students will benefit if you will provide materials, especially worksheets, that have good contrast. If your print is smaller than 12-point type, please enlarge the worksheets 125% for George, Rosie, and Kevin.

Ann's worksheets need to be enlarged 154 percent. I have put 11-x-17– inch paper in the paper tray of the main office copier for this purpose. Additional paper is stored in the phone room next to the nurse's room. When you enlarge material on the 11-x-17–inch paper, please trim pages to a manageable size and staple them.

We've discussed how to enlarge worksheets on your computer. If you want me to enlarge or copy worksheets for you, put black-and-white copies in my mailbox and include <u>your name and the date you will use them in class</u>. Check my Belmont schedule to make sure I'll be there in time to enlarge the work.

I've appreciated your cooperation in returning forms to me. I look forward to working with you this year.

Sincerely,

Jean Olmstead

Jean Olmstead
Itinerant teacher of students with visual impairments
320-4500
jeo@xxx.edu

ers have a workday before students report for school in the fall. You may arrange for a brief meeting on that day to introduce yourself, describe your students' special needs and intervention techniques, and deliver materials and equipment. A conference during which you and your students provide more detailed information can be arranged later.

General In-Service Programs

As a group, the itinerant teachers in a district may choose to present a more elaborate in-service program for classroom teachers, administrators, and support staff involved with visually impaired students. You may be able to reimburse teachers for their attendance or include refreshments to encourage their participation.

If possible, schedule the meeting at a site where much of your adaptive equipment and materials are located. Present general information regarding visual impairments and their impact on students' lives. You can then give the teachers eyeglasses that simulate their students' visual conditions and have them participate in activities that involve reading smudged blackboards, worksheets with poor contrast, and small print, and performing tasks specific to physical education and activities of daily living. Display equipment and devices, such as lamps, reading-writing stands, video magnifiers or closed circuit televisions, magnifiers, examples of assistive technology, and large-print and braille materials. Two or three students with visual impairments can describe their experiences and feelings. In addition, you can discuss the role of the itinerant teacher.

Presenting such an in-service program is a major project, but it is well worth the effort (Hudson, 1997; Holbrook et al., 2000). Keeping good records of organizational details from year to year eases the preparation. Classroom teachers who attend an in-service program are usually more understanding of their students' needs, more responsible about providing materials for transcribing, and more open to suggestions. They also may develop a heightened awareness of visual impairments, which may generate more referrals to your program.

Other In-Service Arrangements

The Students' Classmates

Another type of program can be provided to the students' classmates (especially at the elementary school level), who may be curious about the special materials in the classroom. Gear the program to the academic level of the class, and involve your student in the presentation—according to his or her abilities—to give the students experience and expertise in talking about their visual needs. The presentation may include a description of how the unimpaired eye works, information about how the students' eyes work, an explanation and demonstration of adaptive materials and techniques, suggestions for how the class members can be helpful, discussion of what the itinerant teacher and the students work on together, and time to answer classmates' questions. Elementary school students with access to computers can gain an understanding of braille in an enjoyable way at AFB's Braille Bug web site, designed especially for children (www.afb.org/braillebug).

Other School Staff

Your students will be interacting with other members of the school staff. Provide information or in-service training for administrators, counselors, secretaries and clerks, cafeteria workers, yard supervisors, and bus drivers about how the students' visual functioning will affect their interactions with staff members.

The Students' Families and Guardians

Sharing pertinent information with the students' families or guardians is always important, as is gathering information from them. They need to understand the implications of each individual student's visual condition, be aware of the materials and techniques used at school, and encourage the use of adaptations and special materials in all aspects of the student's life. Families know more about their children than anyone, and there is much you can learn about your student from family members. You can discuss information during telephone calls or home visits, at the IEP meeting, or at formally arranged meetings with the student's family.

These contacts are also an important time for you to learn about how the students function as a family member, taking part in the daily routine, leisure and activities of daily living skills, and other activities. Acknowledge the family's efforts in sharing the information and make suggestions and give information using a nonthreatening tone of voice and vocabulary.

Community Groups

The suggestions presented for in-service programs for other groups will assist you in presenting programs to interested community groups and organizations, such as parent-teacher associations and service organizations such as the Lions Club, Rotary Club, Kiwanis, or others. Showing videotapes or slides of different aspects of your program can enhance your presentation.

CREATING IEPS

An IEP for every student with visual impairments was originally mandated by the Education for All Handicapped Children Act (P.L. 94-142), which became law in 1975. The law is now referred to as IDEA, but the IEP continues to be the document that clearly delineates the type and amount of services your students will receive. The similar plan required for very young children who receive services from birth to age 3, the individualized family service plan, is discussed in Chapter 5. Because an IEP is the basis of educational programming for a student with special needs, and because addressing special needs typically requires the expertise of several individuals, the involvement of an educational team in creating an IEP is also mandated by law. (For more on collaborating with other members of the educational team, see Chapter 4, and; information about the IEP process from an O&M specialist's perspective can be found in Chapter 9.)

In the case of students for whom you provide the only special education service, you are the case manager and responsible for assessing students' needs and abilities, writing the IEP with input from all relevant parties, and arranging for and leading the IEP meeting. In the case of students who receive services from more than one special education teacher, the teachers responsible for what is considered the students' impairment with the greatest impact on their education assume these duties, with input from the other specialist teachers involved with the students. In these instances, your role is to provide pertinent information on areas that relate to and are affected by the students' visual conditions, write goals and objectives, provide consultation, and attend the IEP meeting. If the students receive only monitoring services from you, you may not write your own goals and objectives since the special accommodations you recommend, such as preferential seating or being able to focus longer on objects, should be used on a continuing basis. The classroom teachers should schedule a meeting with the students' educational team before the IEP is written to collaborate on appropriate goals for students. The classroom teacher can then write the goals and objectives and add your name to the appropriate page of the IEP.

IEP meetings must be scheduled at a time when the students' parents or guardians will be able to attend. A special education administrator or on-site administrator should also attend the meetings. The students' classroom teachers should be invited; it is now mandatory that at least one general education teacher be present at the meeting. The students should be present when their participation is appropriate.

Each district has its own requirements and deadlines for IEP conferences. Preparation for conferences and compilation of input for IEPs are both time-consuming and important. Therefore, if your conferences are scheduled for November, begin your assessments as soon as school starts in the fall.

To expedite the process, establish priorities among the areas to be assessed, using information from previous IEPs, observations, and input from teachers. Focus on the students' immediate needs and functional levels. For example, if a student's IEP indicates that a particular skill has been mastered, assess that area again in the fall to determine whether the student is still competent at it. Important information can also be obtained from observing the student in school activities and consulting with other members of the school staff and the student's parents or guardians.

You and the IEP team need to work together to set realistic goals and benchmarks. Remember that the classroom teachers are responsible for the bulk of your students' instruction and that your role is to provide services related to the students' needs that result from their visual impairments. Sharing the results of your assessments with the teachers in either written or verbal form can help them provide appropriate activities and instruction for the visually impaired students. (Assessments are discussed in later sections of this chapter.)

The following list of sample annual goals, and the short-term objectives relating to them, can assist you in writing your own:

Sample Goals and Objectives

Goal: The student will demonstrate the ability to use adaptive materials and equipment.

Objectives: The student will

1. locate information in a 12-volume thesaurus, a 24-volume dictionary, and a 10-volume encyclopedia (or a 7-volume math book) . . . by [date] with 100 percent accuracy over five consecutive sessions.
2. operate a video magnifier for reading and writing . . . by [date] with 100 percent accuracy over seven consecutive sessions.
3. demonstrate the ability to enlarge materials on a copier . . . by [date] with 100 percent accuracy over seven consecutive sessions.

Goal: The student will demonstrate the proper care of eyeglasses.

Objectives: The student will

1. clean the eyeglasses with an appropriate amount of solution, using the cleaning cloth correctly . . . by [date] with 100 percent accuracy over five consecutive sessions.
2. demonstrate the proper way to place eyeglasses on a surface . . . by [date] with 100 percent accuracy over five consecutive sessions.

Goal: The student will demonstrate knowledge of eye care.

Objectives: The student will

1. describe the roles of an ophthalmologist, an optometrist, and an optician . . . by [date] with 100 percent accuracy over seven consecutive sessions.
2. describe a typical eye examination . . . by [date] with 100 percent accuracy over five consecutive sessions.
3. list pertinent information to give and questions to ask an ophthalmologist or optometrist . . . by [date] with 100 percent accuracy over eight consecutive sessions.
4. demonstrate the ability to interpret data on an eye report . . . by [date] with 100 percent accuracy over 10 consecutive sessions.

5. maintain records of his or her eye care . . . by [date] with 100 percent accuracy over five consecutive sessions.

Goal: The student will begin to plan for transition from high school.

Objectives: The student will

1. enroll with the state department of rehabilitation and list [number] ways in which the department can provide assistance . . . by [date] with 100 percent accuracy over five consecutive sessions.
2. begin a personal file of important information, telephone numbers and addresses of agencies, resources, and the like . . . by [date] with 100 percent accuracy over seven consecutive sessions.
3. obtain information about services for people with visual impairments at four colleges . . . by [date] with 100 percent accuracy over five consecutive sessions.

At the IEP meeting, discuss the student's progress in attaining the goals from the previous IEP. The information should be readily available on the progress report cards or report cards you've sent home according to your district's policies. This discussion will lead to the unattained goals being carried over, if they are still considered appropriate, and new ones being added to the IEP.

The amount of time required to provide services to the student will be determined and documented on the IEP form at the meeting. This and the type of services provided will vary according to the assessed needs of the student and should reflect the time required to achieve the goals agreed on by the IEP team.

Some students with visual impairments may require only minimal intervention. Monitoring services may be specified for periods such as 60 minutes a month or even as little as 20 minutes a quarter. Monitoring students entails utilizing the specified time to adapt materials as necessary; observe the students in different activities; and consult with school personnel, the students' families or guardians, eye care specialists, and community resources regarding the students' special needs.

Other students will need direct contact with the itinerant teacher in addition to monitoring. The time required to achieve the IEP goals can vary from 45 minutes a quarter to two or more hours every day. For these students, specify minutes for monitoring on the IEP in addition to the minutes specified for direct services. The number of minutes for monitoring should reflect the time needed to adapt class materials; to observe the student in all aspects of school activities; and to consult with school personnel, the students' families, and eye care specialists. It is essential to protect the time for providing these services to ensure proper support for the student in his or her daily activities. If a transcriber or program assistant is available to adapt most of the materials, the total minutes for monitoring will be fewer than if you are directly responsible for brailling, enlarging, or taping the materials.

For an elementary school student who is academically oriented and reading braille, learning pertinent skills may entail two hours of direct service per day and an additional 80 minutes of monitoring per day. This amount of time may seem excessive to other school personnel, but the concentrated instruction at this stage can be conducive to learning many of the skills necessary for more independence in later years.

For students who receive other special education services or are enrolled in special classes, their case managers coordinate the creation of the IEP and subsequent conferences. Because these teachers usually have to coordinate the IEP conference with many people, you should let them know when you will be available for the conference (you can use a form similar to the one in Figure 3.10). More information on serving students with visual and multiple impairments can be found in Chapter 6.

In some districts, all elementary school teachers are required to have a conference with each parent in the fall. Whenever possible, schedule your IEP conference in conjunction with the meeting about the student's first report card.

FIGURE 3.10

To Ms. Collins

Re IEP for Bert Phillips

Date 2/27/06

I need to be present at the IEP conference.

If possible, please consider these preferences when scheduling the conference:

Best times: Wednesdays before 9

Mondays between 1 and 2

Please avoid Thursdays after 2:30.

Out of town at a conference: March 15-18

Please let me know as soon as the IEP date, time, and site have been confirmed.
Thanks for your consideration.

Jean

Jean Olmstead
Itinerant teacher of students with visual impairments
320-4500
jeo@xxx.edu

You will learn more about the student's progress, the classroom teacher will learn about the IEP's goals and objectives, and the parent or guardian will have to attend only one meeting to hear what both of you have to say.

Having all the students' teachers present at the IEP conference may not always be feasible, particularly at the secondary school level. Therefore, the teachers' completion of the form in Figure 3.11 can provide important information for those present at the conference. It is, however, mandated that at least one general education teacher attend the meeting.

The requirements of the IEP may have specific implications when a student enters your program in the middle of the year. When a new student begins a special class or resource room program midyear, he or she can be more easily absorbed into the existing structure. However, in an itinerant program, adding a student may entail the teacher traveling to a new site and scheduling additional time for direct instruction or monitoring services, or both: adaptation of materials, consultation, and observations. In larger programs, teachers may be able to adjust their schedules as a group so that a new student can be absorbed with no disruption of service to other students. However, difficulties can arise if the student is entering a program served by one itinerant teacher whose schedule is full.

The members of the IEP team have a mandated responsibility to plan services according to the assessed needs of each student. IEPs should indicate the actual amount of support and instruction required for the student's successful participation in the classroom and attainment of competence in the specific skills related to his or her visual impairment, rather than reflect how much time the itinerant teacher has available considering the other demands on his or her time. When students' needs require more time than you have, hiring additional support for the program (such as a part-time itinerant teacher or a transcriber) or providing placement in an alternative program for students with visual impairments is necessary.

ASSESSING REFERRALS

Itinerant teachers typically are responsible for assessing referrals to the program for students with visual impairments. Referrals may come from several sources: parents, eye care specialists, school committees, or casual conversations with members of the school staff.

Each school district has its own regulations about paper work for handling referrals. Be sure that you understand and follow those rules so that there is no invasion of a student's privacy and any required consent from a parent or guardian is obtained in a timely fashion. The following description of the process may or may not be applicable to your district's policies.

The student's file or cumulative folder may yield some information about his or her vision screenings and perhaps even referrals to eye care specialists. It is helpful to have a form such as the one in Figure 3.12 to summarize and stan-

FIGURE 3.11

To Mrs. Smith

Re Roy Grey

Date 1/7/06

An IEP meeting for Roy Grey is scheduled for Monday, Jan. 17 at 1:00 in Room 209. I realize it may be difficult for you to attend but please provide information to Roy's parent(s) about his participation in your class.

Indicate below if you plan to attend the meeting and add pertinent comments. Please return this form to my mailbox by 10 a.m., Monday, January 17.

Thank you,

Jean Olmstead

Jean Olmstead
Itinerant teacher of students with visual impairments
320-4500
jeo@xxx.edu

Sorry I can't be at the meeting. Roy seems to be a smart kid who works below his ability. He needs to stop getting plugged into the taunting of his peers. Absences and incomplete assignments are affecting his grade.

Current grade: D+

Mrs. Grey should contact me for a conference.

J. Smith

FIGURE 3.12

Referral Intake Form

Student's name Matthew Takemoto Date of birth 4/16/92

Grade 4 Social Security no. 222-34-5667

School Hillbridge Referred by Mrs. Takemoto Telephone no. 333-7788

Year 2003-04 Counselor/teacher Mr. Webster Room no. 17

Aide none Nurse Hilda Chan Investigating teacher J. Olmstead

Parents'/guardians' names George and Mary Takemoto

Address 8822 Westchester Ave., Smalton, VA 34327 Telephone no. 333-7788

Mother's work phone 777-2334 (cell) Father's work phone 322-5893

Physician Dr. Manson Eye care specialist Dr. Elizabeth Bench

Address 834 9th Street, Smalton Address 3375 Hillside Blvd., Hangton

Telephone no. 333-5912 Telephone no. 544-7926

Low vision clinic n/a

Address n/a Telephone no. n/a

Date of last eye exam 11/4/03 Eye report requested on 11/20/03 (by nurse)

Visual condition myopia (?)

Visual acuity

Uncorrected		Corrected		Field	
O.D.	20/350	O.D.	20/80	O.D.	full
O.S.	20/400	O.S.	20/100	O.S.	full
O.U.	20/350	O.U.	20/100	O.U.	full

Information from parents/guardians, school personnel, doctors, cumulative and health folders (specify source and date)

10/15/03 Ms. Takemoto called Hilda with concern that Matthew said it was hard to "see" things at school. Hilda asked that Matthew have an eye exam. Hilda left me a note re: Matthew's referral.

(continued)

FIGURE 3.12 (continued)

Case Recording

Student's name Matthew Takemoto Teacher J. Olmstead Page 2

Date	*Comments*
1/30	Cumulative folder
	2/98 M. in school in Alabama. M. referred for assessment: possible learning disability. Not working up to potential.
	6/98 Assessment: no learning disability. "Possible underachiever."
	6/99 M. to repeat 1st grade.
	9/02 M. enrolls at Hillbridge Report cards indicate average grades except for high marks in math. Satisfactory marks in behavior.
	Health folder
	2/98 Vision screening: reduced acuity
	2/99 Vision screening: M. now wearing glasses. Acuities noted as listed above.
11/2	Phone call to Mrs. Takemoto. Her concerns: M. sometimes got closer to things than seemed normal, but parents didn't think it was a major problem. This year for first time M. seemed to have more problems, complaining now and then about things being hard to see at school. Glad that she's taking M. to eye doctor. Told her we need to know that M. has best possible correction. Talked about process and time lines for functional vision assessment. Once we receive a vision report from this exam, we'll have information about whether or not to conduct FVA. If we do the FVA, an IEP meeting will be held and we can discuss then how we might assist M. in the school setting.
12/14	Call to Hilda; vision report not received yet. H. to call dr. to remind about importance of report.

dardize the information you find as you peruse the records and obtain additional information from sources such as parents or guardians, school staff, and physicians. Basic information should include the student's name; birth date; address; home number; grade; school; teacher's or counselor's name; names of parents or guardians, their addresses, and home and work phone numbers; results of vision screenings; names, phone numbers and addresses of the physician and eye care specialist; and the date of the referral. At the end of the form you can jot down comments and other pertinent information, such as current IEPs and highlights of the student's participation in school activities.

If the information in a student's file indicates the possibility that the student will be eligible for your services, ask the nurse to request a vision report. If this is not possible, you may need to request the report, although this may not be the preferred practice in your district. To do so, contact the parents or guardians yourself, explain the situation, and have them complete a release of information form for the eye care specialist so that you can request a report (your district will have its own release of information form). Mail it to the eye care specialist with your state's vision report form. It is essential that you obtain this report to ensure that the student is currently wearing the best possible correction.

If the vision report indicates that the student has reduced visual functioning after the best possible correction, complete your district's form for permission to conduct an assessment and send it home for the parent or guardian to sign. Once the form has been returned to you, you have a specified number of calendar days, depending on your district, to complete the assessment and conduct an IEP meeting to discuss the results. Just because you, an itinerant teacher of visually impaired students, are conducting the assessment does not necessarily mean that the student will be best served in his or her home school. The IEP team may recommend placement in a resource room program or a state school for visually impaired students.

Once the assessment plan is completed, make arrangements with the classroom teacher for an observation. It's preferable to ask the teacher not to tell the student that you're there to observe him or her. This ensures that the student will not be uncomfortable while you're in the classroom and may follow his or her more usual routine. After this anonymous observation you can begin the standardized functional vision assessment.

If the IEP team determines that the student is not eligible for services from the program for visually impaired students, file the paperwork in your office files with that of similar students. It is not uncommon for a student to be referred again; and being able to consult the original records can be helpful.

Conducting Functional Vision Assessments

Functional vision assessments are conducted to assess students' current visual function and determine the need for adaptations or instruction, or both, to improve participation in classroom activities. These assessments are currently mandated for placement in the program for visually impaired students and every three years thereafter. If the student is receiving additional special education services, it's helpful to coordinate the functional vision assessments performed every three years with other such evaluations.

Each established program for students with visual impairments has its own procedure for conducting the assessments. If you are the only teacher in the district, you can use the assessment forms and procedures you received in your teacher training course until you are ready to create your own.

In a new program you will need to purchase different acuity charts for near, 10 feet, and 20 feet, some with letters and some with symbols. It is helpful to have continuous reading cards with different type sizes. Other equipment required includes penlights, occluders, and tests for color vision and stereopsis. Items such as windup toys or pompoms are useful for assessing tracking. Peruse catalogs to find items helpful in assessing a student with limited communication skills. Purchase a tote bag or light crate to carry all the supplies to your teaching sites.

You probably have sample functional vision assessment protocols from your teacher training program, or your district may have its own form. Make a template of the form you prefer to make it easier to write the reports. Store written functional vision assessments in your computer. Doing so can make report writing less complicated. You can copy descriptions of conditions and other standard information from a report for a student with an eye condition similar to the one you're assessing now. Specific information will be different for each individual, but this is nevertheless simpler than starting from the beginning for each report. (For detailed information about conducting functional vision assessments, see Anthony, 2000, and Koenig et al., 2000.) Conduct the indoor part of the assessment in a room with lighting conditions similar to those of the student's classroom. It should also be large enough to measure off 20 feet for the distance assessment. Wear plain, dark-colored clothing that won't distract from the objects you want the student to observe. Conduct the outside assessment more than once, in different levels of light, observing how the student gathers important information around the school's building or campus. Assessment performed at the student's home can also provide pertinent, helpful information.

Many factors are involved when conducting functional vision assessments. Using a form such as the Status of Functional Vision Assessment (see Figure 3.13) enables you to check at a glance the areas completed, those partly done, and those not yet addressed. You can easily add or delete sections of this form as needed. Additional hints for conducting functional vision assessments can be found in Chapter 13.

Conducting Learning Media Assessments

Learning media assessments are conducted to determine what sensory channels, methods, and materials for gathering information and accomplishing learning

FIGURE 3.13

Status of Functional Vision Assessment

Name Raymond Tan Year 2005-06

	Assess	Done
Condition/Appearance		
Glasses	✓	✓
Health	✓	✓
Visual abnormalities	✓	✓
Muscle imbalance		
Basic Responses		
Abnormal visual behavior	✓	
Reaction to light	✓	
Blink	✓	✓
Pupillary response	✓	✓
Eye preference/dominance		✓
Attending to environment	✓	✓
Fixation and Localization		
Eye contact	✓	✓
Patterns	✓	
Horizontal	✓	
Vertical	✓	
Circular	✓	
Oblique	✓	
Toward/away	✓	
Scanning	✓	
Fields		
Peripheral	✓	✓
Central	✓	✓
Stereopsis/Binocularity		
Depth perception	✓	
Suppression	✓	
Color Vision		
Match/Holmgren		
Name		
Ishihara		
Mobility		
Balance/posture/gait		
Independence		
Settings		
Routes/reversals		
Follow directions		
Depth perception		
Travel aids		

	Assess	Done
Acuity		
With correction		
Distance	✓	✓
Intermediate	✓	✓
Near	✓	✓
Without correction		
Distance	✓	✓
Intermediate	✓	✓
Near	✓	✓
School setting		
Distance	✓	✓
Intermediate	✓	✓
Near	✓	✓
Reading		
Print size	✓	
Angle and distance	✓	
Level	✓	
Length of attending	✓	
Visual Discrimination		
Size	✓	
Shape	✓	
Outlines	✓	
Classification	✓	
Picture details	✓	
Visual Perception		
Figure/ground		
Form constancy		
Shape	✓	
Size	✓	
Position	✓	
Visual Motor		
Fine eye/hand	✓	
Writing	✓	
Gross eye/foot		
Illumination		
Indoors	✓	
Outdoors	✓	
Time of day	✓	
Photophobia/glare	✓	
Light adaptation	✓	
Night vision		

tasks are best suited to the student's needs and abilities. A learning media assessment will provide information about the student's most efficient means of gathering information: visual, tactile, or auditory; the media the student will use to accomplish learning tasks; and the media to be used for reading and writing. Conduct these assessments carefully over time and at different times of the day. You may find that at the end of the day a student exhibits visual fatigue not evident in assessments conducted earlier in the day. Involve the student's parents or guardians in the process; interviewing them can provide valuable observations about the student's visual functioning.

Learning media assessments are mandated in IDEA and provide critical information for the student, the family or guardians, the classroom teachers, and you. If your assessment indicates no need for instruction in reading braille, you will need to document that information generally on the signature page of the IEP. You will conduct formal learning media assessments according to your district's time frame, but more informal assessments on a continuing basis are necessary to ensure that students are using the media best suited to their visual functioning needs. (For detailed information on learning media assessments, see Koenig et al., 2000, and Koenig and Holbrook, 1995.)

Reporting Assessment Results

When all portions of a student's assessment are complete, the results need to be converted into recommendations for the student's educational program and for specific services to be provided to the student. The Assessed Needs Checklist shown in Figure 3.14 provides a simple way to summarize and present the recommendations to the IEP team.

ARRANGING FOR STANDARDIZED TESTS

Arrange to have your district's testing office automatically send you each year a copy of the testing schedule or schedules so that you will know when standardized tests will be administered to your students' classes. The accommodations used during standardized testing must be ones that the student routinely uses for classroom work. Some visually impaired students can take the tests with their classmates without affecting their scores. For others, it's important to delineate any modifications to the standardized testing arrangements on each student's IEP. Make arrangements with the testing office to have the tests available in braille, large print, tape, or other form desirable for your student and provide for extended testing time. A general rule of thumb is to allow one-and-a-half times the usual amount of time for students using large print and twice the usual time for students using braille. When possible, your students should be tested at the same time as their peers. In most instances, the students should not use the an-

FIGURE 3.14

Assessed Needs Checklist

Student Virgil Costos Birthdate 7/20/99

Assessed by J. Olmstead Assessment dates 10/20, 10/23, 10/28, 2005

This student has an assessed need for the following services, methods, media, materials, and equipment, in order to access core and/or alternative curriculum, and to meet unique needs as addressed in IEP goals.

V.I. program option for least restrictive environment: ✓ Itinerant __ Resource room __ Special day class for visually impaired students __ Special school

Services: ✓ Teacher of the visually impaired __ O&M specialist __ Transcriber __ Notetaker __ Describer __ Reader __ Paraeducator __ Assistive technology service

Literacy medium (P-primary, S-secondary): __ Braille P Print (best size: 20 point) __ Nonreader

Learning medium (P-primary, S-secondary): __ Tactile __ Auditory P Visual

Instructional strategies: __ One-on-one __ Small group __ Concrete experiences

Instructional materials: __ Manipulatives __ Models __ Real objects __ Raised-line drawings __ Accessible books __ Recordings __ Switches P Reading/writing aids __ Organizational aids

Specialized paper: __ Raised-line ✓ Dark-line __ NCR __ Braille __ Tactile imaging __ Slate __ Computer ✓ Nonglare __ Hi-contrast __ Low-contrast __ Colored

Specialized instructional materials for: __ Concept development __ Sensory development ✓ Academics ✓ Communication __ Visual efficiency __ Listening skills __ Technology __ Leisure skills __ Orientation & Mobility __ Physical education __ Social development __ Functional curriculum __ Daily living __ Vocational skills __ Music/art

Low-vision and visual efficiency aids: ✓ Rx lenses ✓ Magnifiers __ Monocular/telescope __ Binoculars __ Special lights & lighting __ Light box ✓ Desktop easel __ Tilt desk __ Marking pens

Travel aids: __ Long white cane __ Electronic travel aid __ Sunglasses __ Visor/hat __ Maps __ Compass

Equipment and access technology: __ Braillewriter ✓ Video magnifier
✓ Computer (__ laptop ✓ desktop) ✓ Monitor __ Printer __ Talking software
__ Screen access software/hardware __ Braille translation software/hardware
__ Braille display __ Braille input device __ Braille embosser __ Scanner __ OCR
__ Braille notetaker __ External disk drive __ Talking book player __ CD playback device
__ Tape recorder/player (__ regular __ adapted __ 4-track __ voice-activated __ switch-activated)
__ Calculator (__ regular __ large print __ voice output __ scientific) __ Electronic references
__ Other: ______________________________

Source: Adapted with permission from the Oakland, California, Unified School District.

swer sheets provided by the district's testing office. They should mark their answers directly on the adapted copy of the test or use a special answer sheet in braille or large print. You or another adult, such as a paraeducator, will need to transfer the responses to the original answer sheet. Any special accommodations should be noted in the students' folders with the scores.

Secondary school students may take tests such as the SAT or ACT, which may not be listed on the testing schedule because they are not administered by the district's testing office. At each site, consult with the school's testing coordinator so that provisions can be made with the proper agency for your students to be tested. You may be expected to send with the registration forms a copy of the student's IEP that spells out the special accommodations you're requesting. In most instances you will be responsible for arranging and administering these tests. If the testing is done on a school day, the student will not be attending classes. You may choose to give the test on another day, such as a Saturday; if so, you'll need to arrange for an appropriate testing site. Also arrange with your supervisor for taking compensatory time off or being paid at your per diem rate for this additional time.

DEVELOPING TRANSITION PLANS

Transition services promote movement from school to postschool activities, involving advanced education or training, integrated or supported employment, independent living, and community participation. IEPs for students must include a statement of needed transition services at an age determined by your district policies or by the IEP team. The planning process focuses on the unique needs and goals of the students regarding further education or training, employment outcomes, housing options, and social networks.

Transition IEPs must usually be devised when students are in 11th grade unless your district guidelines are different. The transition IEP includes planning components and timelines for activities. As with the IEPs, it must be reviewed at least annually. Transition IEPs indicate the people responsible for these activities, including students and their parents or guardians.

Your school district may have a transition department or unit; you should notify the department when the students are at the appropriate age to begin planning. You have information about some options available to visually impaired students; members of the transition department generally have a wealth of additional information and suggestions to share. They will usually conduct the transition IEP meetings. The department may also offer an employability assessment to determine students' abilities and interests. If your district has no transition department, counselors from your state department of rehabilitation could be helpful partners in creating transition IEPs.

If students have continuing transition needs, they can remain in school through age 21. Their IEPs should reflect goals for the attainment of the necessary skills. These students will receive their diplomas when they have acquired the skills and are ready to leave the district; some districts allow the students to walk through graduation with their peers, even though they will not receive a diploma until later. For those students who need many hours of service from the itinerant teacher, this option should be presented to and discussed with the students and their families or guardians as early as possible: at least by the ninth grade.

The transition process will certainly be eased if the students have been gradually taking responsibility for their special needs, such as participating with teachers in in-service training, ordering adapted texts, and acquiring daily living skills. It is very helpful if students have observed or shadowed adults with visual impairments at work before the transition process begins. These observations—arranged by you as study trips—enable students to have more understanding about how they can use adaptations on the job. Additional resources for helping students learn about jobs performed by people who are blind or visually impaired and acquire job-related skills include AFB's CareerConnect web site (www.afb.org/careerconnect) and *The Transition Tote System* (Wolffe & Johnson, 1997).

PERFORMING UNSCHEDULED ACTIVITIES

Your regular schedule will need to be interrupted occasionally for activities such as attending IEP conferences and administering standardized tests. Flexibility is crucial for an itinerant teacher. Adjustments may also need to be made for spending extensive time with a student, conducting home visits, attending eye examinations with students, and going on study trips.

These necessary special activities often conflict with scheduled time with other students. You and the other teachers in your program should, along with your supervisor, adopt a rule about whether or not these missed sessions should be rescheduled. In general, this is not valuable: if you have to make up all the missed sessions, you could find yourself doing only make-up lessons, and therefore missing more sessions with other students. Since this could be a very vicious circle, it's usually best not to reschedule missed sessions.

Visits to Schools and Homes

Observing each of your students is necessary to facilitate their participation in school activities. It may be advisable to spend a week or so, usually at the beginning of the school year, in the classroom of one or more of your students whose impairments necessitate a high level of adaptation. Your interventions and observations at this time can be crucial in assisting students to form good habits regarding the proper use of materials, equipment, and adaptive techniques. You can also model for school personnel, especially paraeducators, appropriate techniques for assisting the students. Your understanding of and involvement in students' daily activities will enable you to make suggestions and answer questions from a practical viewpoint. In the ideal situation, your interaction with the students should taper off so that at the end of this period you can withdraw, assured that students are participating as fully as possible in their classes' activities.

A home visit may be a comfortable way to share observations and information with your students' parents or guardians. You may also choose to deliver bulky items, including reading-writing stands or volumes of books lent to the students for the year, and in that way also observe students interacting at home.

Eye Examinations

Attending eye examinations with your students and their parents or guardians can provide you with important information that is usually not available in written reports. A general rule is to attend at least one eye examination and all low vision examinations with each student. During the examinations, take notes, ask questions, and discuss your observations of the students' visual functioning with the eye care specialist.

Specific suggestions for maximizing your participation, as well as your students' and their families, include the following:

Hints for Eye Examinations

- Tell parents that you wish to be notified when an eye examination is scheduled, so you can accompany them or obtain a report.
- Be prepared for a student's eye examination. Collect notes regarding the student's visual functioning, and make a list of questions you may want to ask the eye care specialist.
- Prepare your student for the examination. Explain the purpose and procedures, and elicit his or her cooperation. Guide the student in formulating questions, and help the student to verbalize his or her abilities and needs (especially before a low vision examination).
- Prepare the student's parents or guardians for the examination by encouraging them to list their observations and concerns.
- For some students, especially those with multiple impairments, ask school staff members for their lists of observations and questions about the students' visual functioning.
- Bring classroom materials to examinations so that students can use them to demonstrate their abilities in a classroom situation.

- Sometimes an audiotape of an examination is helpful for the student and his or her family or guardian to review; be certain to get participants' permission to make a tape.
- Ophthalmologists and optometrists are busy; sometimes it can take weeks to receive a written report. If your district uses a standardized eye report form, take it with you to the appointment; most eye care specialists are willing to complete a form on the spot if they are asked to do so. Bring a stamped, preaddressed envelope to leave with the receptionist in case they cannot complete the form the same day.
- Do not hesitate to call an eye care specialist for clarification if you need it, but be sure a signed form for the release of information is in the specialist's file on the student.
- Call or visit the student's home a few days after the appointment to discuss the examination with your student and his or her parents or guardians. You may be able to answer their questions or alleviate their concerns.

Study Trips

Often there is only one visually impaired student in each school. Taking the students from different schools in the itinerant program on group study trips allows them to get to know each other. When study trips are scheduled frequently (five to seven a year), a healthy sense of camaraderie may develop among the students. Trips may also be scheduled for individual students for various reasons, such as exploring a particular job or participating in orientation to a new school.

When these trips are specially arranged with the visually impaired students in mind, they can be of immense value. The needs of your group may lead you to visit community and private organizations, local attractions, companies that employ visually impaired workers, or facilities that serve visually impaired people. You may also choose to schedule group meetings at which students can interact with a visually impaired adult who is a positive role model or participate in group counseling or recreational activities.

Be aware that many special activities require transportation. Some itinerant teachers transport students in their own cars. If you decide to do so, make sure you clearly understand your district's insurance coverage and arrangements concerning legal liability while traveling, both inside and outside the district, with students in your car. If you are concerned about the legal ramifications of using your car for this purpose, you should arrange alternative modes of transportation for such trips.

PERFORMING END-OF-YEAR ACTIVITIES

Performing certain activities at the end of each school year will be to your benefit and that of your students and will help you prepare for the following school year. Among these activities are the following:

End-of-the-Year Tasks

- Get lists of textbooks to be used for the coming year, as described in the section Providing Textbooks.
- Consult with appropriate school personnel regarding visually impaired students' placements for the coming year. Elementary school administrators can be helpful in assigning students to teachers whose classroom structures will facilitate inclusion. Occasionally, you may be able to influence secondary school students' schedules at this time, but usually special arrangements cannot be made until about two weeks before school starts in the fall, when the schools' master schedules are finalized.
- Meet with the other itinerant teachers in the program, and the appropriate administrator if necessary, to determine caseloads for the coming year, as discussed in the section Establishing Caseloads. If your caseload for the coming year includes students who were not on your caseload for the year that is ending, have conferences with the students' current teachers of students who are visually impaired to discuss the students' abilities and special needs.
- During the last month of school, gradually take materials that are not being used to your office. Doing so will reduce the number of items you have to transport during the last days.
- Allot time during the last two weeks to collect remaining materials and equipment and return them to your office or storage area. Some items may be left in the students' homes or at the schools for summer school use. Returning all other materials ensures that they will be available for use during the following year.
- Some high schools have a special examination schedule. Get the closing bulletins from your secondary schools so that you can adjust your schedule accordingly.
- Allow time to update files and forms so that students' records will be organized for the beginning of the next school year.
- Acknowledge school staff and classroom teachers' efforts on behalf of the visually impaired students. Thank the teachers for their cooperation in getting materials to you to be transcribed and for utilizing adaptive techniques in the classrooms. Recognition of their acceptance and help can foster their willingness to assist other students who are visually impaired.

Although this chapter contains what may seem like an overwhelming number of suggestions for activities encountered during a typical school year, remember that these activities are scattered over a long period of time. As you gain experience as an itinerant teacher, you will become more comfortable in performing these activities as a regular part of your role.

REFERENCES

AFB Directory of services for blind and visually impaired persons in the United States and Canada (27th ed.). (2005). New York: American Foundation for the Blind.

Anthony, T. A. (2000). Performing a functional low vision assessment. In D'Andrea, F. M., & Farrenkopf, C. (Eds.). *Looking to learn: Promoting literacy for students with low vision.* New York: AFB Press.

Holbrook, M. C., Croft, J., & Kline, C. (2000). Presenting information to the general public. In Koenig, A. J., & Holbrook, M. C. (Eds.). *Foundations of education* (2nd ed.). Volume II: *Instructional strategies for teaching children and youths with visual impairments* (pp. 753–770). New York: AFB Press.

Hudson, L. J. (1997). *Classroom collaboration.* Watertown, MA: Perkins School for the Blind.

Koenig, A. J., & Holbrook, M. C. (1995). *Learning media assessment of students with visual impairments: A resource guide for teachers* (2nd ed.). Austin, TX: Texas School for the Blind and Visually Impaired.

Koenig, A. J., Holbrook, M. C., Corn, A. L., DePriest, L. B., Erin, J. N., & Presley, I. (2000). Specialized assessments for student with visual impairments. In Koenig, A. J., & Holbrook, M. C. (Eds.). *Foundations of education* (2nd ed.). Volume II: *Instructional strategies for teaching children and youths with visual impairments* (pp. 103–172). New York: AFB Press.

Lewis, S., & Allman, C. B. (2000). *Seeing eye to eye: An administrator's guide to students with low vision.* New York: AFB Press.

What do you do when you see a blind person? [videotape]. (2000). New York: AFB Press.

When you have a visually impaired student in your classroom. (2002). New York: AFB Press.

Wolfe, K. E., & Johnson, D. (1997). *The transition tote system: Navigating the rapids of life.* Louisville, KY: American Printing House for the Blind.

CHAPTER 4

Facilitating Participation in Educational Activities

Students who are visually impaired who receive assistance from an itinerant teacher are usually enrolled in their own neighborhood schools or bused to other schools with special education classes. They are enrolled in these schools because they can benefit from extensive participation in the schools' activities and have the necessary skills to utilize special materials and techniques to meet their visual and other learning needs when the itinerant teacher is not at the school. The students' successful integration depends, in part, on the schools' commitment to inclusion and on the effective intervention of the itinerant teacher. The school has the primary responsibility for the visually impaired student; you give specialized support by providing individualized instruction, adapted materials, and specialized equipment; observing the student periodically and sharing conclusions based on your observations; and consulting with other school personnel.

INDIVIDUALIZED INSTRUCTION

The amount of time you spend with a visually impaired student depends on his or her needs. Careful assessment, which includes observation, consultation with school personnel and the family, and the use of checklists and evaluation tools, provides the data for the IEP team to determine the amount of time you will

---

The section in this chapter on working with paraeducators was contributed by Lori Cassels; information on music education was contributed by Frances Mary D'Andrea; and material on adapted physical education was contributed by Mary Alice Ross.

work with the student. You may see one student once a week for 30 minutes and another student for two hours each day.

When and where you see the student depends on the student's schedule and the availability of school facilities. Sometimes working in the classroom is appropriate; in that instance, you will want to be aware that the classroom teacher is in charge and you are there as support for the student who is visually impaired. This arrangement works best when your lessons dovetail with the class's activities. In other situations, you and the student will work in another room assigned by a school administrator.

Before the advent of IEPs, the development of the concept of low vision and all it entails, and the creation of a compensatory curriculum in the form of the extended core curriculum, teachers of students with visual impairments often assumed responsibility for teaching their students subjects such as reading, math, or spelling. Now, however, this has changed in most instances. In most cases you will not have the time to provide instruction in areas that can be easily addressed by other school staff members. Your role is to provide instruction in areas related to and affected by the student's visual impairment. The content of your lessons depends on the assessed needs of the student in the following areas: compensatory academic skills including communication modes, social interaction skills, recreation and leisure skills, independent living skills, career education, use of assistive technology, visual efficiency skills, and orientation and mobility (O&M). You are not responsible for teaching math. However, you may be involved in the math class to teach new symbols to a student who reads in braille. When teaching other skills, you will want to take advantage of opportunities to incorporate current class assignments. For example, when teaching a student to copy from the board, use the vocabulary words that the class is studying to enhance your student's familiarity with the words. The exception to this rule, however, is teaching braille reading and writing; as noted earlier, this instruction cannot be separated from direct instruction in the reading and writing process (see, for example, Wormsley & D'Andrea, 1997).

Flexibility is an important attribute of the itinerant teacher. You may be prepared to present a specific lesson only to discover that providing instruction in or assistance with a concept or assignment introduced in the student's class is more important. If the student requires more on-the-spot instruction than you anticipated, a reassessment is indicated. If the student's needs seem to be related to or caused by the visual impairment, it is advisable that you increase your time with the student or even consider alternative placement. If his or her needs appear to stem from causes unrelated to vision, the IEP team should consider other sources of extra support in the district, such as the use of peer tutors or placement in a resource specialist program, if one exists.

The need for flexibility also extends into other areas. For example, you may arrive at a school and discover that you have not received prior notification about an activity, such as an assembly or special program, scheduled at the time during which you work with your student. If the special activity seems less

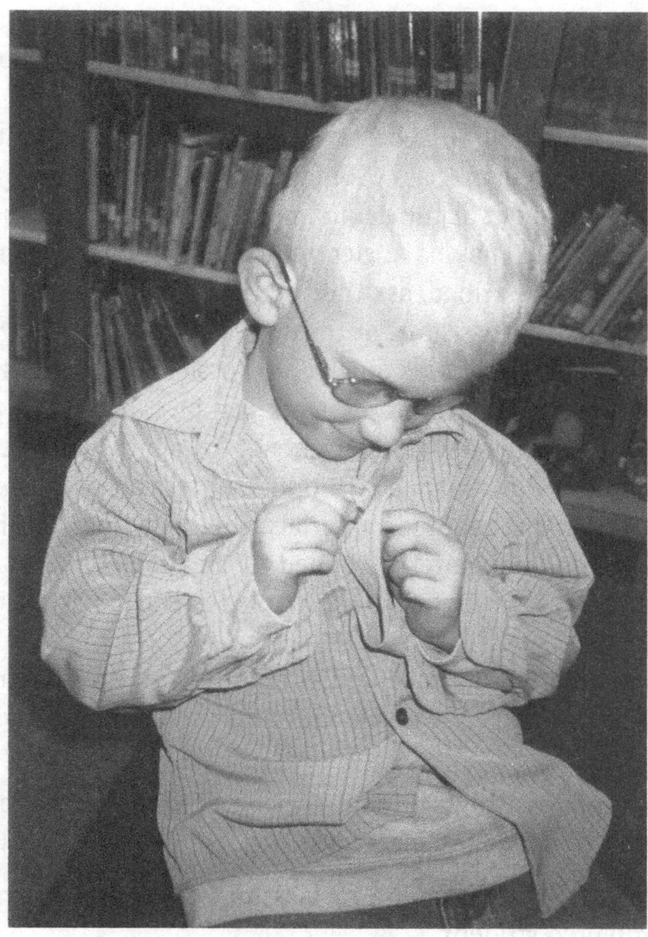

Independent living skills, such as buttoning a shirt, are part of the expanded core curriculum taught by teachers of visually impaired students.

Jean E. Olmstead

meaningful to the student than your lesson, you should work with him or her. When the activity is one the student should not miss, you have several options: you can participate in the activity with the student and provide appropriate interventions, such as describing what is occurring on the stage during an assembly; you can observe from a distance the student's participation in and use of special equipment and techniques during the activity; while the student participates in the activity you can remain at the school to confer with personnel, check records, make telephone calls, or complete paperwork; or you can drive to another site where work needs to be done. Such flexibility will also be required if a student you expected to work with is absent. If you have a student who is chronically absent, make it a point to call ahead to check whether he or she is in school before arriving there yourself.

ADAPTED MATERIALS

Ideally, at the beginning of the year you will be able to deliver books in braille or electronic form, in large print, or on tape to the school for your student's use. During the year, however, additional material typically needs to be adapted. With the student and classroom teacher, you will need to be creative about devising methods and utilizing resources to enable the student to participate as fully as possible in his or her class's activities.

An organized classroom teacher may give you, on request, work to be adapted before it is used in class. Some textbook series have accompanying worksheets that you can get at the beginning of the year to be brailled, enlarged, or taped; some publishers may have electronic versions of these materials. When worksheets are to be transcribed, ask the teachers to give you the darkest, clearest copy, so that you or an assistant or transcriber can braille, tape record, or enlarge the worksheet as easily and quickly as possible. If the classroom teacher prepares material on the computer, the work can be e-mailed to the transcriber or teacher of students with visual impairments for almost instant adaptation to braille or large print or downloaded to a braille notetaker or other device.

When you deliver the adapted materials, the classroom teacher will find it helpful to have the original material clipped to the brailled or enlarged copy. Always write identifying information on a brailled sheet in case it becomes separated from its print version.

Handouts prepared at the last minute, board work, transparencies for overhead projectors, and so forth are challenges that can be met in a variety of ways:

Options for Adapting Last-Minute Materials

- You, a program assistant, or transcriber can visit the school first thing in the morning to adapt the materials.
- A paraeducator, older student, or classmate can read the material to the visually impaired student.
- Students with low vision might access work at a distance by standing or sitting close to the chalkboard or transparency screen or by using distance optical devices (such as handheld telescopes, video magnifiers with swivel cameras, or one of the new head-mounted electronic telescopes) if they're adept at using these special aides. However, standing in front of distance work for any length of time blocks the view of other students and handheld telescopes are generally efficient for reading and copying only short pieces of information such as homework assignments. In some secondary schools, classmates of the student may be hired as notetakers for extensive work at a distance such as on the chalkboard or overhead transparencies. The notetakers will copy only written information; your student will be taking his or her own notes on class lectures or discussions, either on paper or using an electronic notetaker. Give the person taking notes lined carbonless copy paper to write on; the student with low vision gets the top copy and the notetaker keeps the fainter, lower page. Funding to pay notetakers may come from a category established for that purpose in the budget for the program for visually impaired students or from other district programs, such as those relating to work experience.

- The classroom teacher, a paraeducator, or a responsible student can tape record a description of the visual information.
- An enlarging copier at the school can be used to prepare large-print copies of handouts for students with low vision for whom they are appropriate. Various people can be responsible for enlarging handouts: the classroom teacher, a paraeducator, another adult, such as the secretary, or the student if he or she is reliable. Emphasize your willingness to teach any one of these people how to enlarge materials using the copier. Provide paper in appropriate sizes and make sure that whoever does the enlarging is aware of the optimal print size for the student.

SPECIALIZED EQUIPMENT

Providing the specialized equipment a student needs—whether a reading stand, bold felt-tip marker, computer with a speech synthesizer, or braille notetaker and braille embosser—is an important part of your job. Sometimes the special devices and equipment for one student will fill your car. You may find it helpful to use a luggage cart when delivering materials. It is wise in some instances, particularly with bulky items, to request assistance from the custodian with a flatbed dolly. In some schools driving right up to the classroom door is a possibility; be absolutely sure that you do so at a time that is completely safe.

Work with each student to determine which types of devices and equipment best suit his or her needs. You should have enough of the heavier, bulky items, such as reading or writing stands and braillers, so that one can be left at each site where the student will need them: classrooms, your workspace, and the student's home.

Assistive technology can be of immense value to your students. Chapter 9 provides detailed information about assistive technology. You will find it advisable to keep abreast of the latest advances in technology and computer hardware and software by attending conferences and receiving brochures and announcements by mail. Being knowledgeable about the operation and capabilities of each device allows you to recommend the purchase of equipment best suited to the needs of your students. When possible, do business with companies that lend equipment for a trial period so that you and your student can determine its effectiveness.

Apply creativity to the school's resources. For example, if an elementary school class has access to a computer, providing a voice synthesizer may be all a student who is visually impaired needs at a particular time. However, additional specialized equipment may need to be purchased at some time and delivered to the site for the student's instruction and use. Once a student is proficient with the special devices, duplicates of those that are not portable should be available for the student's use at home.

FIGURE 4.1

Video Magnifier Contract

I understand that using the video magnifier when no adult is present is a privilege granted to me that may be denied if I am not responsible about following these rules:

1. I will remember to turn off the light and make certain the doors are closed and locked each time I leave the room.
2. I will return the key to the secretary each time I leave.
3. I will use the video magnifier according to instructions. If the machine appears to be broken, I will stop using it and leave a note about the problem in the main office.
4. I will not bring anyone else to the room.
5. I will not bring food into the room.

Marsha Kelley	10/5/05
Student's signature	Date
Sara Kelley	10/5/05
Parent's signature	Date
Jean Olmstead	10/5/05
Teacher's signature	Date

In elementary schools, the equipment may be left in the classroom. You and your student can demonstrate for the classroom teacher how the equipment works and discuss the situations in which the student will use the equipment. In secondary schools, some equipment may be left in classrooms, such as an English class, where extensive reading and writing are required. Sometimes a student may carry devices from class to class; in that case, it may be advisable to transport equipment and materials in a backpack or suitcase with wheels. It is necessary to find alternative sites for devices that are not portable, but such sites will depend on what is available at the school. The room should be either open all day and staffed by an adult or locked but easily accessible with a key: a library, media center, or computer room may be appropriate. The arrangements need to be flexible enough to allow the student to use the equipment when he or she needs it.

Having students and their parents sign a contract similar to the sample video magnifier contract presented in Figure 4.1 helps to encourage the responsible use of devices. In the case of secondary school students, you may also choose to write a letter to inform the students' classroom teachers of the arrangement to use the equipment (see the sample letter in Figure 4.2). You may wish to have the teachers complete a questionnaire attached to your letter to determine whether

FIGURE 4.2

Date October 9, 2005

To teachers of Dale Mitchell,

A video magnifier is located in Room E for Dale's use. To use this device, one places regular print material under a magnifying camera, and it is displayed enlarged on a screen.

Dale is proficient in the use of the video magnifier and now has my permission to use the machine during your class periods when students are working independently and books or worksheets have not been enlarged for him. At appropriate times, please send him with a hall pass to the main office so he will be able to complete his assignments more easily.

Please make sure that substitute teachers are aware of this arrangement.

Please return the attached slip to me.

I appreciate your cooperation.

Sincerely,

Jean Olmstead

Jean Olmstead
Itinerant teacher of students with visual impairments
320-4500
jeo@xxx.edu

Please check the appropriate choices and return this slip to my mailbox by 5th period, Oct. 11th.
Thank you.

Jean Olmstead

1. Dale Mitchell will probably leave my class to use the video magnifier:

    ____ never

    ____ rarely

    ✓ 2-3 times a week

    ____ 4-5 times a week

2. ✓ I would like a demonstration of the video magnifier.

    ____ I would not like a demonstration of this device.

3. ✓ Please contact me to answer my questions about this arrangement.

Peter Daniels
Signature

they understand the purpose of and the arrangements for a specific student's use of the machine.

STUDENT OBSERVATIONS

As the school year progresses, assessment tools and consultation are effective means for judging students' performance. To ensure successful inclusion and integration of students, periodic observation is also essential. Time to perform these observations should be protected in the monitoring minutes specified on the students' IEPs.

Observe the students at different times of the day. Visit their classes during academic periods to see how they are using their materials and equipment when you are not directly involved. Watch them during art, music, and physical education classes, on the playground, and at lunch. These observations will provide invaluable feedback for assessing students' successes, as well as indicating areas that may require further intervention. Observations also enable you to evaluate the students' social skills. You can see how often they interact with their peers and adults and whether these interactions are appropriate. For those who are isolated or brusque with other students, intervention in the form of role-playing or small group activities may enhance students' relationships with others.

Observing students performing chores, studying at home, or participating in community programs is also helpful. You may be able to demonstrate or suggest strategies to enhance their use of effective techniques. Overall, periodic observations on a continuing basis enable you to recommend or provide interventions that facilitate the development of the competencies needed by your students to become contributing members of society.

COLLABORATION WITH SCHOOL PERSONNEL

Being an itinerant teacher means interacting with a range of people effectively and communicating frequently in a collaborative way. In many cases your students' level of educational services will be enhanced by your ability to consult and collaborate. At the start of any year, it is important to make contact with the major contributors to your students' educational program, as described in the section on Information Sharing in Chapter 3. You will also need to collaborate and maintain contact with most of them throughout the school year.

Collaboration can take many forms. It can be as formal as a meeting of all the students' caregivers and service providers or as informal as a note or e-mail message. When communicating by writing a note or letter, it's helpful to use carbon paper or carbonless copy paper, or to keep a photocopy for the students' files.

In some instances collaboration may be relatively simple. If students are enrolled in general education classes, itinerant teachers provide the information to the classroom teachers and other staff members with whom the students have contact, including the school secretaries, lunchroom personnel, bus drivers, and yard supervisors.

For students enrolled in other special education classes, such as those with multiple impairments, collaboration may be more complicated. In addition to the special class teachers, students may receive services from other designated providers. These providers may be itinerant, too, and will often be at sites when the teachers of students with visual impairments are elsewhere. Conferring by telephone, e-mail, or in writing may be sufficient most of the time, but certainly meetings should be held during which all specialized personnel and classroom teachers, and the students' parents or guardians when appropriate, discuss appropriate adaptations for students. Such a meeting is helpful at the beginning of the school year or just before an IEP meeting. The teacher of students with visual impairments can work with other IEP team members to facilitate assessment, prioritize and write integrated goals and objectives, prioritize activities, choose appropriate settings, and decide on effective instructional approaches, as well as demonstrating adaptations to the people who will be implementing the instruction. They can respond to other members of the IEP team who may be concerned about the impact of students' visual, auditory, or tactile issues when they are designing interventions. Teachers of students with visual impairments can get help from other IEP team members when communication, motor, or other issues affect interventions they are designing for the student.

Communication books can foster collaboration. With this method, school staff and specialized service providers write important information in one notebook for the student, and the book is sent home daily for family members or guardians to review. The classroom teacher is generally in charge of providing access to the notebook, sending them home with the student every afternoon, and receiving them in the morning. The student's parents or guardians can monitor the remarks and add their own. The communication book should be kept in a central location so that providers can access it easily to review the comments of others and add their own. In other instances members of the IEP team and the student's parents or guardians may find using e-mail an easy way to collaborate. Messages may be kept in an electronic file or hard copies may be stored with the student's other records.

Collaboration with the student's family or guardian is very important. Productive professional relationships between parents and professionals provide an exchange of pertinent, helpful information, resulting in greater consistency in the student's two most important environments, increased opportunities for learning and growth, and expanded access to resources and services. Home visits help parents or guardians implement instruction at home. During these visits, discuss how the student functions at school. Ask the parents or guardians to describe how the student does homework and chores at home as well as how his or her leisure time is spent. You might also arrange observation visits when the student is home. A supportive, nonjudgmental approach will lead to increased communication with the parents and other family members.

In-service programs and other communication with school personnel at the beginning of the year (see Chapter 3) should be followed by continuing contact, which will provide invaluable information about students' academic progress and social skills. You may also need to observe or consult with classroom teachers about students' participation in such activities as art, physical education, assemblies, and study trips and to confer with other staff members, including secretaries, recess and yard supervisors, bus drivers, and cafeteria workers.

In some schools, especially at the secondary level, you should arrange to receive copies of the weekly schedule and learn the location of the master calendar (usually on a wall in the administrative office) that lists special activities for a month or whole year. Check the calendar frequently: at least once a week. Keeping abreast of students' interactions at school and arranging for needed support when you are not at a school are important. At the same time, you need to remember that your students are served on an itinerant basis because they can adapt to less than ideal situations and can take some responsibility for their own special needs. It is essential to maintain a balance between providing appropriate assistance and smothering students with excessive attention.

In a hurried day of traveling, it is usually difficult to find time to spend in the faculty room or other common meeting places, but casual encounters with school staff can result in a helpful exchange of information. One option is to eat lunch at various schools during the week. By being available in the lunchroom, you can establish a closer relationship with the staff, who will have the opportunity to share pertinent information on a spontaneous basis.

Conferring with a number of teachers at several sites can be accomplished in several ways. You may be able to contact teachers in the classroom or faculty room at lunchtime, recess, or before or after school. Some teachers prefer that more formal appointments be made to discuss students' progress.

Have teachers of secondary school students complete a form similar to the one in Figure 4.3, which will provide pertinent information. Using the form or a comparable checklist can save time because you will need to have conferences only with the teachers in whose classes students are experiencing difficulty.

Develop good consultation skills. Keep notes of issues and questions for discussion during meetings with school personnel. At the meetings, take notes on carbonless copy paper to give copies to the other staff members involved so that they will have written reinforcement of the points discussed. Keep your remarks succinct. Do not be surprised if you need to reinforce key issues you addressed at the information sharing or in-service program you provided at the beginning of the year. Stay informed of upcoming school events so that you and the teachers

FIGURE 4.3

To Mrs. Watson

Re Martha Snyder

Date 9/15/05

Please return this questionnaire to me by 4th period, September 24

Thank you,

Jean Olmstead

Jean Olmstead
Itinerant teacher of students with visual impairments
320-4500
jeo@xxx.edu

1. Please evaluate Martha's participation in your class.

   Very poor.

2. Have you noticed Martha having any problems seeing materials, such as texts, worksheets, or board work? Yes ✓ No ____

   Please specify:

   Martha is not able to operate a sewing machine. She can only do hand sewing. She has tried to thread the hand sewing needle but usually my T.A. threads her needle. I usually put the knot at the end. She can't take out a knot—no motor skills.

3. Would you like me to contact you personally regarding Martha? Yes ✓ No ____

   If yes, what is a good time for me to contact you?

   7th period in class or 4th or 8th period are my conference periods.

4. Other comments:

   I've talked to Mrs. Snyder. She wants Martha to stay in sewing, but her success will be almost 0 because she needs more help than we can give. She needs almost a one-to-one situation.

can discuss, if necessary, students' participation in special activities. Listen for subtle clues, such as less than enthusiastic responses, and offhand remarks that may indicate areas that require trouble-shooting. Equally important is your acknowledgment of the staff's efforts on behalf of students.

People coming into contact with visually impaired students should have information about their students' functional vision, how they use it, and what adaptations will enable them to participate successfully in various activities. One of the more important roles for teachers of students with visual impairments is to convey that information while educating the students to be their own advocates. When the students have absorbed the information and practiced communicating it to adults and their peers, the students can take primary responsibility for this role. Additional suggestions about sharing information with school personnel can be found in Chapter 3.

Itinerant teachers often collaborate with eye care specialists during eye examinations and by calling for clarification if questions arise at a later time. Maintaining contact with community resources, such as groups providing appropriate services, is also important; this contact keeps you abreast of the services offered and can lead you to make timely referrals for your students and their families. Being aware of state and national resources can also keep the itinerant teacher abreast of recent developments and of government- and organization-sponsored programs of benefit to people with visual impairments. (See Appendix B for information on these organizations.) The American Foundation for the Blind (AFB) provides many resources and publications as well as advocacy for people with visual impairments; its *AFB Directory of Services for Blind and Visually Impaired Persons in the United States and Canada* (2005) provides helpful information on pertinent agencies. The Association for Education and Rehabilitation of the Blind and Visually Impaired (AER) has divisions that address particular concerns, such as Division 16 for Itinerant Personnel. AER also sponsors international and regional conferences as well as publishing newsletters. There may also be a professional organization in your state. As our roles become more complicated, a wise teacher will seek assistance from mentors at the local, state, and national levels.

Qualities of successful collaborators include self-confidence, an appreciation of self-awareness and growth, and being open to other perspectives. Collaborators have clear values and see themselves as part of a family, community, and society. They can tolerate ambiguous situations; are flexible; can negotiate in conflicts; have good observation, helping, and communication skills; and understand group processes. They also maintain membership in pertinent organizations and regularly access the Internet for the latest information on electronic discussion groups and web sites, such as those of the organizations listed in Appendix B.

Because of its importance, collaboration is mentioned often in other sections of this book, wherever consultation and providing information or in-service workshops are discussed.

WORKING WITH PARAEDUCATORS

Teacher assistants or aides have long been used to work with teachers of students with visual impairments and with the students themselves. Some teacher assistants are assigned to a special educator or resource room teacher and usually serve any of the students on their supervising teacher's caseload. They perform a variety of tasks and essentially are supervised by the teacher to whose class they are assigned. These assistants perform duties such as enlarging materials and reinforcing good study habits. A variety of terms are used to describe this support person: teacher assistant, paraprofessional, one-to-one-aide, and, in the case of students who are deaf-blind, intervener. A more recent term is paraeducator, which will be used in this chapter.

Paraeducators are often used to augment or support the services of an itinerant teacher of visually impaired students. This may be a logical deployment of personnel, given that itinerant teachers may visit several schools in one day depending on their caseloads, while the paraeducator often remains at the school site and can work on a daily basis with a particular student. However, the role of paraeducators and the activities they undertake vary considerably from district to district or even school to school. Their role is a topic of continuing debate among educators.

In some schools, you may find that a paraeducator has been assigned to an individual student rather than to a classroom and is working one-on-one with that student. Among the reasons for this may be staff shortages and the concerns of parents and the school district. Whatever the reasons, there are ways in which paraeducators need to work with visually impaired students, and the teacher of students with visual impairments needs to explain and oversee that work. A paraeducator should only provide instruction that is sanctioned by the IEP team.

It is possible, if not probable, that if a student needs the assistance of a paraeducator to participate fully in the educational program, a resource room program for visually impaired students might be a more appropriate placement for the student. There, with a teacher of visually impaired students on campus all day, he or she could concentrate on honing various skills in order to achieve additional independence. However, in some communities, a resource room for students with visual impairments is not available. There may not be enough students to support a full resource class. The level of services needed by the student that a specialized teacher can provide may be under dispute and additional student support may be delivered by a paraeducator based on cost rather than educational factors. If the IEP team does not agree that a student would benefit from attending the state school for students with visual impairments, in

Paraeducators need to understand how to support students' development of skills without encouraging dependence.

Rona Shaw

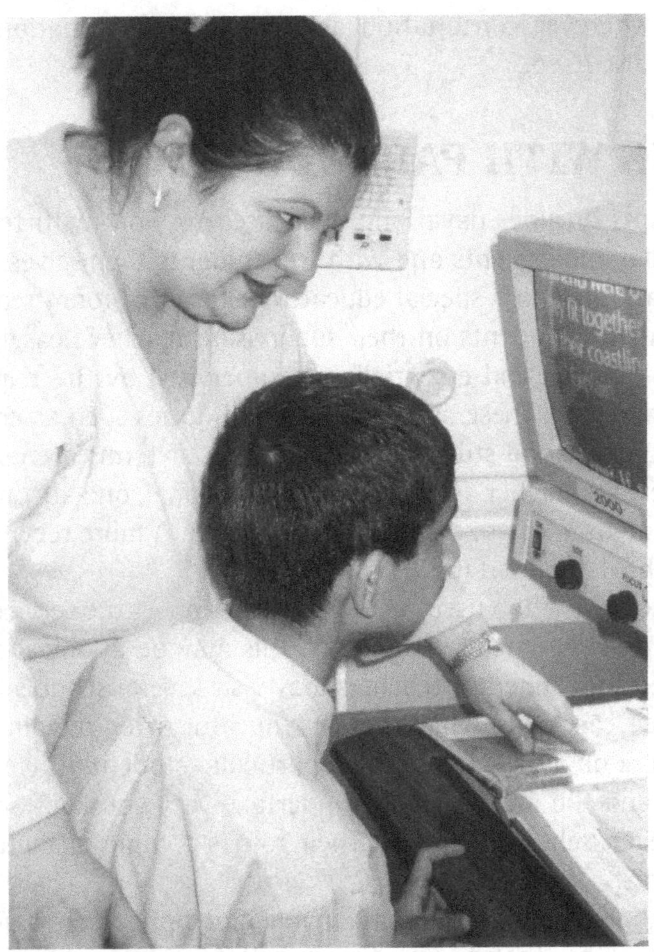

some instances various parties may believe the best option is to provide a paraeducator to the student together with services provided by you. This may occur because a student lacks the ability to be independent when you are not at the site or when the size of your caseload or other factors prevent you from having time to provide individual services to the student.

When a paraeducator is part of the IEP plan, the student is not, in a sense, participating in a pure itinerant program; nor is the student fully included in the strictest sense of the expression. The student is in what might be called a supported inclusion program. In such circumstances, it is important for the teacher of students with visual impairments to assess the strengths and needs of the student and to advocate with school administrators, parents, and the rest of the IEP team for appropriate placement.

The Role of Paraeducators

When students work with paraeducators, the students are still your responsibility as well as that of the classroom teacher. It is important to make that clear from the first day of school. When you contact the teacher at the beginning of the school year, it is important to discuss the duties of the paraeducator. Ask the classroom teacher about the class structure, and discuss how the paraeducator can best support the student in that setting and what activities it is appropriate for the paraeducator to perform. A meeting at the start of school that includes the paraeducator, classroom teacher, and you to spell out the specific roles and duties of the paraeducator is also important. Above all, the classroom teacher needs to know that he or she is responsible for meeting the instructional guidelines of the curriculum as mandated by the school district or state and that your role is to address the needs of the student as they relate to his or her visual impairment. The paraeducator, who may feel eager to teach and help, needs to adjust to working as a mediator or assistant, supporting the classroom teacher's role as the educator. It is essential for both classroom teacher and paraeducator to understand the sensitive issues involved in working with a student who is visually impaired in a way that supports the student's development of skills but does not encourage his or her dependence or overinvolvement with the paraeducator.

Paraeducators, it could be said, serve as the extended arms of the itinerant teacher, providing support to the student when the itinerant teacher is not at the site. They can assist in obtaining materials in the student's preferred learning or reading medium. They often interact with the classroom teacher, you, and other specialists on the IEP team, such as physical, speech, or occupational therapists. In doing so, they may assist with communication among the members of the IEP team. One of the paraeducators' most important roles is to enhance the student's attainment of independence, such as by shadowing while the student practices an O&M technique on a school route. You (or an O&M instructor) provide the instruction for needed skills and the paraeducator reinforces and monitors their attainment on a daily basis. A tool such as the Paraeducator's Tasks form (see Figure 4.4) can be useful during discussions about a paraeducator's role in working with a student who is visually impaired. The paraeducator and the classroom teacher can each complete the form, with paraeducators checking the tasks for which they take responsibility and teachers indicating the tasks they plan to assign to the paraeducator. When they are finished, meet with both of them to discuss the results. If there are discrepancies in expectations, work with them to clarify the duties of the paraeducator. Having a clear understanding of the paraeducator's role can enhance the partnership between the classroom teacher and the paraeducator.

Training Paraeducators

The success of students who work with paraeducators depends in large part on the quality of the training provided to the paraeducators, which should be comprehensive and continuing. Paraeducators should clearly understand their duties and be trained in communicating with teachers, students, parents, and school

FIGURE 4.4

Paraeducator's Tasks

Listed below are a number of tasks that a paraeducator may perform. If you are a paraeducator, mark with a "p" those activities that you would be comfortable doing. If you are a teacher, use another form and mark with a "t" those areas in which you intend to make use of a paraeducator. Compare and discuss your lists.

Adaptation of materials

___ 1. Adapt materials to large print.

___ 2. Adapt materials to braille.

___ 3. Tape record written work.

___ 4. Make tactile drawings.

Orientation & Mobility

___ 5. Use human (sighted) guide technique when walking with student.

___ 6. Follow student quietly on familiar routes.

___ 7. Allow student to get confused on familiar routes and give the student time to correct the mistake.

___ 8. Be alert and warn student of any danger en route.

Support

___ 9. Allow student to make mistakes on class assignments.

___ 10. Let the student ask the teacher or peers questions about class work or activities.

___ 11. Maintain a distance from the student unless working directly with him or her.

___ 12. Let the student pick up dropped objects.

___ 13. If the student is working with a group of peers, withdraw to a distance when possible.

___ 14. Stay at a distance when the student is eating lunch.

___ 15. When a student has mastered a task, such as putting on a coat, allow him or her to complete the task independently even if it seems to take too long.

___ 16. When in doubt, do nothing; intervene only when necessary.

Classroom activities

___ 17. Reinforce concepts already presented by teacher in small groups or with individual students.

___ 18. Listen to students read.

___ 19. Read to students.

FIGURE 4.4 (continued)

____ 20. Supervise small groups of students in independent or group work.

____ 21. Modify written materials (i.e., rewrite at an easier level).

____ 22. Help students work on assignments and projects.

____ 23. Assist physically disabled students.

Behavior management support

____ 24. Provide or supervise earned reinforcement.

____ 25. Supervise time-outs.

____ 26. Be a resource for students who are experiencing stress.

____ 27. Monitor progress on behavior contracts.

____ 28. Provide positive feedback and encouragement.

Diagnostic support

____ 29. Correct and grade assigned activities.

____ 30. Observe and record academic behavior and progress.

____ 31. Observe and record social behaviors.

____ 32. Administer informal assessments.

Classroom organization

____ 33. Make instructional games.

____ 34. Develop and manage learning centers.

____ 35. Prepare displays.

____ 36. Locate instructional materials.

Clerical support

____ 37. Type or use the computer as directed.

____ 38. Duplicate materials.

____ 39. Record grades.

personnel. The paraeducator is there to assist and provide adaptations but not to replace either the classroom teacher or you.

You are responsible for the training. At the beginning of the school year when you give the classroom teachers concise information about a student's visual impairment and specific instructional strategies, give the same information to the paraeducator. (See the discussions on collaboration and sharing information in this and the previous chapter.) Try not to overwhelm the paraeducator with too much information at first. The first weeks of a school year can be daunting. After he or she gets to know the student, questions will follow. You can share the publications *When You Have a Visually Impaired Student in Your Classroom: A Guide for Paraeducators* (2004) and *When You Have a Visually Impaired Student in Your Classroom: A Guide for Teachers* (2002) as well as discussing issues relating to the visual environment of the classroom: lighting, seating, and presentation of materials.

For a paraeducator who is new to assisting students with visual impairments, it will be extremely helpful for you to spend the first few days in the classroom, modeling how to fulfill the role. Assume the role of the paraeducator for a time and then discuss with the paraeducator why you did things a certain way. Gradually withdraw, letting the paraeducator assume the role.

Observing an experienced paraeducator in the beginning of the year is also very helpful. It is best to be able to suggest more productive ways to work with a student as soon as possible. Remember to give praise for work well done. Being present during class time should be augmented by observing the student and paraeducator at all times of the day: from drop-off point to first class and from last class to pick-up, lunch time, recess, and breaks between classes. Sometimes you may spend two or more days observing to determine how the paraeducator and student are interacting in the school environment until you are sure that the relationships among the classroom teacher, the paraeducator, and the student are appropriate. Making the student as independent as possible, by promoting the student's self-sufficiency, is one example of being appropriate. Therefore, ongoing observations should continue through the year to ensure the student's development of the greatest possible level of independence. In addition to the direct instruction minutes specified on the student's IEP, the itinerant teacher needs to have monitoring minutes adequate for observing and consulting regularly with the paraeducator and the classroom teacher, as well as performing all the necessary peripheral duties, such as adapting materials and consulting with families or guardians, physicians and eye care specialists, and community resources.

As a new teacher you may find that one of the students on your caseload already has a paraeducator with whom he or she has been working. Discuss with the paraeducator and the classroom teacher the paraeducator's experience in working with persons with visual impairments. Then provide additional training, as necessary, to ensure that the paraeducator will be providing assistance appropriately to your student.

Training Recommendations

How you provide training to a paraeducator can be as varied as your time and energy permit. For example, you might give an in-service session (see the "Sample In-Service Suggestions"), drop off weekly or monthly reading materials (see the box on "Working with Students with Visual Impairments: A Guide for Paraeducators"), or provide a video containing pertinent information. Some school districts provide staff development time that could be a perfect opportunity to provide an in-service session for one or a group of paraeducators. It is very important that time for this training be specified and protected by the student's IEP; insufficient and ineffective training can result in inappropriate interventions on the paraeducator's part. The bulk of the training will no doubt occur at the beginning of the school year, but contact between the teacher and the paraeducator should continue on a regular basis throughout the year.

Overall, the paraeducator's training should include pertinent areas of awareness of visual impairments, academic adaptations, and communication strategies. The list of training topics provided in the accompanying box is just a starting point: feel free to add any topics that would be meaningful, depending on the particular issues and concerns specific to the individual students on your caseload. Additional training can be provided using information sheets, in-service meetings, and other meetings throughout the school year.

If the student receives O&M instruction, the O&M specialist will also provide in-service training to the paraeducator about the student's abilities and needs and how to encourage his or her independence. If the student uses a cane, the O&M specialist can demonstrate techniques such as human (sighted) guide and clarify issues such as when the student should be using the cane instead of a guide. It is also important for the O&M instructor to attend at least some of the meetings with the paraeducator, you, and the classroom teacher, as well as observing the paraeducator working with the student during different times of the day and throughout the school year. The O&M specialist can reinforce the information he or she has provided to the teacher and the paraeducator by giving them copies of the O&M-Specific Skills form (see Figure 4.5), which provides information about travel skills the student has already learned and new ones to be monitored.

In addition, it is essential to keep in mind the following points when working with paraeducators:

Working with Paraeducators

- Keep meeting with the paraeducator until you are sure that he or she completely understands and fulfills his or her exact roles and duties.
- Ensure that the paraeducator has a complete understanding and knowledge of the student's visual impairment and visual functioning.
- Establish a daily schedule for the paraeducator based on the student's program. Be mindful that scheduling may need to be flexible and that you,

Sample In-Service Suggestions

Conveying information to classroom teachers, paraeducators, and other IEP team members and school personnel can be done effectively via in-service training. The following outline can be used to organize information-sharing meetings that cover topics of fundamental importance.

Working with Students with Visual Impairments

1. Introductions
2. Common visual impairments and their implications for education
3. Suggested classroom modifications
4. Do's and don'ts: Hints for working with visually impaired students
5. O&M pointers
6. Role play travel in school using a blindfold
7. Showing of the video *Oh, I See*
8. Questions and feedback

In addition, the following points are helpful to keep in mind:

- You can bring all the paraeducators for students on your caseload together and discuss issues relating to visual impairment, modifications, and suggestions. Distribute the pamphlet, *When You Have a Visually Impaired Student in Your Classroom: A Guide for Paraeducators* (2004) and show the video *Oh, I See* (Longuil, 1991), both available from AFB Press.
- Also share with paraeducators the publication: *Paraprofessional's Handbook for Working with Students Who Are Visually Impaired* (Miller & Levack, 1997), available from the Texas School for the Blind and Visually Impaired. If possible, order a copy for the paraeducators.
- Provide a question and answer sheet or list of suggestions regarding working with visually impaired students (see the sidebar on "Working with Students with Visual Impairments: A Guide for Paraeducators").
- Whenever possible, provide in-service training on a monthly or quarterly basis. Some suggested topics are technology, O&M, communication skills, living skills, social skills, and academic modifications.
- Remind everyone that you are available to discuss sensitive issues: what to do if other students ask questions such as "What's wrong with him or her?" or how to react when visually impaired students will not use devices or adapted materials because they do not want to feel conspicuous.

Working with Students with Visual Impairments: A Guide for Paraeducators

Congratulations! As a paraeducator, you are going to be working with a great student this year. Your student has a visual impairment, and listed here for you are some guidelines to use when working with students with vision impairments.

Do:

- provide respect and encouragement.
- listen to your students.
- tell the students the names of peers who are in a group the students are joining.
- keep the environment safe and uncluttered. For example, remove any unnecessary equipment. Remind students to move any chairs that are in the middle of the floor.
- adapt students school materials as directed by the teacher. For example, make tactile drawings, record information, read aloud, or enlarge materials.
- allow students to communicate their needs directly to appropriate adults. Expect students to speak to classroom teachers.
- expect students to work hard.
- allow enough time for students to complete their work.
- allow students to make mistakes.
- let students solve problems by themselves. Resist rescuing them.
- expect visually impaired students to interact with other students socially during lunch and recess times and at other appropriate occasions.
- ask yourself if you could be doing less.

Don't:

- do the students' work for them. Your role is to provide appropriate assistance.
- talk for your students. They are capable of communicating for themselves.
- talk about your students in their presence as if they aren't there.
- hover; move away when not directly needed and give them space to feel self-sufficient.
- be afraid to use the words "look" or "see."
- leave your blind or visually impaired students alone in open space; move them into contact with a wall or object if you are leaving them, even for a brief time.
- walk away without letting them know that you are leaving.

Training Topics for Paraeducators

The following list suggests some of the many possible topics to consider for training sessions with paraeducators in the basic areas of awareness of visual impairments, academic adaptations, and communication strategies.

Disability Awareness

- information about the student's visual condition
- information about the student's functional vision
- environmental adaptations
- how to interact with a student with visual impairments
- how to encourage independence
- O&M pointers
- hints for working with a student with visual impairments

Academic Adaptations

- learning media
- expanded core curriculum
- procedures for enlarging materials
- braille use and techniques
- taping materials
- tactile graphics
- assistive technology
- use of materials in electronic form

Effective Communication Strategies

- documenting students' progress
- appropriate communication with you
- conferring with the classroom teachers and students
- conferring with the IEP team members
- appropriate communication with parents or guardians

the paraeducator, and classroom teacher should discuss any changes that may be needed.

It is also important to orient the student to the paraeducator's role. Be clear about when the student should ask for help from the classroom teacher or peers and when to ask the paraeducator. The student needs to understand that the paraeducator is not there as a teacher, servant, parent, or buddy. For example, when appropriate, the student should be responsible for keeping materials orga-

FIGURE 4.5

Orientation & Mobility–Specific Skills

Student	Roger Higgins	Grade	4
School year	2003	School	Mountain View
Classroom number	17	Teacher	Mr. Smith
Itinerant teacher	Jean Olmstead	O&M specialist	Mary Jones
Telephone	320-4500	Telephone	320-4500
E-mail	jeo@xxx.edu	E-mail	mbj@xxx.edu

The above student has completed instruction toward the following orientation & mobility goals in order to promote self-sufficiency and independent travel. School personnel should allow the student to travel independently in the following settings:

Last year Roger could independently follow the route between his classroom and the boys' restroom and the route between his classroom and the lunchroom. He could also reverse the routes. After youve observed him following the routes five times without problem,you may stop monitoring him on these routes.

The following goals are being taught during this school year. School personnel should reinforce and monitor the student's use of these techniques and routes.

Roger will be learning the routes from the bus to his classroom and vice versa and from his classroom to the office and reverse. As of this date he can walk independently from the bus to the school door. Beyond that point he should walk using the human (sighted) guide technique. I will advise you when he has mastered the second step of this route.

Sometimes Roger uses a cane arc that is too wide. When you are walking behind him,please remind him to narrow his arc if it can be seen to extend about 4 inches beyond either foot.

The student needs to be monitored and supervised in the following settings and routes.

Please supervise Roger to and from the following areas: play yard,computer room,motor room, and other unfamiliar destinations. He will also need supervision in those areas as well as the lunchroom.

Please dont hesitate to contact me if you have questions or concerns.

Thanks,

Mary

nized, for carrying the materials, and for getting from one site to another independently. To maintain the appropriate relationship, paraeducators should be addressed by their surnames, not their first names. If the paraeducators have desks in students' classrooms, the desks should be at a distance from the students with visual impairments to reduce fostering too much dependence on the paraeducators.

Remember to introduce yourself at the start of the year to the principal or other administrators in the school, describe your duties, and how you and the paraeducator will be assisting the staff in working with the student with visual impairments. Keep the appropriate administrator informed, especially if issues arise with the classroom teacher, paraeducator, student, or parents.

Some Final Thoughts

Keep in mind these concepts as you continue to work with students and their paraeducators:

More Tips for Working with Paraeducators

- Maintain a professional relationship with paraeducators and encourage them to do the same with you.
- Discourage them from becoming the best buddy of the student to whom they are assigned.
- When working with an older student, it may be preferable that the paraeducator be of the same gender.
- Because of his or her daily contact with the student, the paraeducator should have input in the IEP process as a member of the IEP team. If that is not possible, make sure the paraeducator receives all information regarding the goals for his or her student.
- Maximizing the student's independence is the ultimate goal of all members of the IEP team. The paraeducator's most important work is to encourage the student's attainment of independence so that eventually he or she can participate in school activities without a paraeducator's support.
- Classroom teachers, you, and paraeducators should meet on a regular basis (and, at least occasionally, with the O&M specialist) to discuss progress and instructional strategies that promote the student's success.
- Both the classroom educators and the paraeducators must understand that the teachers are in charge of most teaching. It may be easy to have the paraeducator work solely with the student, but that is not an appropriate role. Paraeducators are there to provide adaptations for instruction and to interact with the students as outlined in the IEP and agreed upon by you and the O&M specialist. It's best if paraeducators and students are not always working together. Sometimes, perhaps more often than not, it is ap-

propriate for the paraeducators to work with other students in the classroom or perform chores for the classroom teacher while discretely monitoring the visually impaired student from a distance.

- Be creative when scheduling appropriate times for paraeducators to take lunch and other breaks. Giving them breaks when the students are with you or the O&M specialist can be tempting, but it is more helpful if the paraeducators are willing to be flexible about their break times, so that sometimes they can observe how you and the O&M specialist work with the students.
- A poster called "*Nineteen Ways to Step Back*" is available from AFB that provides appropriate reinforcements of crucial training issues for paraeducators and teachers as well.

The use of support from a paraeducator is determined by the IEP team. The team needs to ensure that the provision of a paraeducator serves the best interests of the student with visual impairments and that the paraeducator is not provided solely because of a request from the classroom teacher, the student's parents or guardians, or because of other circumstances. The IEP team also must monitor the success or failure of the use of a paraeducator and make corrections swiftly if problems occur. Some school districts have developed criteria for implementing the use of a paraeducator, and mandate reviews of the paraeducator's effectiveness every six months. An adult hovering over an already sensitive student can cause havoc with the student's social interactions and self-esteem. The assistance of a properly trained paraeducator, however, can be effective in promoting the educational success of a student with visual impairments.

INTEGRATION AND SUBJECT AREAS

Facilitating the integration of students who are visually impaired into nonacademic school activities and programs can require other specialized adaptations. Adapted techniques and materials may need to be used in order for students to participate in continuing activities. The value of their participation will be seen in many aspects of the students' experience, ranging from increasing confidence and social relationships to enhanced academic performance. Physical education and music are two examples of such subjects. Information on adaptations is provided here to help readers support students' participation in them and to serve as models for adapting other subjects as well.

Adapted Physical Education

IDEA mandates that physical education (PE) be available to all students with disabilities. PE makes valuable contributions to students' psychomotor, cognitive, and affective development. However, because of factors such as lack of motivation, lack of opportunities for movement, the inability to imitate actions observed visually, and, in some instances, overprotection, some students who are visually impaired lead a sedentary life. In some cases PE classes get little attention for students who need high levels of support. As a result, students may lack vitality and stamina and have compromised posture, as well as experiencing other negative effects. For them, PE can provide physical fitness and motor skills needed for activities and O&M, a more positive self-concept and sense of self worth, as well as skills to use during leisure time. For example, arm strength and endurance are necessary for using a long cane successfully. Vestibular and sensory motor skills need to be developed from an early age, and need to progress with age and growth.

Students with visual impairments who have participated in PE classes have reported a range of reactions, from "You're blind, you can't participate in physical education" and "Sit on the sideline and learn the rules or keep score" to "Let's work together so that you can succeed in this class." In the area of PE in general, it is important that the teacher of students with visual impairments and the O&M specialist, as needed, be involved with suggesting adaptations for the students' successful participation in the class activities.

Since adapted physical education involves adapting, modifying, and changing an activity so that all students can be successful preparing to adapt a PE program, it's important to learn about the student, his or her impairment, and visual functioning. Does he or she have light perception? See faces? See shadows? Does his or her vision change from day to day? Knowing a student has detached retinas, for example, is very important information; any activity that includes jarring or building pressure (lifting heavy weights) should be avoided to prevent further retinal detachment and additional vision loss. When beginning new physical activities, it is always a good idea to check with the student's eye care specialist and physician to determine if there are any contraindications.

It is recommended that students who are visually impaired attend the general PE classes. Adaptations for activities can be provided or suggested by the teacher of visually impaired students, the PE teacher, O&M specialist, or an adapted PE specialist. When appropriate, adapted PE services can be specified on the students' IEP to ensure continued assistance. Some students have additional disabilities, such as a hearing loss or a physical impairment such as cerebral palsy. Students with multiple impairments can attend a general PE class with modifications or attend an adapted PE class if available.

Once a basic approach or PE placement has been decided for a student, assess the environment. Check the safety of the gym or other area where PE classes are held, and availability of landmarks and cues. In particular look for the wires that support gymnastics equipment; they can be very difficult to detect. If there is little contrast in the gymnasium, colored tape and brighter lighting may be helpful to some students. After that assessment, orient the student and encourage

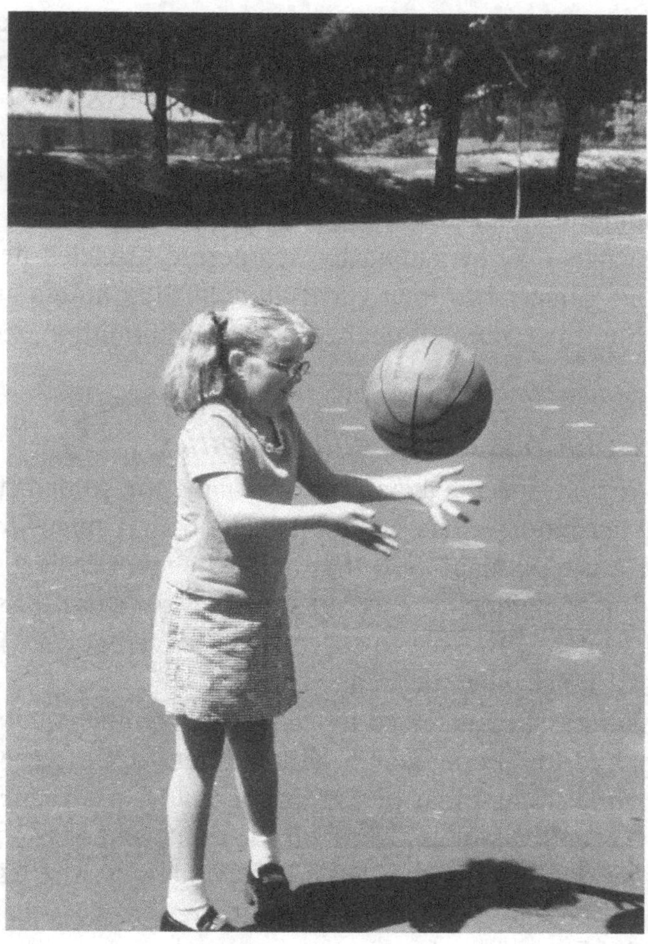

Physical education supports the development of motor skills needed for activities and O&M, as well as physical fitness, a more positive self-concept, and leisure skills.

Jean E. Olmstead

him or her to use all other senses to stay oriented. If available, the O&M specialist could help.

Evaluate each PE activity and determine whether modifications are necessary for the student. There is usually a creative solution to all challenges. These include peer assistance and adapting equipment or rules, such as modifying distance, time, or space. One example is to let students use two hands instead of one during some activities. Use a voice call in activities, for example when the students are on scooters, so they will hear which direction to go. The voice call—for instance, "Keep going Jim, over here"—could be continuous or at intervals. Keep directions clear, concise, and accurate. Use directions that make use of a clock face ("point the scooters at 12 o'clock").

Specific examples of adapted materials include using beep balls, bell balls, large brightly colored balls, and hard or soft balls. Cones that are bright orange or color-coded can be used for boundary lines. Using beeping targets or ones that make noise when hit may help. Sometimes students may need a simple adaptation, such as moving out of glare into a shady area for better contrast, or using a Velcro mitt and ball to work on object control and throwing skills.

When an activity is being introduced, verbal instructions should be detailed.

Physical assistance and coactive movement can be useful. For example, for fitness training in the weight room the student should be oriented in the room and know where the equipment is located. The student needs to know the proper technique for lifting weights, the correct amount to lift, and number or repetitions to be completed. An adapted PE teacher should help the student with specific fitness training techniques.

Some PE teachers may be willing to incorporate so-called new games (also called cooperative games) into their curriculum. In these stated activities everyone works together to accomplish goals. (For more information, see, for example, Orlick, 1982.)

Suggested Adaptations for Specific Activities

Some activities require specific adaptations to allow the student to succeed. For example, when teaching archery, a bright balloon that pops when hit by the arrow would be a useful adaptation that helps the student hear that he or she has succeeded. The technique of teaching archery is the same for sighted and visually impaired students. The key to success will be verbal cues for aiming and some physical assistance when needed.

For in-line skating, students need to learn to put on the equipment, the rules for safe skating, and the proper way to fall and get up. Once the skates are on, the visually impaired student may be assigned a buddy. In a defined area, skating in the same direction (the wall is always on the right) and hearing auditory cues such as, "The gym door, where the music is playing, is on the left side and the bathrooms are on the right side," are important for success. It may not be feasible to modify all PE activities for visually impaired students in school. In such cases, appropriate alternatives, such as weight training or aerobic training on a treadmill or exercise bike, should be available.

Specialized Games

Some adapted PE and general education PE teachers meet their high school students at the local "Y" or fitness club three times a week for swimming, aerobics, or weight lifting. However, when encouraging students with visual impairments to participate in activities, local organizations that serve people who are blind or visually impaired can be excellent resources, as well as sources of information. Having the right equipment is a crucial component (see Appendix A for some sources of adaptive gym equipment). If braille is needed—to label the information on the treadmill, for example—the managers are usually more than happy to comply.

Goal ball and beep baseball are two sports specifically designed for visually impaired athletes. Goal ball is an indoor game, played by two teams of three players each on a volleyball court. The object of the game is for each team to roll the bell ball across the opponent's goal line, while the other team tries to prevent it from going past the end line. Beep baseball is played outside on a baseball field. Several modifications have been established: the softball-sized ball beeps, two bases (first and third) emit a buzzing sound, and the pitcher is sighted. Using a batting tee rather than a sighted pitcher can be a good adaptation.

The United States Association for Blind Athletes has information about these games and local sources for these and other activities (see Appendix B for information on this and other organizations related to sports and other activities for individuals with visual impairments). Encourage students to get involved.

Visually impaired students can and do participate in physical education, fitness activities, and leisure sports: swimming, weight lifting, wrestling, hiking, horseback riding, rock climbing, kayaking, rowing, self-defense, in-line skating, water skiing, and downhill skiing. Students might not perform the activity in exactly the same way as individuals who are sighted, but if everyone is involved and learning, the experience is usually a success.

Music

Music instruction can offer opportunities for participation by and integration of students with visual impairments. Public schools often schedule classes in music for all students, and many public schools also have well-established programs in voice and instrumental music. Despite the recent emphasis on academic subjects, research indicates that students who study music and art are more successful in school in general. Students with visual impairments should have the same opportunities to learn these special skills as their sighted peers. Participation in vocal and instrumental music ensembles provide students with visual impairments expanded opportunities for social interaction. Students in middle and high school often find these groups a great place to develop and improve their social skills in an environment where they can excel and minimize the impact of their visual impairment.

Making adaptations for music instruction works best through collaboration among the student, parents or guardians, the school (or outside) music teacher, and the teacher of visually impaired students. If the teacher of students with visual impairments is inexperienced at reading print music, perhaps the music teacher at the school could give a quick lesson or two on the rudiments of music that an elementary school student would be learning: time signatures, whole notes, half notes, quarter notes, and the scale. Look at what concepts sighted students are learning in the music classes and teach students with visual impairments these rudiments of music so that they can keep up with their peers.

Some students who wish to participate in the school's music program will need few adaptations. They may be able to use their prescribed optical devices as in the classroom. Other students may benefit from a prescribed optical device, such as a spectacle-mounted telescopic lens system, that will be used specifically in music class. Selecting and acquiring such a system reinforces the necessity and benefit of ensuring that each student with low vision receives a clinical low vision evaluation from a qualified eye care specialist. Some students with low vision who play a musical instrument may prefer to use large-print music, since their hands will be occupied as they play. In addition, good posture is needed in music performance for muscle and breath control, and stamina, and having large-print music may allow students to sit farther away from the music stand, or to hold choral music away from the body. In some situations, students will want to memorize their music (especially if they are in marching band, which would make large-print music or optical devices more difficult to manipulate). Some students may benefit from learning braille music.

One of the challenges of being an itinerant teacher of visually impaired chil-

Sources for Braille Music

A variety of code books are available from the American Printing House for the Blind (APH) for teachers who want to learn more about braille music (see Appendix A). One of the most practical and easiest to use is the *Primer of Braille Music*, by Edward Jenkins (San Diego, CA: Opus Technologies, 1971), which is available in both print and braille, containing most of the basic signs used in the braille music code. Other books are available that have more detailed information on braille music transcription. APH is also a source of braille music scores, as is the National Library Service for the Blind and Physically Handicapped.

How to Read Braille Music, by Bettye Krolick (San Diego, CA: Opus Technologies, 1999), a handbook written for teachers, parents, and students who are blind or visually impaired, is available in print, braille, and on CD-ROM.

They Shall Have Music, by Dorothy Dykema (San Diego, CA: Opus Technologies, 1986), is a slim volume designed for sighted individuals such as music teachers, teachers, parents, and others who are teaching music to students who can't read print. While it stresses the importance of braille music, there are also hints and strategies for all aspects of music instruction.

Who's Afraid of Braille Music? A Short Introduction and Resource Handbook for Parents and Students, by Richard Taesch and William McCann (Valley Forge, PA: Dancing Dots, 2004), is a highly readable manual that gives a short overview of the braille music code. *An Introduction to Music for the Blind Student: A Course in Braille Music Reading*, by Richard Taesch (Valley Forge, PA: Dancing Dots, 2001), is a course in music fundamentals, using the braille music code as the medium.

The National Resource Center for Blind Musicians (www.blindmusicstudent.org) and the Music Education Network for the Visually Impaired (www.superior-software.com/menvi/index.htm) are among the organizations specializing in assisting families and educators of students who are blind or visually impaired who want to participate in music programs (see Appendix B).

dren is trying to fit in yet another activity or adaptation. However, braille music is a special skill that can enrich a student's life, foster integration with peers, and even lead to further study and life interest. Whether or not your student wants to become a musician, learning to read music can have a positive impact on his or her learning and self-esteem. Although students learning braille music eventually have to memorize the music anyway, learning to read the music can give the student instant, independent access to the notes and the other musical markings that denote tempo, loudness, length of the note, and other important details. Having the braille music available as a reference will help the student learn the music more accurately. Additional information is provided in the accompanying box, "Sources for Braille Music."

CONCLUSION

An itinerant teacher wears many hats: teacher, collaborator, skilled observer, provider of creative adaptations of materials and environment, and enabler, to name only a few. However, you generally only have to wear one hat at a time. By keeping in mind the importance of your work to the well-being of your students, having confidence in your ability to problem solve and refine your own skills, and making use of the suggestions provided here and by helpful colleagues, your capacity for selecting and coordinating those hats will continue to grow to the benefit of your students and yourself.

REFERENCES

AFB Directory of services for blind and visually impaired persons in the United States and Canada (27th ed.). (2005). New York: AFB Press.

Longuil, C. (1991). *Oh, I see* [videotape]. New York: AFB Press.

Miller, C., & Levack, N. (1997). *Paraprofessional's handbook for working with students who are visually impaired.* Austin: Texas School for the Blind and Visually Impaired.

Orlick, T. (1982). *The second cooperative sports and games book: Over two hundred noncompetitive games for kids and adults both.* New York: Pantheon.

When you have a visually impaired student in your classroom: A guide for paraeducators. (2004). New York: AFB Press.

When you have a visually impaired student in your classroom: A guide for teachers. (2002). New York: AFB Press.

Wormsley, D. P., & D'Andrea, F. M. (1997). *Instructional strategies for braille literacy.* New York: AFB Press.

CHAPTER

5

Providing Services for Infants and Their Families

Cinda Wert Rapp

Working with infants and young children with visual impairments offers a different set of opportunities than does working with older children. It also involves a service system and philosophy that differ from the way in which we serve students from ages 3 through 21. Children ages 3 and over are covered under Part B of the Individuals with Disabilities Education Act (IDEA), whereas children birth to age 3 years are covered under Part C. However, many of the principles underlying services to infants and those relating to older children are the same, including the need to individualize services and review the plan frequently. Teachers and administrators working with young children also have the mandate to provide a free, appropriate public education for children with disabilities, including those with low-incidence disabilities such as visual impairments, through local school districts.

Although all special educational services must include family members, early intervention emphasizes the essential importance of the family's needs and concerns in determining a child's educational program. Under IDEA Part C, early intervention specialists devise a program to assist these children with their development and interactions with their physical and social environments. However, they also need to network with the larger community of professionals and toddler programs to help families find all appropriate early intervention services. Instead of an individualized education program (IEP), the team creates an individualized family service plan (IFSP). A baby's needs cannot be separated from his or her family's needs. Intervention specialists must be good observers and listeners to understand the situation of the entire family and to direct them to agencies that can help to meet their needs.

Early intervention services emphasize the essential importance of the family's needs and concerns in determining a child's educational program.

Vincent G. Fazzi

At its best, early intervention identifies a child in need of special services as early as possible in order to support and promote the child's development. It includes assessment by professionals trained in disciplines based on the child's disabilities as well as the coordination of services that will meet the family's needs. For example, if a family is in need of housing assistance, referrals need to be made to local agencies that can help; the teacher is a primary source of information and available resources.

As part of the assessment of a child, it is essential for you to ask the family about their priorities and goals for their family and for their child's development. In working with families, you can model new ways of encouraging language or movement. Some teachers bring toys and ideas to home visits with a family; others may use the toys or objects already in the home so the family may learn to view everyday objects in a new way. In either case, the family should be observed and supported for what they already do with their child and be given new ideas to allow them to stretch in new directions.

Respect for cultural diversity is a vital part of service delivery. Be prepared to work with the child and family while honoring their culture, morals, and perspective. On a visit to one family you may be expected to leave shoes behind shoji doors and be treated to tea and cookies. A visit to another home may involve driving to an apartment with sparse furniture and few comforts in an unfamiliar inner-city neighborhood. Each family has its own unique strengths and needs that contribute to their baby's well-being.

REFERRAL AND ASSESSMENT

Referral

Services to very young children begin with a referral. Referrals can be made by anyone who is aware of the child and his or her possible need for service. Referrals can come from the pediatrician, another agency, a relative, a teacher, or an acquaintance in the park who is aware of early intervention services. From identification (awareness of the child) to referral the time elapsed is usually 2 days. From referral to implementation (or the first IFSP meeting), the time elapsed is usually 45 calendar days. Every school district's telephone operator should be able to route callers to the number for the early intervention program.

Assessment

Children referred to special education from the ages of 3 and older are tested in the areas in which impairment is suspected. In infant programs, babies are assessed in all areas of development: cognitive, social, communication, physical status (including vision and hearing), adaptive (self–help), and gross and fine motor skills. Eligibility for services is based on risk factors for developmental delay (including vision or hearing loss that put a child at risk for a delay) or a demonstrated delay, or both, as assessed by the personnel qualified in that area. The child is eligible for early intervention services with delays (as measured by comparison with typically developing babies at similar age levels) in two of the eligibility areas or a 50 percent delay in one area. The percentage of delay that determines eligibility for services varies among states. In some it may be 25 percent delays in two areas, and in others it is 33 percent. In others, the delay or risk for delay can also be determined based on the team's professional opinion.

When assessing children under age 3, two or more qualified professionals are required to conduct the assessment together. In the ideal situation, assessment of a child with a visual impairment would be conducted by a transdisciplinary assessment team consisting of a teacher of students with visual impairments who conducts the functional vision assessment and an additional specialist (such as a speech and language pathologist or special education teacher) who perform other assessments together, accommodating for the vision loss. In addition to observation and interviews with family members and caregivers, assessors may use formalized assessments, such as the Hawaii Early Learning Profile (0–3) (Parks, 1997) with appropriate adaptations or the Oregon Project (Oregon Project for Visually Impaired and Blind Preschool Children, 1991), or the assessment team may determine that services are needed based on their experience.

THE IFSP

Once the assessment is complete, an IFSP team creates a plan for the child and his or her family. The team would include the parents or guardians, anyone the family chooses to bring, such as grandparents, friends, or others; service providers (occupational or physical therapists, speech therapist, a teacher of students with visual impairments, or others); and anyone the school district or other agencies involved require (such as an administrator). In some cases, the family may meet with one service coordinator, and the service providers who cannot attend are represented in their written reports. These meetings should be conducted at a place and time convenient to the family, which is most likely at home. Experienced teachers in diverse communities have conducted IFSP meetings in fast food restaurants, parks, a parent's office during lunch, grandparents' houses, as well as at the center or agency providing service. Because the role of the family is crucial in an infant's life, the plan reflects information about the entire family. Some agencies may use a family questionnaire, which would document where family members spend their time, or ask in what activities the family participates. This would enable the team to determine the natural environment,

As a natural environment for a toddler, preschool is an appropriate setting for services, in which children can be observed in their everyday activities to make sure their vision-related needs are addressed within their usual routines.

Jean E. Olmstead

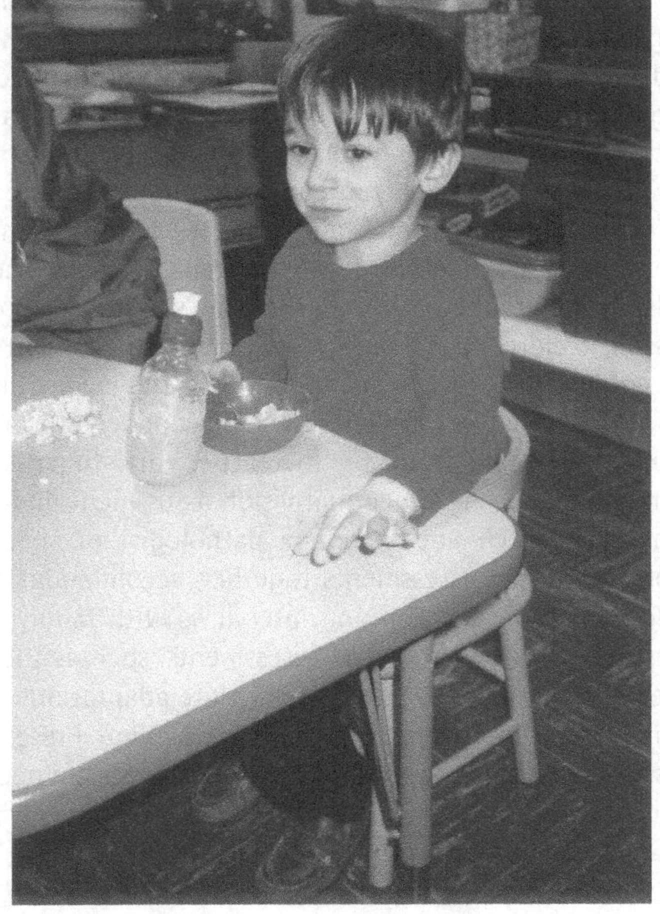

or where the child spends his or her time. Determining where the family and baby spend their time is important because current law states that all services should be provided in the child's natural environment (see the following section on Natural Environments). If the child is in day care, for example, it would be important that the early intervention specialist see the child there to help consider the child's needs and to ensure that the child's vision-related needs are acknowledged and addressed within his or her usual routines.

The IFSP consists of home and family data, the child's eligibility and who will be the service coordinator, the child's age and present level of development, and his or her health status. The family is asked about their family resources, for example: Who helps? They are asked about their concerns, priorities, and needs. This is very important for the family, as every concern should be addressed in the desired outcomes, as well as the services (whether or not required under Part C of IDEA) that will help meet those desired outcomes, concerns, and priorities. For example, the family may be concerned that the child has global delays and is not yet moving independently. When the team asks the parent a question, such as, "What would you like to see happen for your family and child?" The answer might be, "I just want my baby to be ready for kindergarten when he's 5." The professional will acknowledge the parent's concern and write an appropriate goal for what needs to happen next to work toward that goal based on the assessments results, such as, "When lying on his tummy on Mom's chest, Joey will pick up his head as she calls his name."

Babies grow and change often. The child is assessed annually, but the plan is reviewed every six months. An infant beginning an early intervention program at 3 months of age has a minimum of nine meetings throughout an infant program before the creation of his or her first IEP at 3 years of age. After the initial referral and assessments, the typical progression for such a child includes the following team meetings:

Time Lines for IFSP Meetings

- Initial IFSP meeting, which starts the provision of services.
- Periodic review, 6 months after the initial IFSP. The desired outcomes are reviewed and progress is noted, as well as any other information in the IFSP that needs updating, such as the parents' concerns, the child's health, or others.
- First annual IFSP meeting, held 1 year after the initial IFSP in this example, when the child is 15 months old. Every page of the document is rewritten and updated, with new or current assessment results reported.
- Periodic review meeting, held 6 months after the annual IFSP, when the child is 21 months old.
- Second annual IFSP meeting, when the child is 27 months old.
- Periodic review, when the child is 33 months old.

- Transition plan meeting, held 3 to 6 months before the child's third birthday.
- Final IFSP meeting.
- Initial IEP meeting, if the child is eligible for services under IDEA Part B.

The final IFSP meeting can be held at the same time as the initial IEP meeting. The desired outcomes are reviewed and any determined to be incomplete may be added to the IEP standards and benchmarks. The family needs to know that when their child turns 3, early intervention services end and services will continue via the IEP process. Besides these meetings, regular vision and hearing screenings or updates of the functional vision or hearing assessments are held.

Families have rights and responsibilities under IDEA Part C legislation. These rights and their interpretation change often, so it is wise to check the latest regulations frequently. Among the most basic of these are that families have the right to give their consent before any assessments are made and to have adequate notice before any meetings are held regarding their children. No services are provided without the parents' or guardians' consent.

NATURAL ENVIRONMENTS

Under current federal requirements, the setting for early intervention infant services is supposed to be, as much as is feasible, the child's natural environments: places where typically developing babies, toddlers, and preschoolers are usually found. This concept is the approximate equivalent of the mandate to educate older children with special needs in the least restrictive environment possible. Natural environments include children's homes, day care settings, preschool and toddler programs sponsored by Head Start or school districts, or other state programs for a child's age group. Story time at local libraries, parent and child exercise or activity programs, zoos, and parks are other examples of natural environments.

In the past, services that addressed the unique needs of infants and young children with visual impairments were more commonly provided in segregated or specialized environments. Federal regulations currently reflect a philosophy that placement with typically developing children is preferred. To balance placement in integrated settings with work with specialized professionals trained in providing services to students with visual impairment, you must be creative to determine the means to meet the child's needs within this framework.

The first step is to conduct an interview to discover the family's normal routines. Using an interview form (see Figure 5.1) to help the family articulate what they do during the day will help the team determine appropriate procedures that will help the family accomplish the desired outcomes on the IFSP. Families are unique, so the natural environment interview must be especially flexible. It should permit you to ask generalized questions about typical routines, but be open enough to address any significant concerns in more detail.

FIGURE 5.1

Natural Environment Interview

Child's name ___David M.___ Parents' name ___Sarah & David M.___

Interviewer ___Cinda Wert Rapp___ Date of interview ___5/23/05___

Children have opportunities to learn in a variety of community and family settings. Please list or check places where your family goes and what your family does. The list will provide information that will help us help you see learning opportunities for your child.

Include things as routine as car or bus rides, window shopping, department or grocery stores, and walking around your neighborhood. Remember occasional things such as swimming, visiting friends, malls, outdoor playgrounds, petting zoos, restaurants, relatives' homes. Include special trips such as to theme parks, Halloween carnivals, reunions, picnics, the beach, and so on.

Family Life

__✓__ **Routines**

____ Bathing –loves his bath

____ Cooking ✗

__✓__ Driving

__✓__ Eating

____ Eats pureed food

"I have no child care and I drive a school bus –he rides with me all day."

Mom feeds him – eats before family does–No one sits together at one time.

__✓__ **Entertainment activities**

____ TV

__✓__ Videos

____ Movies ✗

____ Looking at books

____ Local children's theater ✗

____ Sports ✗

Doesn't care

Watches baby music videos sitting in walker right up against TV!

__✓__ **Socialization activities**

____ Play groups

____ Family gatherings

____ Mother's groups ✗

Family comes to visit here only because the rest of the family smokes and Mom can't expose his lungs there.

____ **Gardening** ✗

__✓__ **Family rituals or celebrations** ___Go for a walk every Sunday.___

__✓__ **Physical play** ___Loves being thrown in the air by Dad.___

Community Life

____ **Family outings** ___"Since we drive all week, we stay home on Saturdays and Sundays"___

____ **Children's attractions** ___Not yet___

____ **Church/religious groups** ___No___

____ **Community events** ___Can't go because of germs.___

____ **Early childhood programs (describe)** ___None - home only wanted.___

One area of the interview form should include home routines: eating, bathing, cooking, gardening, toileting, and the like. During the interview, these routines would be discussed with the family as appropriate. For example, if a family had no garden or houseplants, the teacher would skip the section on gardening and cross it off on the form.

It is best if the natural environment interview takes place during the intake interview. If this information is obtained at intake, outcomes can be written to include these natural settings. For example, one teacher read that all the children and babies in Sophie's family go to church every day for an hour. When the occupational therapist reported that child needed to work on hand release, the goal became: "Sophie will put the offering in the basket during church."

However, the intake and assessment process can be lengthy and overwhelming for families if it involves too many questions. In that case, you may ask the questions from the natural environment interview at the first home visit. The interview would attempt to document pertinent details about everyday routines such as eating, bathing, and bedtime. For example, you might ask, "How does Joey enjoy bathing?" "Do you use the big tub or the sink?" "Does he bathe with his siblings?" This information can then be used to suggest ways to incorporate intervention into the child's daily life. If Joey loves his bath, that could be noted, and in future home visits ideas could be given to family members who could use that time for naming body parts, pouring for fun, or other activities. If Maria cries during towel drying, this could cue you to other assessments that may need to be done, such as sensory integration assessments with an occupational therapist. If Casey is upset by bubbles in the tub or by someone singing in the bathroom, the team would be aware that they should avoid suggesting interventions using such stimuli as bubbles and singing, or give ideas to incorporate them slowly into other parts of the child's day until they are accepted.

PROVIDING VISION INTERVENTION SERVICES TO BABIES

Most programs for infants are home based, in recognition of the fact that serving babies apart from their primary caregivers minimizes the effects of those services. Families who are supported with information and assistance are better able to care for and teach their children. An important focus for service coordinators and providers is to help families meet their needs and understand the suggested interventions so that families are able to implement the interventions themselves throughout the weeks and months ahead.

Home and Other Visits

The structure of home visits is individualized according to the child's and family's needs. Visits can be weekly, biweekly, or any number of times up to eight per week, and can involve direct service, consultation, or both. They usually last an hour each, but this is also individualized.

A typical home visit may include greetings and updates on what's happening in the family, then updates on what the family may have practiced or continued since the previous visit, the introduction of new ideas or perhaps old ideas in a new way, a time for questions from the family, and the presentation of what the teacher did in response to last week's questions. One routine that has helped some families is to bring the "HELP at Home activity sheets" from the Hawaii Early Learning Profile (Parks, 1997), go over them and place them in a notebook that has been organized into sections for each of the child's areas of development (cognitive, communication, motor, and so forth).

Some visits might involve attending an appointment with an eye care specialist with the family to help them understand the results of a vision examination or to answer questions derived from discussions with the family during previous home visits. Another visit might entail observing several day care sites to determine their appropriateness for the child, if that is the family's primary concern. If the child is having difficulty sitting in a shopping cart at the supermarket with her parent, you might go shopping with them to help troubleshoot problems, and make suggestions so the parent and baby can make trips together more successfully. Observe the child objectively as the parent shops; then you and the parent can brainstorm ideas together for making future trips a success. Such ideas might include shopping for a smaller number of items at one time, shortening the trip, or going to a smaller store initially. The parent might give the child something interesting and desirable to hold while in the store. Trips to the store could also be an opportunity for you to discuss the benefits of naming foods, describing hot or cold areas of the store, talking about the various food sections, or other activities.

Home visits allow for endless creativity. One child became depressed when the teacher took back the toys she had brought with her. Some toys had been donated to the child, but were immediately broken, sold, or lost. The teacher then looked around the apartment for what the family did have. She spotted a blue plastic milk crate in the corner of the living room. She placed the child inside the crate, and practiced saying "Go!" (a new word for him), after which he got a ride in the crate around the living room. He was given choices, such as "Fast?" or "Slow?" with body movements representing those choices that he could imitate. He never wanted it to go slowly, so he quickly learned to imitate her movement for fast.

Record Keeping

Keeping a record of home visits will provide a journal and history of intervention. If the forms are on carbonless copy paper, the parent can be given a completed copy at the end of the meeting, and can maintain this written documentation of

FIGURE 5.2

Home Visit Record

Child's name Samantha Q. Date of visit 10/4/05

People present Social worker, Dad, Teacher, Samantha

The social worker, Sarah G., scheduled to come during the home visit to discuss openly with Mom and teacher that Mom has not been showing up for her drug tests. Since she has missed two, there may be a possibility that Samantha will be removed from home if Mom misses again.

We discussed Samantha's development, good weight gain. She has accomplished 3 out of 8 goals in two months!

Mom hasn't yet scheduled the eye doctor's appointment, but promised to call this week.

We exchanged phone numbers and will meet again all together in three months to talk about results of doctor's visits.

Next home visit 10/11/05

the baby's progress and ideas. Giving written notes can also help the parent share the information with other family members. Two forms could be used. One home visit record could simply state the baby's name, the date, and who was at the visit at the top, and then provide a blank page to write whatever is appropriate (see Figure 5.2). Another variation of the form could have the same information with additional categories, such as "What worked from last week?" "Interventions suggested and child's response" or "Resources/activities to bring for next visit," or, as in the version shown in Figure 5.3, "Materials brought," "Child's response," "Parent's concerns," "Suggestions," "Teacher follow-up," and "Parent follow-up." Forms help you and your families plan for the next visit and provide natural, nonthreatening accountability for all participants.

A Family's Other Concerns

Although the primary function of an early intervention specialist is to work with the child and family to enhance the child's development, parents may not always want suggestions or information about their child. During some visits they may just want to talk about their frustrations or experiences. In such situations, you might write in the record, "Parent talked about her frustrations this week," and

FIGURE 5.3

Home Visit Record

Child's name David M. Date of visit 9/16/05

People present Mom, Cinda, David

Comments from last visit

New nightlight in David's bedroom has helped stop the crying at night. When he wakes up, he goes back to sleep now.

Materials brought

Began functional vision (annual) assessment. Documentation on protocol.

Child's response

David enjoyed the "games."

Parent's concerns

David doesn't seem to be eating much lately. Tongue pushes food out. Doctor is concerned about poor weight gain. Started choking on "Toddler 2" foods.

Suggestions

Ask doctor for oral-motor evaluation through insurance. Encourage lip closure by holding spoon on tongue for a moment.

Teacher follow-up

Bring information regarding feeding issues.

Parent follow-up

Try not scraping spoon on teeth to release food. Hold spoon lightly on tongue to encourage lip closure.

Source: Developed by Kathy Fields, Rose Stamm, Nancy Dolphin, Julie Nesnansky, Cinda Wert Rapp, Sandra Hagood, Kyle McKune-Santos, Frances Delacio.

include details if appropriate. The specialist doesn't need to include personal complaints, such as "My husband doesn't change diapers," since intervention for such a situation is inappropriate and not part of the specialist's role. You may want to tell the family about child and elderly abuse laws and let them know of your responsibilities if you hear or see any abuse in the home. As the family goes through the process of accepting their child's special needs, the specialist may provide materials about community resources (including family resource centers). A teacher can easily get involved in conflicts outside of his or her expertise. She or he will need to be able to access resources for the family instead of solving the problems personally.

Home visits are intimate experiences; it requires a great deal of trust on the family's part to permit a stranger to come into their home and talk about something that may be difficult: their baby with special needs. A valuable resource for dealing with such issues is the PAVII Project (Parents and Visually Impaired Infants), in particular, "The Art of Home Visiting" (Calvello, 1990).

If a parent asks for materials, such as information about typical childhood development, the teacher can bring the requested items with him or her on the next visit. If the family feels that they are never able to get out of the house, a note might be made to call other support services and to schedule the six-month periodic review (a meeting to review the family's concerns and the child's development and services that is held between annual IFSP meetings), which may result in adding respite services to the services already provided to the family.

MANAGING AN EARLY INTERVENTION CASELOAD

Keeping records organized involves careful planning. For example, how does a teacher keep track of all the children on his or her caseload and know whose review is coming up next? The simplest method is sometimes the best, such as a calendar form that can be pinned to the wall at a teacher's desk (see Figure 5.4 for an example). When filled out at the beginning of the year in pencil, it can serve as a rotating, dynamic reminder throughout the year of upcoming meetings for each child. For busy teachers, a quick glance at the yearly calendar above a desk is helpful in planning.

Some agencies schedule IFSP meetings well before the due date: at a child's birthday or a month before the actual meeting is due, for example, to make sure that if there is a cancellation, illness, or other reason, there will be time to reschedule. A teacher can add to the calendar as needed. For example, if Joey's annual IFSP meeting is due May 12th, an entry for April 12th might read, "Assess and schedule Joey's annual."

When on the telephone discussing issues with families or other agencies, having a quick reference can help you to make sure no reviews are missed. Meet-

FIGURE 5.4

Cinda's Meetings
2005–2006 School Year

August	September	October	November	December
David—Annual 31st	Samantha— periodic review 15th	Cindy— Annual 4th	José— 6 months' vision evaluation	
January	**February**	**March**	**April**	**May**
José— periodic review 11th	David— periodic review 31st Samantha— begin assessment	Samantha— annual transition plan 15th	Cindy— periodic review transition plan 4th	

FIGURE 5.5

Early Intervention History

Child's name José Gonzales Date of birth 6/22/05

Service coordinator's name Cinda

Previous services/programs? Yes If so, where and dates of IFSP San Francisco, 9-29-05

Referral date to our program 10-4-05

Last IFSP? San Francisco Date 9-21-05

Service coordinator Jane Smith

Date of initial IFSP to our program 10-21-05

Services provided home visits Parent Education Vision

Periodic review date 3-14-06

Changes to IFSP? Add respite

Annual IFSP date 9-16-06

Services provided Same

Periodic review date 3-10-07

Changes to IFSP? Add toddler group Add busing – Mom will ride too

Annual IFSP date 9-15-07

Services provided Home visits, bus, toddler group, respite, speech and language consultant

Periodic review date 3-16-08

Changes to IFSP? No

Transition plan meeting 12-21-07

Final IFSP date 5-30-08 IEP date 5-30-08

Notes José will be going to Jane Dunham's preschool class for visually impaired toddlers, with inclusion in general education preschool next door.

ings for incoming infants' assessments, reviews and meetings can be added throughout the year.

Given the complexity of IFSPs, with their multiple addenda, it can take time to leaf through them to get an idea of a child's background history. It can be helpful to have at the front of the teacher's working file for each child a summary of key information about the child's experience in early intervention activities, such as meetings, services provided, and changes in staffing. Figure 5.5 provides an example of a form that can help organize this information. In addition to organizing the whole year, the form can be expanded in a variety of ways to include other service providers and consultations (informal or not) made on behalf of a child. For example, information about when busing was added, or when the child had surgery and missed three weeks of programming, or when the mother had a second baby and needed to take a break from services can all be documented.

MAKING A LASTING IMPACT

Perhaps there is no greater joy than working with families who have young babies. Serving this population provides a wonderful opportunity for your personal and professional growth in learning to listen; leave your personal biases or agendas at the door, and be open to the challenging, interesting world of diverse families with the youngest children with special needs. Working effectively with a very young child and his or her family can have the most profound impact on the course of the child's subsequent development and thereby offer you great professional satisfaction.

REFERENCES

Calvello, G. (1990). The art of home visiting. In D. Chen, C.T. Friedman, & G. Calvello (Eds.), *Parents and visually impaired infants.* Louisville, KY: PAVII Project and American Printing House for the Blind.

Oregon Project for Visually Impaired and Blind Preschool Children (5th ed.). (1991). Medford, OR: Southern Oregon Education Service District.

Parks, S. (1997). *Hawaii early learning profile.* Palo Alto, CA: VORT Corporation.

CHAPTER

6

Working with Students Who Have Visual and Multiple Impairments

Jane N. Erin and Jean E. Olmstead

Although beginning teachers of students with visual impairments have usually had some instruction and experience with students who have multiple disabilities, they often find it difficult to understand their role with students who have different rates and ways of learning and work efficiently with them. Some students may be able to read and write, while others are learning to use gestures or objects to communicate. Some can walk independently but cannot keep themselves safe, while others can move their arms or legs but cannot move forward to locate a toy.

Students with multiple disabilities have a wide range of physical and behavioral differences, and their extensive needs evoke different reactions from people who interact with them. Students who are tube fed or are unable to move their limbs may appear helpless. Many new professionals working with them may sometimes feel daunted, discouraged, or even depressed until they learn to recognize the signs and rates of progress. If you find yourself reacting in this way, seek out your experienced peers or others who have worked with students who have multiple disabilities, and talk with them about what you are feeling. To be successful with your students, it is important that you feel comfortable with their ways of learning and your abilities to support them, and that you also recognize their abilities as well as their disabilities.

It is important to recognize the abilities of students who are multiply disabled. These students are playing traffic sign bingo.

Jean E. Olmstead

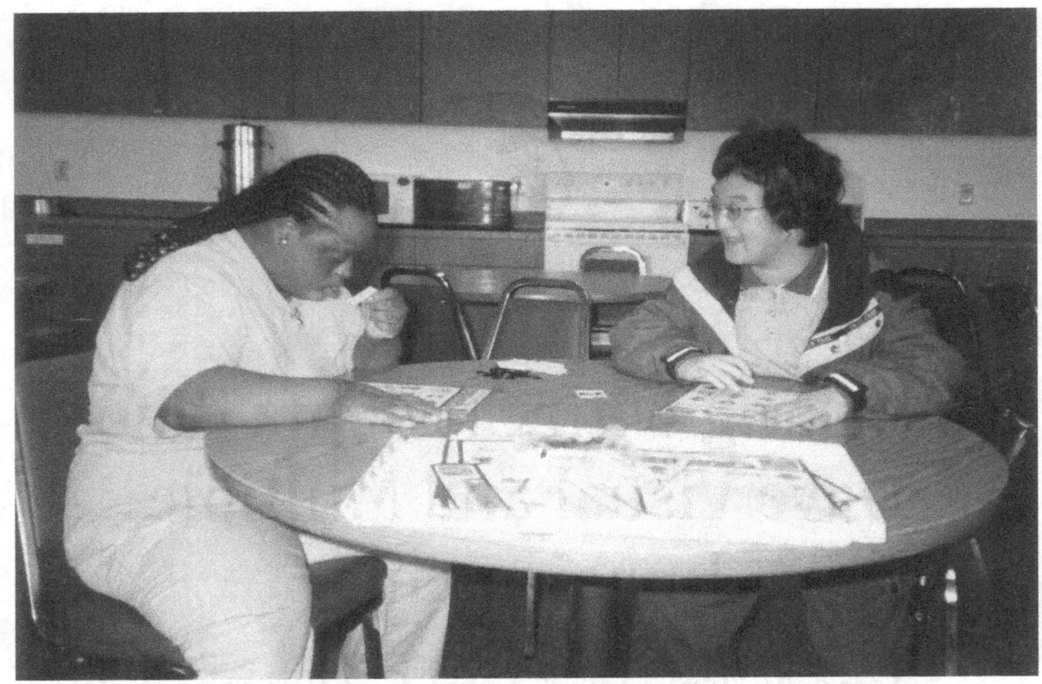

GETTING ORGANIZED

Scheduling

What strategies can you use to support the education of a student with multiple disabilities? First, because multiply disabled students usually need a more consistent program than others, it may be counterproductive for an unfamiliar adult to instruct them only once or twice a week. They must practice a skill regularly, often several times a day, to learn that skill effectively. Students who are medically fragile may sleep more than their unimpaired peers or may miss school often due to medical treatments. Because of these learning patterns and physical characteristics, it's advisable that your services be flexible and involve the adults who work regularly with the student. The following arrangements may be considered:

Service Options

- Clustered services, in which a block of time is designated for students in the same class or school. Activities can be varied week to week according to the students' needs and availability.
- Group services, in which two or three students with similar needs learn in a small group with you.
- Consultation, in which you work with the classroom staff to make sure that students' needs related to visual impairment are being met. Sometimes time can be scheduled to consult at the same time as other specialists, such as physical therapists, so that students' physical and visual needs can be integrated in the most appropriate way.

- Adapted instructional times to provide services for time periods and specific times when learning is most appropriate. For students with limited attention spans, a short session of 15 or 20 minutes a day each day may be ideal. Sometimes you can alter your daily schedule to see a student before or after the school day to work on specialized skills such as dressing, food preparation, or recreational activities; however, the need to change the student's busing schedule may preclude such a plan.

Collaboration and Communication

Although flexibility in schedules and services can seem ideal for the student, it can seem hectic for you as the teacher of visually impaired students since you are working to address the needs of many students in different places. Often the best solution is working closely with parents or guardians, classroom teachers, and paraeducators to ensure that skills are practiced regularly in familiar settings. In this case, you will serve as a consultant to provide feedback on a student's needs related to visual impairment.

Scheduling and service options should be discussed with the educational team, especially the family. The terms "monitor" or "consultation" can mean one thing to you and something entirely different to a family. Some people view a consultant as an outside expert who occasionally stops to observe, while others assume that this person will work regularly with the classroom team. Still others think that a consultant will only be involved when a question arises. It is important that the team participates in the discussion of what services the student needs and why, and that there is a clear understanding of how special services will be provided.

Each person on the educational team should be informed about the student's visual functioning and what adaptive techniques and materials will enhance his or her participation in activities. This includes other related service providers, such as speech therapists, adapted physical education teachers, physical and occupational therapists, and O&M specialists. It is ideal if the team can meet as a group at the beginning of each school year.

At these meetings, share the results of the students' functional vision assessment reports and also interpret reports from eye care specialists. Talk about any special equipment and techniques for each student. Bring to the group any questions you may have about the student's other abilities and disabilities. For example, many students have head tilts or posture that may be due to visual disabilities, physical disabilities, or both. Talking to other team members can help you decide what causes the head tilt and whether it is helping the student to adapt or interfering with learning. It is also useful for you to have the opportunity to observe the other specialists such as the occupational therapist working with the student. Other specialists on the team can provide a new perspective. A notebook or handheld digital notetaker to record ideas for later follow-up is a great help at a fast-paced meeting.

During the school year, keep in touch with this core group. Most itinerant teachers have few opportunities for organized face-to-face meetings with other members of the IEP team. More often, communication consists of a hallway conversation, a quick cup of coffee in the teachers' lounge, or an exchange of e-mails. Especially when contacting parents and classroom teachers by telephone, it is important to find out when and how it is most convenient to contact them. A parent who gets an unexpected call while cooking dinner for three children will not be as receptive as one who is expecting a call that comes at 9:00 p.m. after the children are in bed. Some parents will appreciate and welcome a visit to the home, and it may provide you with some insight to understand how the family manages the student's extensive needs. Keeping a written notebook for each student is helpful because staff can describe the student's activities and make suggestions for other team members (see Chapter 3). The classroom teacher is in charge of this book, which is usually sent home daily with the student so that parents or guardians can read the notes and respond when appropriate. Many students with multiple disabilities cannot describe what they have learned or experienced. A notebook gives others a way to comment on something that has happened or encourage the student to show something new he or she has learned. In some instances, e-mail messages to the parents and other IEP team members can replace the use of a notebook.

Because your services may be variable (that is, on a consultant, or monitoring, basis) and may not involve regular contact with a student, it is important to document your visits, meetings, and time spent in related activities such as phone calls. Since your role may often be behind the scenes, misunderstandings can occur. For legal reasons you should have a record of what you have done to support the student's learning, even if you were not instructing the student directly.

Teachers of students who are visually impaired can play an important role in describing what developmental and learning delays are typical for young visually impaired students, and different members of the team may help the family understand the nature and extent of the student's other disabilities. Most families appreciate direct, descriptive information, but keep in mind that your role is not to diagnose other disabilities. It takes great tact and sensitivity to encourage a parent to seek other assistance without overstepping your role: "Samantha is having more trouble using and understanding words than most students who are visually impaired. I think it would be a good idea to ask the psychologist and the speech therapist to observe her and let us know if anything other than a visual impairment could be affecting her learning."

Creating IEPs

The IEP meeting is especially important for a student with multiple disabilities because often several related service providers are involved. The family and other team members must have a clear understanding of instructional priorities and teaching procedures in each area. The meeting is an opportunity to discuss the student's progress and the next levels of achievement to be targeted.

Your role in the creation of the IEP for a student with multiple disabilities may be different than for other visually impaired students. The student may have specific goals and objectives that you will implement, such as braille instruction or work on picture identification. Other goals will be implemented through different activities and by various instructors. Specific goals and objectives for the students who receive only monitoring or consultative services are not often recommended by the teacher of students with visual impairments. These students often require environmental adaptations such as being placed on their backs or sides for the best use of their vision. These adaptations cannot be identified as benchmarks in the student's IEP since they are continuing. For these students, you may meet with the classroom team and develop preliminary goals cooperatively. Your name will be included on the IEP form as one who participated in setting those goals. Although you and other members of the team may suggest learning goals and strategies to the team, the family and the team will consider and approve them before they are established as educational goals.

IEP forms and procedures can vary by location. Some school districts have eliminated a section for recording a student's present levels of functioning as a separate IEP page. If this is the case in the area in which you teach, the only reference to the students' visual impairments in the IEP may be the service in visual impairment listed on the designated pages for your signature or the form in use. You may therefore find it beneficial to include the summary and recommendations from the students' functional vision assessments on an IEP meeting notes page, especially when the student is moving to a new grade or classroom.

MAKING APPROPRIATE ADAPTATIONS

The Visual Environment

One of the most important things you can do for students with low vision is to help to create the best environment for their learning. Many students with multiple disabilities do not know that they can change their world in order to see better. They cannot move to another seat, put the window blind down, decide to wear a hat, or place materials against a contrasting background. Some are unresponsive to visual changes, and others startle or become upset when small features of their environment change. Those around them sometimes ignore their responses because they may be subtle or not clearly communicated.

As a professional who does not regularly work in the classroom, you may provide a fresh perspective on how a visually impaired student understands the learning space. Shelves with many colorful objects, crowded furniture, and carpets or surface changes on the floor may pose difficulties for visually impaired students, while others in the class notice and anticipate these variations.

You are also experienced in noticing visual responses that others may overlook. One of your first roles with a new student will be to observe him or her in the typical school setting. A comment such as, "I notice that he turns his head to the left every time he wants to look for something on the table" can draw staff members' attention to a student's visual behaviors so that they will consider what the student sees. Basic recommendations such as "He might be able to see the white cup better against a dark placemat" will call attention to ways of encouraging the student's use of vision.

Encourage staff to consider how the world looks from the student's point of view. Asking students about whether the light is too bright or there is glare on the picture will help some students begin to realize that they have choices about where they sit and how they position materials. When students have physical disabilities, consider how things look from where they sit or lie. Lying on a student's floor mat can reveal that he or she is looking directly into a light or can see only the tops of the heads of nearby people because of his or her head position.

Comments and suggestions should be given sparingly and at a time when staff can be attentive. Recommendations should reflect respect for the staff members who will implement them. If paraeducators feel that they are being directed by someone from outside the class, they may not cooperate. However, if they feel that they are important participants in the fascinating process of teaching, they are likely to try the suggestions and generate some of their own. In general, clarifying the roles of the classroom teacher, the teacher of students with visual impairments, and the paraeducator assigned to a class is an important part of planning effective services for a student (see Chapter 4).

The Learning Environment

Classroom staff may be familiar with the organization of a school setting for students with multiple disabilities, but they may never have considered how the experience is different for students who are blind or visually impaired. One key factor is the student's ability to anticipate events and make sense of the entire environment if he or she cannot see it and does not understand words.

You may find it helpful to represent the daily schedule through a calendar system or calendar box and use touch cues to help the student anticipate a change in events, positions, or activities. In addition, you may be able to find ways of making different areas of the room distinctive through the use of carpets, wall surfaces, low-volume sound sources, and other sources of information that will help the multiply disabled student remain oriented and understand where he or she is when moved from place to place.

Learning Materials

Students with multiple disabilities use the same objects every day for daily routines. Objects such as cups, spoons, orthopedic devices, wheelchairs, and eyeglasses are the most important materials for learning because the student sees them every day. You can suggest visual adaptations to make these materials easier to see: contrasting or bright colors can enhance visibility and also mark the materials as belonging to that student.

Remind classroom staff to let the student view an object before it is used in a routine (e.g., looking at a shoe before it is placed on his or her foot) because this helps connect the object with the routine to follow. Some simple adaptations to materials can improve the student's independence in regular routines. For example, to reduce figure-versus-ground-confusion for students in wheelchairs with clear trays, cover their trays with nonglare paper when items are presented on the trays; the paper should be light for dark items and vice versa. Dishes and plates of several colors allow contrast with the food that is served, and placemats with solid backgrounds will serve the same purpose for finger food.

Classroom teachers may regard the teacher of visually impaired students as someone with specialized knowledge about materials, and they may not realize that the arrangement and presentation of *ordinary* materials is the most appropriate and flexible approach to varying the visual environment. New classroom materials such as light boxes or tactile object displays can add interest and encourage different ways of thinking. However often your most important role with materials is to find ways to make everyday objects visible or meaningful to the students who use them.

Students with very limited or inconsistent responses may respond to sensory materials such as vibrating pillows, mirrors, and switch toys that involve movement, noise, or light. Scented oils may be used for massages. A young student could be placed under a small plastic sawhorse from which dangling objects may stimulate visual interest; a small fan can be used to move the objects slowly. These materials should not be used passively. Introduction of a sensory material should involve pauses and turn-taking so that the student can indicate interest or aversion. When possible, the student should be able to control and explore the material independently. With some students, stimulating materials such as flashing lights can provoke seizures; these materials should be introduced gradually to check for aversive reactions.

Technology

Many students with visual and multiple disabilities benefit from adaptive technology used for communication, mobility, life activities, or academic skills. You can be an effective source of information about the visual and tactile aspects of these devices. The appropriate size and contrast of pictures, the student's scanning ability, the placement of controls for visual access, and the use of tactile cues are features that you may evaluate (see Kreuzer & King). You may make recommendations related to positioning, glare, and image size with computers as a member of the team planning for a student's technological needs. In selecting technology, work closely with other specialists to find ways for the student to function best with available sensory, physical, and intellectual abilities.

In identifying the appropriate technology, the student's immediate functional needs should be of the highest priority (see Chapter 9 for additional information on technology). A complex communication device will be ineffective if it is not regularly available or if it is difficult to program and use. Sometimes families or other team members become interested in the use of complex technology such as braille notetakers or computers, and you will be a key participant in deciding whether a student can use such devices purposefully. For students who are able to learn reading and writing, it will be your role to explore adapted devices when a student has multiple disabilities; for example, the use of extension keys or one-handed braillewriters may be helpful for braille readers who have physical disabilities. *Braille Literacy: A Functional Approach* (Wormsley, 2004) is a comprehensive resource for teaching braille to students who have multiple disabilities or other learning difficulties.

PROVIDING MONITORING SERVICES

Since almost all multiply disabled students have monitoring time specified on their IEPs, you will be spending at least some of that time in the special education or general education classroom to observe, make suggestions, or demonstrate techniques. You may discover a great difference between special education classes and general education classes. Students in general education classrooms will have lessons in certain academic areas; curriculum in special education classrooms may vary according to the students' abilities and the teachers' discretion. Some multiply disabled students will be included full- or part-time in regular classes. Others may be involved in community-based activities and others may spend most of their time in the special education classrooms.

Your role in monitoring students' work is to ensure that their needs as visually impaired learners are being met. This may involve providing materials, suggesting techniques, working directly with students, or providing feedback to others working with students. The goal may be to enhance the students' use of vision in functional situations, or to help the students use other senses to carry out a task or interact with others. Special education class teachers are the specialists in instruction of students with multiple learning needs, and they are responsible for providing appropriate curricula. If these teachers ask about suitable activities, you may provide some suggestions. However, you can also ask, "If the students weren't visually impaired and were operating at this level, what lessons would you provide?" Once the teachers list some activities, work with them to adapt the lessons according to the students' visual needs. A useful resource for special and regular educators who work with students who have multiple and visual impairments is *When You Have a Visually Impaired Child with Multiple Disabilities in Your Classroom: A Guide for Teachers* (2004).

Many students with multiple disabilities are educated along with their nondisabled peers for part or all of the day. When this is the case, the classroom teacher will be interested in ways of making a lesson appropriate for a student's sensory abilities and his or her cognitive level. You may be concerned if you are asked to provide input on curricular questions that may not seem to relate directly to the student's visual impairment. For example, if a second-grade teacher asks how to involve a student who has severe retardation and blindness in a lesson on addition, should you suggest the type and use of materials or just the appropriate sensory qualities of any materials intended for use by this student? While many questions are likely to be answered more appropriately by other special educators, explain what materials are appropriate for students of varying abilities. You would not recommend an abacus for a student who is at a developmental age of about 18 months; instead, you could guide the teacher to find interesting groups of objects that could be manipulated by the student and to confer with the appropriate special educator regarding an effective math curriculum for the student.

INSTRUCTING THE STUDENT

Adapting Instruction to Individual Needs

There are wide variations in needs and abilities among students with multiple disabilities. In order to adapt instruction for a particular student, you will need to have information about the student's communication abilities, physical abilities, sensory responses, social responses, and typical behaviors. Arrange to observe the student in familiar and unfamiliar situations before assessment begins; also talk with the student's parents or guardians about what concerns they have related to the student's vision.

Although you will conduct functional vision evaluations and learning media assessments just as you would with any student, you may need to rely more on observation of the student in daily routines and activities. Many students with multiple disabilities cannot respond to formal evaluations such as the Snellen eye chart for acuity assessment. Even though the assessment process may need to be less formal with some multiply disabled students, it should still be an objective report of responses and, whenever possible it should include measurable data such as frequency, time, and distance to describe the student's behaviors (see Erin, 1996, for more information). With students who show very few observable behaviors, it may be helpful to ask the family and regular staff to videotape the student in several activities so that you will see a representative cross-section of behaviors.

Instruction in the Use of Vision

Like all students who are visually impaired, those with multiple disabilities may benefit from encouragement to use vision in daily tasks. Because their vision may be affected by neurological conditions, multiply disabled students may have different visual responses than other students or may be attentive to different visual phenomena than those without multiple disabilities. You may be most helpful in recommending ways to prompt visual responses, such as auditory prompting (for example, tapping a spoon on the table to get the student's visual attention) or visual prompting (e.g., moving a target object in front of the student). Guiding other staff to incorporate the most appropriate prompts into the student's regular routines such as eating or locating the sink will allow greater independence for a student who may continue to need assistance for activities of daily living.

Some students with multiple disabilities have distinctive visual behaviors that should be considered in instruction. For instance, many students with cortical visual impairment appear to be unable to look at objects and pick them up or touch them at the same time. They may look quickly at an object, look away, and then pick it up. Prompting them to look at objects may be counterproductive because they cannot tolerate or integrate the sensory input; however, this decision can only be made after the students have been prompted and reinforced for visual responses.

For a student with cognitive limitations, visual instruction may include association of symbols or language with visual experiences. For example, a student who heads toward the window when asked to go to the restroom may have visual difficulties locating the bathroom or may not understand the meaning of the words used. Some difficulties in orientation, localizing, or object recognition are a result of the student's incomplete understanding of the meaning of what he or she sees. Only regular visual experiences paired with consistent language will allow the student to anticipate and respond to objects and concepts that are a regular part of the environment.

Instruction for Blind Students

Students who are blind often need support in alternative communication, ranging from the use of object symbols to the use of braille. Students who will not become braille readers may still need tactile symbols to help in organizing their world, such as swatches of fabric on drawers to suggest the contents or raised tactile symbols to indicate events or experiences. You can often suggest resources to speech and language therapists and special educators to help them in developing a system that will add meaning to the student's world. *Teaching Students with Visual and Multiple Impairments: A Resource Guide* (Smith & Levack, 1996) provides extensive detail about communication and other educational needs of multiply disabled students in a context that can be applied by itinerant teachers.

Students who are blind may also need specialized intervention in O&M skills. They may be overlooked for O&M training because others assume they will not be independent travelers. However, most students can improve their travel skills or their ability to monitor their own travel through instruction. Sometimes traditional O&M techniques are varied for multiply disabled students to meet their individual abilities. For example, a student with a physical disability may lean on the forearm of the guide for additional stability, and a student who uses a wheelchair may use voice prompts as cues for forward movement. These decisions require collaboration with an O&M specialist and a physical or occupational therapist. You may need to facilitate the communication among these specialists.

Shaping the Instructional Process

When working directly with the student, decide how much assistance to give in teaching a skill. Too little assistance does not provide a framework for learning; too much assistance stifles the student's initiative. Familiarize yourself with various levels of prompting and prompt only when the student fails to respond after a specific period of time. Because many multiply disabled students have learned that others will do things for them, it may take intensive work to encourage them to take initiative in routines or interactions. Even though you may be working to elicit a particular behavior, be responsive to any initiative from the student that may be interpreted as a communication or response.

Keep in mind, however, that sometimes other people use regular verbal prompting to help a student learn a task, and they may continue to prompt when it is no longer necessary. Students may assume that the prompting is actually part of the activity, and will not go ahead with the next step unless the prompt is given. When this occurs, teachers must find a way to fade the prompts by using fewer words, a sound cue, a longer period of time between prompting, or another approach to make sure that the student is not depending on an adult's directions to complete a task that he or she is capable of doing independently.

Students are often more responsive when a task includes a reward, and those with multiple disabilities may be rewarded by different things than are nondisabled learners. A sensory effect such as a pleasant odor or a raucous song may motivate some students, while others respond to social praise or the opportunity to have a special experience such as going outdoors. Talking with the families or classroom staff can help you to understand what is rewarding for the student, especially if you are working with him or her infrequently.

If a student has behavioral difficulties, you may want to work with a paraprofessional or someone who knows the student very well, at least for initial lessons. In this way, you can learn what strategies are used to respond to inappropriate behaviors in the classroom, and you can begin to incorporate these responses into your own work with the student. You can also help to develop strategies to address unusual behaviors by reminding the team of how visual impairment might affect a student's ability to follow social expectations; for example, a student's mannerisms or reluctance to wear clothing may be related to the inability to see how others act and dress.

You can be effective in direct instruction with multiply disabled students if the sessions are consistent and the skills are generalized to the regular classroom. If you teach a student to select his own coat from a hook or use a tissue to blow her nose, staff should reinforce the same skill throughout the day when appropriate. Only with a plan for generalization will the student begin to regard that skill as part of his or her regular routine.

CONCLUSION

To be effective in working with multiply disabled students, teachers need to be creative, flexible, and organized. On some days, this seems like an impossible task; on others, you will realize that working with students with multiple disabilities can be the most rewarding part of your work. The key is to focus on your role as the person who addresses the student's needs as they relate to his or her visual impairment, and also to view yourself as a member of a team that must work together for progress to occur. With clear goals and a consistent program, your students may accomplish more than you anticipated. In return, you will gain an understanding of the wide variety of ways in which students learn and grow and an appreciation of your own skills in helping them.

REFERENCES

Erin, J. (1996). Functional vision assessment and instruction of children and youths with multiple disabilities. In A. L. Corn & A. J. Koenig (Eds.), *Foundations of low vision: Clinical and functional perspectives* (pp. 221–245). New York: AFB Press.

Erin, J. (2004). *When you have a visually impaired child with multiple disabilities in your classroom: A guide for teachers.* New York: AFB Press.

Kreuzer, D. T., & King, J. Guidelines for customizing visual displays for students with visual impairments who have severe speech and physical impairments. In A. H. Lueck (Ed.), *Functional vision: A practitioner's guide to evaluation and intervention* (pp. 343–350). New York: AFB Press.

Smith, M., & Levack, N. (1996). *Teaching students with visual and multiple impairments.* Austin: Texas School for the Blind and Visually Impaired.

Wormsley, D. P. (2004). *Braille literacy: A functional approach.* New York: AFB Press.

CHAPTER

7

Orientation and Mobility and the Itinerant Teacher

Faith Dunham-Sims

Like teachers of students with visual impairments, orientation and mobility (O&M) specialists frequently work in itinerant programs, and they share many of the same needs and encounter similar situations because of their itinerant status. However, other issues for O&M specialists pertain more directly to their role as teachers of specialized travel and mobility skills who work with students in a variety of settings. This chapter provides an overview of the role of O&M specialists as itinerant professionals.

Teachers who work with students with visual impairments may work as teachers of students with visual impairments, O&M specialists, or as dually credentialed in both areas. Although the two roles overlap somewhat, legally, no teacher can formally assume one of the roles without having the proper credential. For every program designed to serve visually impaired students, there must be both a teacher specializing in work with visually impaired students and an O&M specialist. When one person fills both roles, he or she will need to have adequate time available to provide appropriate services in each role to his or her students. The topics addressed in this chapter pertain to both the itinerant O&M specialist and the dually credentialed teacher.

In instances in which two or more people each hold only one of the credentials, they need to collaborate frequently about the needs and abilities of the students they share. Students will benefit from this collaboration; it allows each teacher to reinforce important concepts. Because there is some overlap between the role of the teacher of students with visual impairments and the O&M specialist, each can work with the students to use adaptive equipment such as monoculars and to demonstrate appropriate travel skills during the course of the lessons. Having different teachers for these roles can be beneficial to the student, who will hear important concepts being voiced and reiterated by two people. However, in some instances, such as when a student would have both a new teacher of students with visual impairments and a new O&M specialist for the upcoming year, it may be advantageous to have a dually credentialed teacher provide both services to help reduce the possibility of anxiety associated with transitions.

Training to be an O&M specialist or a teacher of students with visual impairments includes learning about such topics as how visual impairments affect learning, independent travel, and participation in school activities; how to teach street crossing skills; the use of adaptive equipment; cane skills; and the intricacies of visual conditions and special education law, as well as how to be sensitive to the needs of multicultural students. However, very little time is devoted to learning how to teach in an itinerant program. Discussing it briefly during training and doing it are two very different things.

PROFESSIONAL SUPPORT

Professional support is crucial for all professionals and particularly for itinerant teachers. Making use of all the lines of professional support available to you is an important survival skill.

The itinerant O&M or dually certified professional spends the vast majority of his or her time in the field serving students. This presents a unique set of challenges. There may not be a centralized office where you have a desk, prepare lesson plans, and put together lesson materials. Offices may be mobile as many itinerant O&M professionals work out of their cars a good deal of the time, and you may or may not have access to clerical assistance. You will need answers to questions about district policy, help with students with unusually complex needs, and assistance in locating specific teaching materials. You may find yourself in a wide variety of environments in the course of your work week. Working conditions certainly are not typical of classroom teachers.

The foundation of your professional support system will often be your immediate co-workers and program supervisor. Co-workers can be the best resource for day-to-day support. The program supervisor, on the other hand, should be available to assist with more complicated issues, including but not limited to those that are specific to your district, sensitive, or problematic.

In the ideal work environment, co-workers and the program supervisor are very supportive and are able to provide all the assistance you may need. However, if this support system is not accessible, you can draw on many other resources to obtain assistance. Do not hesitate to enlist and make the most of these potential sources of professional support:

This confident cane user is practicing during an O&M lesson.

Jean E. Olmstead

Support Systems

- the master teachers from your university teacher preparation program under whom you worked while fulfilling your student teaching requirements
- program instructors from your university teacher preparation program
- classmates from your university teacher preparation program
- colleagues, including those in related fields
- special education and general education teachers you work with in your district
- electronic discussion lists—there is one for just about every topic you can imagine
- family and friends for non-work-related support needs (it is important not to overlook your personal needs!)

Working in isolation may stifle creativity and cause poor morale, so make the most of the professional support resources at your disposal.

BEING PREPARED

Part of being an itinerant O&M professional is the inherent unpredictability that comes with the itinerant model of service delivery. To maximize your teaching potential for any given day, be prepared for unexpected changes in your schedule. Absent students, school assemblies, major storms, and severe heat may call for a change of plans. By having a few basic materials on hand, you can be prepared for just about any itinerant contingency. Here are a few basics:

Tips for Being Prepared

- Have alternate lesson plans ready, either student-specific or generic for use with any of your students.
- Keep extra lesson materials in your car such as puzzles, games, maps, Chang Kit, Wheatley Tactile Diagramming Kit (available from the American Printing House for the Blind; see Appendix A), beanbags, balls, manipulatives, or anything that you routinely use with any of your students. The Chang Kit and Wheatley Diagramming Kit are Velcro boards with removable shapes. They are great for creating quick maps and intersection representations, but their potential uses are endless.
- Have your laptop or other record-keeping materials handy to make the best use of downtime. Treat this as an opportunity to catch up on chores such as anecdotal and attendance records. Although downtime is rare, it pays to be prepared to make the most of it.
- Weatherproof your lessons. Keep items such as jackets, rain gear, hats, gloves, and sunscreen in your car, as well as similar items for your students' use. Having a few extra water bottles available is a good idea year round. Don't let the weather become an excuse for not conducting a lesson. After all, students need to learn to travel independently in all kinds of weather. Of course, a lesson may need to be cancelled in cases when weather conditions pose health or safety concerns for you or your students.
- Keep cane repair equipment in your car so that it is available at all times. Basic tools include a wrench, spare cane tips, cane tip tape, elastic cord, duct tape, a bar of soap (to help keep folding cane segments from sticking), scissors, and a screwdriver. Having a variety of types of cane tips available may also come in handy.
- Don't leave for a lesson without your O&M pack. Use a fanny pack, backpack, purse or personal tote of your choice to carry with you on lessons all of the items necessary to be prepared for emergencies (see the Safety and Off-Campus Instruction sections later in this chapter) as well as frequently used equipment such as a compass, miniature cars for use with the Chang Kit or Wheatley, and so forth.

Using a map can be an important part of O&M training.

Jean E. Olmstead

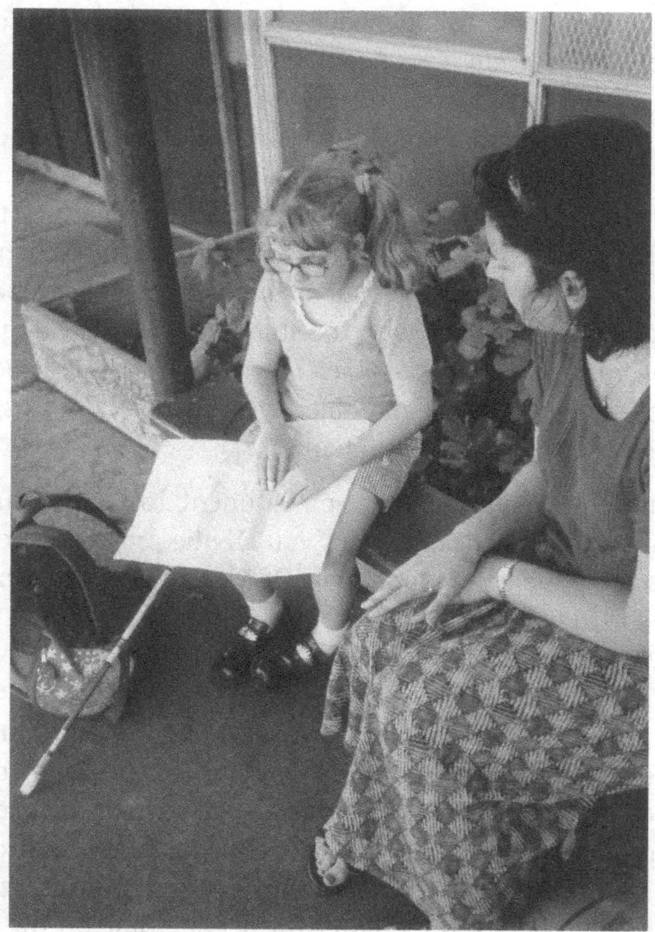

Countless obstacles may arise to thwart the best-laid plans. Being prepared to tackle most of them can turn frustration into success.

SCHEDULING

Caseload scheduling is a crucial and fundamental part of the work of itinerant professionals. As an itinerant O&M or dually certified professional you are responsible for developing and implementing your caseload schedule. The best organizational skills in the world will not be of much use if you are unable to schedule your caseload efficiently. You can learn a few techniques from a book, but you will gain perhaps the most valuable information about caseload scheduling through experience and the process of trial and error.

Developing your caseload schedule can be complicated because you need to work around other teachers' schedules, including classroom teachers and other professionals providing services to each student. To minimize frustration, be prepared to make many changes before your schedule is finalized. The process can be time-consuming, but the following tips may help you with caseload scheduling:

General Scheduling Tips

- Before beginning to build your caseload schedule, it is helpful to gather as much information about your students as possible. At the very minimum you should have a copy of each student's current IEP, including goals related to their visual impairment and O&M needs. Some programs for students who are visually impaired keep an in-house file on each student in the program. If this is the case, review student files to garner pertinent background information and get a feel for your students. If possible, confer with the teacher of students who are visually impaired and the O&M specialist who worked with the students previously to gain as much up-to-date information as possible. This would include progress made toward meeting annual goals and objectives, lesson plan ideas, as well as insightful hints that may come in handy.

- Consider the make-up of your student roster carefully and categorize your students by the services you will be providing: services for students who are visually impaired only, O&M only, or both. Next, set priorities for which students should be scheduled first. Students usually are given priority according to the level and type of services they receive (stated in the IEP). For example, students who receive direct service are given priority ahead of those who receive monitoring and consultation services. Students who receive braille or cane instruction, or both, would be scheduled ahead of those students who are print readers and do not require a mobility device. Let the frequency and duration of service delivery help guide you through the process of prioritizing your students' scheduling needs: the greater the service time on the IEP the greater the priority.

- Next consider all of the students who receive direct service. Contact their teachers to determine possible days and times for your lessons. Using self-stick notes on the schedule form is helpful in firming up your schedule. Write each student's name, school site, and service time on a self-stick note. The notes can then be shuffled around on your schedule form, like puzzle pieces, as you work to place students in ideal daytime slots. Some students may require consultation and collaboration in addition to their direct service time (this is typically indicated in the IEP). Be sure to leave adequate time for consultation and collaboration at each site where they are vital.

- Finally, check with the teachers of those students who receive only monitoring or consultation services. Schedule visits for students receiving weekly monitoring. Others may be seen more infrequently (for example, 30 minutes per semester). You may have a general time on your schedule for seeing those students (for example, you may see a different monitor/consult student in that time slot each week).

- Don't forget to schedule in adequate travel time to commute from site to site.

Other suggestions will be especially helpful for O&M specialists:

Tips for the O&M Specialist

- Make contact with itinerant teachers of students with visual impairments, resource room teachers, and special day class teachers (those with self-contained special education classes) sooner (during the first day or two of school) rather than later. These teachers may be waiting for all of their students' educational team members (including O&M specialists) to approach them with their scheduling requests before making their class activity schedule. This gives you a greater opportunity to choose your desired lesson day and time, rather than trying to fit your lesson into an open time slot.
- Make contact with general education teachers toward the end of the first week of school or beginning of the second week. Often general education teachers are overwhelmed the first few days of the new school year. They are creating their class schedules and dealing with student issues as well as myriad other complications present at the start of the school year. Typically, they are not prepared to respond pragmatically to your scheduling requests during the first school days. Wait a few days and allow them to get their schedules under control. They will be better prepared to receive your lesson proposal, making it more likely that you will be able to schedule the student during your desired time slot.
- Be aware that you may be competing with other service providers for a time slot with a particular student. Many students receive more than one related service (such as vision services, occupational therapy, speech therapy, adaptive physical education, or physical therapy, to name just a few) and these other service providers will be setting up their caseload schedules as well. As a result, conflicts can arise. If two of you are vying for the same time slot with a particular student, do your best to come up with an amicable arrangement. Sometimes you may have more than one student in common and it may just be a matter of comparing schedules and swapping time slots.
- Students may have restrictions on when they can be taken from class to receive related services. For example, a parent or teacher may request that a student not miss class during math period. Occasionally students who receive many related services are pulled from class so often that it may become detrimental to their academic success. Specific requests for after-school lessons or restricted service times are typically stated in the student's IEP and based on an IEP team decision. (If you are required to teach beyond your contractual work day, you should explore receiving per diem pay for the extra time or coming in later or leaving earlier on other days.)

- If you are providing O&M services only, be sure to confer with the teacher of students with visual impairments regarding your students in common. This will eliminate scheduling conflicts.
- Some school districts require teachers to be very specific about where they conduct O&M lessons scheduled off school grounds. In most cases, paperwork related to off-campus instruction needs to be submitted before you start working with the student off campus. Developing an off-campus lesson schedule can be difficult without complete flexibility—that is, the ability to conduct a lesson wherever may be appropriate, without restrictions. One way to approach this challenge is to use a monthly format. For example, you may work at the local mall on the first Monday of the month, at intersections in the school neighborhood on the second and fourth Mondays of the month, at the grocery store on the third Monday of the month, and in the student's home neighborhood on the fifth Monday of the month when applicable. Statements to address contingencies for rainy or hot days can also be included. For example, "In the event of temperatures in excess of 80 degrees or moderate to heavy rain or fog, lesson destinations may be changed to accommodate weather conditions. Changes are limited to those destinations listed on this schedule, or the option of working on campus. Due to safety issues I will not transport students in the event of extreme weather conditions." While not allowing for absolute flexibility, it makes a tough situation workable.

Figure 7.1 shows a typical caseload for an O&M instructor, and Figure 7.2 provides a sample schedule worked out for this teacher's caseload. Additional information about scheduling can be found in Chapter 3

INTERPERSONAL INTERACTIONS

An itinerant O&M or dually certified professional will interact with many different professionals on a regular basis: general education teachers, special education teachers, occupational therapists, physical therapists, adapted physical education teachers, speech therapists, hearing specialists, administrators, school staff, bus drivers, principals, school nurses, parents, and the public. Each one of these interactions is an opportunity to educate them about O&M specifically and services for students with visual impairments in general. Take advantage of every teachable moment and become an O&M ambassador who explains the importance of specialized services for students.

We all understand the importance of having positive interpersonal interactions in our daily lives. Good communication skills are crucial when it comes to the role of an itinerant professional, especially one who is dually certified in teaching students with visual impairments and O&M. Communicative abilities

FIGURE 7.1

2005–06 Orientation & Mobility Caseload for Ms. Rivera

Last Name	*First Name*	*Grade*	*Room*	*Teacher*	*Telephone Number*	*Direct Service Minutes*	*Monitoring Minutes*	*Unit (Week/Quarter/Semester)**
Canterbury School								
Abdul	Mahmood	1	2	Ms. Jones	123-4567	30	20	week
CCC Transition								
Wilson	Toby	13	EC Longs	Mr. Steinfeld	123-8910	120	0	week
DeAnza High School								
Barnaby	Sam	9	152	Ms. Ibey	724-9876	30	10	week
Simpson	Joanna	10	151	Ms. Janey	724-9877	0	6.7	week (60 qtr)
Wagoner	Lisa	10	156	Ms. Janey	724-9877	0	1.7	week (15 qtr)
Ellerhorst Elementary School								
Morgan	Yolanda	5	25	Mr. Barnes	741-2986	60	10	week
Viceroy	Ishmael	2	12	Ms. Tobbler	741-2985	0	1	week (15 sem)
Peres Elementary School – in school 9:30-12:30 Speech M W 10:30								
Gonzales	Maria	Pre-K	27	Ms. Lee	123-2800	0	6.7	week (60 qtr)
Seaview								
Diaz	Juan	Pre-K	Surf	Ms. Escalera	741-2376	60	30	week
Thomas	Julia	Pre-K	Surf	Ms. Escalera	741-2376	60	30	week
Tara Hills Elementary School								
Abbott	Susan	3	20	Mr. Rivers	724-3498	30	10	week
Cravets	Lenny	K	22	Ms. Smiley	724-5680	0	5	week (90 qtr)
Edwards	Alan	4	7	Mr. Clemmons	724-3498	60	10	week
Finkle	Marianna	6	2	Ms. Autum	741-1221	60	10	week
Hinman	Josh	2	20	Ms. Smiley	724-5680	120	20	week
Jiminez	Carmen	3	20	Mr. Kario	724-3498	60	10	week
Kellog	Kathy	6	5	Ms. Smiley	724-5680	60	10	week
					Totals	750	191.1	
					Minutes per week	941.1		
					Minutes per day	188.22		

*Indicates the unit of time used in calculating the caseload. Figures in parentheses refer to the unit used in a student's IEP, if different.

FIGURE 7.2

2005–06 Orientation and Mobility Schedule for Ms. Rivera

Monday		Tuesday		Wednesday		Thursday		Friday		
8:45–9:30	SEAVIEW Juan Diaz Campus routes & consult	8:30–9:10	DE ANZA Sam Barnaby Campus routes & consult Monitors: Joanna Simpson Lisa Wagoner	8:30–9:20	CANTERBURY Mahmood Abdul Canterbury routes & consult	8:30–9:30	Prep 3	8:45–9:30	SEAVIEW Juan Diaz Campus routes & consult	<u>Canterbury</u> M. Abdul <u>Transition</u> T. Wilson <u>DeAnza</u> S. Barnaby J. Simpson L. Wagoner I. Williams <u>Ellerhorst</u> Y. Morgan I. Viceroy <u>Peres</u> M. Gonzales <u>Seaview</u> J. Diaz J. Thomas <u>Tara Hills</u> S. Abbot L. Cravets A. Edwards M. Finkle J. Hinman C. Jiminez K. Kellog
	Travel		Travel		Travel					
10:00–11:00	TARA HILLS Alan Edwards 1 & 3 T.H. routes 2 Appian 80 4 Hilltop Mall 5 Pinole Vista	9:30–10:10	TARA HILLS Susan Abbot Concepts & consult Monitor: Lenny Cravets	9:30–10:40	TARA HILLS Kathy Kellog 1 & 3 T.H. routes 2 Appian 80 4 Hilltop 5 Pinole Vista & consult	9:30–10:30	Prep 4	9:30–10:30	SEAVIEW Julia Thomas 1 & 3 T.H. routes 2 Appian 80 4 Hilltop 5 Pinole Vista & consult	
						10:30–11:30	Prep 5			
					Travel				Travel	
11:00–12:00	TARA HILLS Carmen Jiminez 1 & 3 T.H. routes 2 Appian 80 4 Hilltop Mall 5 Pinole Vista	10:10–12:00	TARA HILLS All consults	11:00–12:00	ELLERHORST Yolanda Morgan 1 & 3 T.H. routes 2 Hilltop Mall 4 Pinole crossings 5 Advanced & consult Monitor: Ishmael Viceroy	11:45–1:30	1st Thursday Visually Impaired Program Staff Meeting / PERES Maria G.	11:00–11:30	CCC TRANSITION Toby Wilson Campus routes	
	Lunch		Lunch		Lunch		Travel	11:30–3:00	Lunch	
1:00–2:00	TARA HILLS Marianna Finkle 1 & 3 T.H. routes 2 Hilltop Mall 4 Appian 80 5 Pinole Vista	1:00–2:00	TARA HILLS Josh Hinman 1 & 3 T.H. routes 2 Hilltop mall 4 Appian 80 5 Pinole Vista	1:30–3:00	CCC TRANSITION Toby Wilson Bus travel		Lunch Travel		Special Consult	
2:15–3:00	Prep 1	2:15–3:00	Prep 2			2:00–3:00	TARA HILLS Josh Hinman Bus travel		Assessments	

can be looked upon as both a skill set and a coping mechanism. Managing difficult personalities while juggling scheduling conflicts is an art.

Some suggestions for making the most of your interactions with other professionals include the following:

Effective Professional Interactions

- Work diligently to establish a good rapport from the beginning. Do so by being sensitive to scheduling concerns and difficulties, offering your assistance in whatever form will help alleviate potential problems, and by making as much personal contact as possible. If you are unable to make personal contact, write a note or e-mail message or make a phone call.
- Personalize your contact by addressing the teacher formally by name (for example, "Ms. Grant"), and introduce yourself informally, by first name.
- When making schedule requests, be assertive but not demanding. Provide teachers with several options to choose from. By offering two or three days and times to them, they can choose the best option to meet the student's needs as well as what fits best into their classroom schedule. Being offered options is always preferred and appreciated.
- Make certain teachers know you are there to support them as well as serve the student.
- Be flexible. No matter how hard you work on your interpersonal communication skills, at some point you are bound to encounter a very inflexible teacher. Be persistent and as assertive as necessary in order to provide an appropriate program for each student, however remaining steadfastly polite and professional.

It is especially helpful to establish a good rapport with the school secretary. This little tip can be very important in having a good experience at a site. The first point of contact when working at a school site will typically be the secretary. You will need to sign in and ask for a campus map, bell schedule, and perhaps directions to a classroom. Also, get to know the principal and as many staff members as possible. Not only will you benefit from these positive interactions but it will also reflect favorably on the program you represent.

ASSESSING STUDENTS

Federal law states that each student who is visually impaired and receiving special education services is eligible for an O&M assessment. Make sure you have a thorough understanding of how the assessment process is handled in your school district before beginning an O&M assessment. Both federal and state laws require that you have a signed and dated assessment plan in order to assess a student. In addition, if you will be assessing a student off campus, make certain you have completed the required paperwork. Once you have the signed and dated assessment plan from the parents or guardians, you have 50 calendar days to complete the assessment and hold an IEP meeting to discuss the findings.

Choosing an appropriate assessment tool is important, and many O&M assessment protocols are available. Your program for visually impaired students may have several assessment tools in stock, such as *TAPS: Teaching Age Appropriate Skills—An Orientation and Mobility Curriculum for Students with Visual Impairments* (Pogrund et al., 1995). If you don't have assessment instruments from your O&M training program or cannot seem to find the perfect assessment protocol to meet your student's needs, you can create your own O&M assessment protocol. You can use an existing format and make modifications to suit your needs or develop a new one. When formulating an off-campus O&M assessment protocol, make sure to include the following elements to help get a thorough picture of the student's abilities:

Elements of Off-Campus O&M Assessments

- *Street furniture.* Make sure the route you travel has plenty of street furniture (such as street sign poles, bus benches, trash receptacles, and newspaper racks) for your student to negotiate.
- *High- and low-contrast signage.* Different types of signs will enable you to learn how your students with low vision function visually.
- *Street crossings.* Include as many simple (four-way stop) and complex crossings (uncontrolled and lighted intersection crossings) as possible.
- *High- and low-contrast pavement.* Some students may find changes in pavement contrast to be a problem.
- *Areas of bright light and shadow.* Changing lighting conditions may affect your student's capabilities.
- *Residential travel and light business travel.* Make sure your route incorporates both types of environments.
- *Orientation elements.* Assess whether the student can recall the route traveled to reach the assessment site and where the car is parked. Assess the student's knowledge of cardinal directions.

You will use the findings from your assessment as the basis for your recommendations for O&M instruction. It is advantageous to gather as much pertinent information about the student as possible. It may also be helpful to confer with a colleague to reinforce the appropriateness of your recommendations. Figure 7.3 presents a sample of a template that can serve as a guide for formatting your assessment report and help to ensure that you address all appropriate skill areas, whether it is an initial assessment or the required triennial reevaluation. This template is annotated to explain how it might best be used in practice.

FIGURE 7.3

Best Ever Unified School District
Program for Students with Visual Impairment
Pupil Services Center
2465 Davis Way
Sunny Town, California 94806
(510) 555-3333

Orientation and Mobility Assessment Report

Date of report ______________

Developed by ____________________________

Purpose of report: *Initial O&M assessment, triennial reevaluation, etc.*

Service delivery: *Direct instruction, monitoring, consultation, etc.*

Identifying Information

Pupil's name ____________________ Birthdate __________ Age ______

Current placement ____________________ Grade __________ Gender ______

Ethnicity ____________________ Primary Language __________

*Assessments**

Assessment	*Administered By*	*Date*	*Score*
List all assessment tools used.			*N/A*

(Typically there is no score associated with an O&M assessment unless you have used a standardized test.)

***In accord with legal mandates, these tests or alternative assessment procedures are valid and reliable for the purposes of this assessment.**

Background Information

Pertinent background information may include, but is not limited to, the following: current school, program placement, grade, relevant medical and behavioral information and any other information that will help the reader understand the student's current status and needs.

Vision

Pertinent vision information may include, but is not limited to, the following: information from a current eye report or functional vision assessment, or both; whether the student wears prescribed spectacles or uses prescribed low vision aids, or both; how the student uses vision in the classroom and for O&M; and any other information that will help the reader understand the student's current status and needs.

(continued)

FIGURE 7.3 (continued)

Assessment Findings

The outline below represents suggested pertinent skill areas that may be included in an O&M assessment. Not all areas will be applicable to all students; other areas may need to be added. You may use a paragraph format or break out each skill as shown.

I. Personal Information
II. Orientation to Environment
    Cardinal directions
    Map use
    Knowledge of location
    Specific destination orientation
    Line of travel
    Midblock position vs. corner position
    Auditory alignment to traffic sounds
III. Use of Sensory Input
    Auditory
    Tactile
    Thermal
    Proprioceptive
    Olfactory
IV. Mobility Techniques
    Trailing techniques
    Curb detection
    Obstacle negotiation
    Sidewalk recovery skills
    Street crossing mechanics
    Street crossing recovery skills
V. Body Image and Related Concepts
    Movements of the body
    Limb movement and spatial awareness
    Laterality
    Objects in relation to body planes
    Laterality in relation to objects
    Laterality of body
    Directionality of other people
    Directionality of objects
    Directionality of others' movements
    Quantitative concepts
    Directional and positional concepts
    Colors
    Geometrical shapes
    Textures (i.e., smooth/rough, hard/soft, etc.)
VI. Auditory Memory
VII. Problem Solving Skills
VIII. Posture, Gait, and Pace
IX. Psychological Factors
X. Visual Capabilities
    Pavement markings
    Signage
    Scanning
    Tracking
    Street crossings

Summary and Recommendations

In this section, sum up the student's performance on the O&M assessment. It is important to list the student's strengths as well as weaknesses (it is gracious to list his or her strengths first). Then list your professional recommendations for the student. It is very important to include a statement such as "The IEP Team will meet to discuss these findings and recommendations."

Validity statement: The tests used in this assessment were individually administered, current, reliable, normed on representative samples, and selected in accordance with the general requirements of the California Education Code. They were appropriate for student's age or grade level, or both, and they were administered in the student's primary language when possible. In my professional judgment, the assessment results are a valid measurement of this student's current levels of functioning.

Respectfully submitted,
Signature
Name
Title
Date

IEPS

Writing an IEP for each student is an important part of the O&M or dually certified professional's job. There is no one way to prepare an IEP, since each school district tends to create its own forms. Keep the following considerations in mind while you're learning the IEP process in your district.

Know Your District's Procedures

Although the IEP process is governed by federal and state guidelines, each school district has some latitude to mandate how its students' IEPs are written, interpreted, and executed. You must be knowledgeable about and understand your school districts' policies regarding IEPs to remain in compliance. Be sure you are using the most current forms available; it is not uncommon for school districts to change their IEP forms from year to year or even during the school year.

Support

In an effort to ensure that teachers are creating effective and compliant IEPs, many school districts publish their version of an IEP manual. There may be mandatory training meetings when the manual is distributed. Your school district may also offer monthly IEP support meetings at which teachers can ask specific questions pertaining to the IEPs they are writing for their students and get answers to questions about the process in general. Be sure to take advantage of these resources if they are available in your school district. The supervisor of your program for visually impaired students should keep you apprised of IEP training workshops and any pertinent literature or manuals that are available.

Other Resources

Sources of assistance in the development of IEPs include the following:

Help for Writing IEPs

- *Previous IEPs.* Reviewing your students' previous IEPs will provide you with background information and give you a sense of how your student has been progressing. You can use the reports and goals and objectives as guidelines in writing your new reports.
- *Co-workers and colleagues.* Take advantage of the years of experience amassed by your co-workers and colleagues. If they offer assistance, accept it. If you are in need of help, ask for it.
- *Coursework.* You may be surprised how helpful textbooks and coursework from your university teacher preparation program can be.
- *Internet sites.* You can download helpful information regarding federal and state regulations pertaining to IEPs at the web site for IDEA Practices

(www.ideapractices.org). In addition, states and school districts may sponsor web sites with links to information pertinent to IEP development.

Once you are familiar with the IEP procedures in your school district, you can begin streamlining the paperwork process. Although each of your students is unique, there will be similarities as you start the process of report writing. One way to create an IEP short cut is through the use of templates. A sample template for an annual O&M report is presented in Figure 7.4 that can serve as a format guide and to help ensure that you address all appropriate skill areas. It is annotated to explain how it might be used in practice.

O&M LESSON STRATEGIES

It is likely that you will encounter a student who is reluctant to participate fully in O&M lessons. The following ideas may encourage that student to be more open to instruction.

Reward Activities

Break down your O&M lesson into three to five mini-assignments (for a one-hour lesson period). Each mini-assignment should have specific rules and criteria for success. The student should repeat aloud the rules, criteria and assignment objectives to the O&M professional. Each successfully completed mini-assignment earns one reward activity. Reward activities can take place immediately after each mini-assignment or be saved until the end of the lesson. Examples of reward activities include but are not limited to

Suggestions for Rewards

- puzzles
- games
- talk time. Some students may prefer to just sit and chat. This is their opportunity to talk about anything they wish.
- manipulatives
- play time—use of a jungle jim or other play structure (most elementary schools have one or more play structures on campus), basketball, bean bags, jump rope, or other equipment
- anything that is highly rewarding to your student

"Brown Bag It"

During the lesson carry your reward activities and lesson materials in a paper shopping bag (or plastic bag, tote, or backpack). Better yet, let your student carry the bag. (Some students have a difficult time carrying things while traveling with

Template for IEP Report

FIGURE 7.4

Best Ever Unified School District
Program for Students with Visual Impairment
Pupil Services Center
2465 Davis Way
Sunny Town, California 94806
(510) 555-3333

Annual Orientation and Mobility Report

Date of report ________________

Developed by ________________________________

Purpose of report: *Annual IEP review, addendum, etc.*

Service delivery: *Direct instruction, monitoring, consultation, etc.*

Identifying Information

Pupil's name ____________________ Birthdate _________ Age _________ Gender _______

School ____ Grade ______________

Program ____

Assessments

Typically, formal or standardized assessments are not used for the annual IEP review. It is helpful to include a sentence conveying this to the reader; for example, "Standardized assessments were not administered for purposes of this annual meeting." If, however, a formal assessment was necessary, list the name of the assessment tool used, the dates administered, and by whom in this section.

Vision

Pertinent vision information may include, but is not limited to, the following: information from a current eye report or functional vision assessment, or both; whether the student wears prescribed spectacles or uses prescribed low vision aids, or both; how the student uses vision in the classroom and for O&M; and any other information that will help the reader understand the student's current status and needs. You can also direct the reader to further information with a statement such as, "For details regarding Roberta's functional vision, please see the Functional Vision Assessment Report prepared by J. Vangard, dated 7/7/05."

Present Levels of Performance

In this section sum up the student's performance over the past year of instruction as it pertains to his or her present levels of performance. The most important areas to cover are those skills specifically addressed in the student's annual goals and objectives. (You may denote these items by using an asterisk to mark the text and a footnote at the bottom of the page to explain the asterisk.)

(continued)

FIGURE 7.4 (continued)

In addition to the specific skills addressed in the student's annual goals and objectives, many other skill areas are typically focused on as well. The outline below represents pertinent skill areas that may be included in an annual O&M IEP review. Not all areas will be applicable to all students; additional areas may need to be added.

- Behavioral considerations
- Body image
- Cane skills
- Community travel
- Home neighborhood travel
- Money skills
- Orientation and mental mapping
- O&M notebook
- Passenger skills
- Personal information
- Poor lighting travel
- *Positional and directional concepts
- Mall travel
- *Map skills
- Posture and gait
- Scanning patterns
- Shopping skills
- *Street crossing skills

*Pertains to current goals and objectives.

Progress Toward Annual Goals and Objectives

In this section you must specifically discuss how the student has progressed over the past year in terms of satisfying his or her annual goals and objectives. You may discuss his or her performance, completion of goals, as well as areas that still need work. It is recommended to include a statement regarding the IEP team such as, "The IEP team will meet to discuss this review."

their canes. This is an opportunity to practice that skill while having fun.) Keeping the activities and materials under wraps may heighten anticipation and increase the student's eagerness to earn a reward activity.

Let Students Think They Are Playing a Game

Games are a great way to reward students for good behavior and effort during their lesson. Many games can accomplish the task of providing an enjoyable activity as well as reinforcing O&M concepts and skills. Many O&M games are available through APH as well as other educational supply companies (such as Exceptional Children and Discovery Toys; see Appendix A). Games are easy to make up or you can modify a popular game to meet your students' needs. When possible, let your students make up a game.

O&M Notebook

An O&M notebook is a great way to help your student keep track of O&M-related materials that you use during lessons. It also teaches organizational skills, increases a student's level of responsibility, and is the perfect opportunity to introduce O&M homework. You provide the materials and let your student put it all together. You will need the following materials to create an O&M notebook:

Making an O&M Notebook

- *Three-ring binder.* Any type will do. This is a great opportunity to reuse old binders.
- *Subject dividers.* These can be made from a variety of materials. Braille paper can be used for the divider page itself and colored construction paper for the subject tabs. A glue stick can be used to glue the tabs to the divider pages.
- *Labeling materials.* Your students with low vision can label the subject tabs with markers, crayons, or the writing instrument of their choice. Students who use braille will need braillable label sheets (available through APH) or some form of tactile labeling that can then be applied to the tab (puff paint also works well).

Next, decide how the notebook is to be organized. Determine this yourself or work out a plan with your student. The subject tabs need to be labeled and the dividers placed in the notebook. Younger students may enjoy decorating the divider pages and the outside of the notebook.

The student is now responsible for organizing and filing O&M lesson materials as well as bringing the notebook on O&M lesson day. Rewards (such as stickers) can be awarded for completed homework assignments and good notebook organization, as well as remembering to bring the notebook without prompting.

Examples of possible subject areas for an O&M notebook include, but are certainly not limited to, the following:

Topics for an O&M Notebook

- routes
- maps
- worksheets
- homework
- O&M journal
- lesson notes
- street crossings
- bus travel
- cane skills
- accomplishments

Sticker Charts

Sticker charts are a great way for a student to monitor his or her progress. You can award one sticker for good effort during a lesson and additional stickers if the student works above and beyond expected performance. To spice things up, a "double sticker challenge" can be proposed to entice greater performance.

It is easy to make large-print grid charts with boxes using your computer. Tactile sticker charts can be made from cardboard or braille graph paper. Always have a variety of stickers to choose from and let your student choose the sticker he or she wants, peel it from the sheet, and place it on his or her chart. Tactile stickers are available through APH or can be made from a variety of materials such as thumb tacks, push pins, raised stickers, modeling dough, or clay.

Prize Page

Sticker charts are a tangible way for your student to track progress, and they can also serve as immediate reinforcers as the student works toward a larger reward. For example, when a student earns 10 stickers, a small prize can be awarded. This can be a surprisingly powerful tool to motivate your students. Use party supply stores as a great place to find bargains on little prizes. Watch for sales when items can be purchased inexpensively. Items such as plastic animals and dinosaurs, mini-squish balls, colorful mini-tops, key rings, fuzzy rings, and finger puppets are popular with younger students. Older students may like mini-note pads or telephone books and colorful pencils or pens.

Lesson Plans

Now that you have devised your lesson strategies, you will need a useful lesson plan to help implement your ideas. A lesson plan can be as simple as a well-thought-out plan in your head or as complex as a full-page written outline of lesson objectives. It is recommended that you write down a lesson plan in some form, but it may not be mandatory. Most important is to devise a lesson plan that works well for you and your style of teaching.

An example of a lesson plan template can be found in Figure 7.5. This format includes all of the pertinent information you may need to help track your students' progress as well as keep track of lesson environments. To use, simply outline the objectives you wish to cover in the Lesson Objectives column. While your student is carrying out the objectives, note his or her performance in the Evaluation of Student's Performance column. Then you can give an overall rating of that objective by using the "–", "√" and "+" symbols to represent poor, satisfactory, good, or any combination thereof. The symbol column provides an at-a-glance summary of how your student performed during the lesson. If ideas for the next lesson pop into your head, jot them down at the bottom of the form. An effective lesson plan helps cut down on recordkeeping time in the long run.

FIGURE 7.5

Lesson Plan

Student name José Date/time 10/15/05 1:00-2:00 p.m.

Route/environment B Street & Stone Avenue Materials needed Map

- ✓ +	*Lesson Objectives*	*Evaluation of Student's Performance*
✓+	Give verbal route	Some prompting required
✓	Trace route on map	Trouble orienting map
✓+	ID masking sounds	Some prompting
+	Cross with All Quiet	Very good! José is very confident
✓	Cross with All Clear	New skill, requires a lot of help
✓+	Crossing 1	Mostly independent
✓-	Crossing 2	Needed help with visibility
✓+	Crossing 3	Mostly independent
+	Crossing 4	Totally independent! Very good!

Next lesson:

- Map work
- Work on visibility

SAFETY

Safety is a consideration for all itinerant teachers. For an itinerant O&M professional who may transport students in a private vehicle and work in the community at large, safety is fundamental.

Safety issues to contend with include that of our students, our personal safety, issues while working on school campuses or off campus, and travel and vehicle safety. The best way to tackle these issues is to understand fully what conditions might be dangerous, as well as to be prepared for emergencies.

Protect Yourself

In today's litigious society, guard, to the best of your ability, against potential worst-case scenarios. Be aware of all of your school district's safety and emergency policies as well as guarding yourself personally. The following sections note specific areas to be aware of.

District Emergency Policy

Every school district has different safety policies, forms, and procedures. Make sure that you have a thorough understanding of these policies and procedures and that you have completed the requisite documentation before taking your students off campus in your private vehicle (or district vehicle). Your supervisor should be able to provide this information. It is essential that you carry with you on lessons current emergency phone numbers and forms giving you permission to authorize emergency medical treatment for each of your students, in the event that parents or guardians cannot be reached immediately.

Chain of Contact

If there is an accident while transporting a student, you need to know the appropriate chain of contact. Some contacts that may be in that chain include (but are not limited to) the following:

Emergency Chain of Contact

- 911
- site administrator (principal)
- parent or guardian
- program supervisor

An accident report should be filed as soon as possible, while the details are fresh in your mind.

Cell Phone

A cellular telephone for emergencies is a worthwhile investment. Be certain to keep the battery charged, or keep a car-adaptable charger in your vehicle, or both.

First Aid Kit

For minor injuries, keep a small first aid kit in your O&M pack and a larger first aid kit in your vehicle.

Professional Liability Insurance

Professional liability insurance is also a worthwhile investment. If you are involved in an accident while with a student, you could be liable personally as well as an employee of your school district. Your school district policy should offer you legal protection as their employee; however, it may not offer assistance on a personal level. This added protection is highly recommended by many professionals in the field.

Professional liability insurance is offered at competitive rates to members of the Association for Education and Rehabilitation of the Blind and Visually Impaired (AER). You can also contact any commercial insurance carrier for information on how to obtain this type of insurance.

Off-Campus Instruction

Off-campus O&M instruction is often mandated in a student's IEP and getting students off campus will likely involve paperwork. Depending on the school district's policies and procedures, ease of communication with students' parents or guardians, timely completion of forms, and scheduling considerations, it may take up to three weeks before you can begin off-campus O&M instruction. Issues related to off-campus O&M instruction are detailed in the following sections.

Paperwork

Almost every school district has transportation and safety policies that must be adhered to and forms that must be filed. Understand those policies and complete the requisite documentation before taking students off campus. Do not overlook this step; paperwork is a vital link between you, your district policies, and your professional liability. Some aspects of this paperwork are detailed here.

District Forms

Complete all the necessary district-mandated forms that relate to off-campus instruction (required forms vary from district to district). These might include forms for parental permission, consent to treat minors, emergency contacts, and driver insurance, as well as a detailed O&M off-campus lesson schedule (including day of the week, time, and lesson destinations).

Copies

If the forms need to be routed to various administrators or departments, they may be misplaced along the way. Make copies of everything and always have a backup copy available if needed.

Once all of the signed and properly filed paperwork related to off-campus instruction has been returned to you, keep copies of this paperwork in your vehicle. This is a precaution in the event that your authority or credentials are ever questioned while you are working in the community with a student.

Keep copies of your students' emergency contact forms on your person when on an off-campus lesson. If a student should experience a medical emergency, use the emergency contact information and your cell phone to summon the appropriate assistance without delay. Use a photocopy machine to reduce emergency contact forms to fit in a small envelope that you keep in your O&M pack at all times.

Automobile Insurance

If you do not have the use of a district vehicle, contact your automobile insurance carrier to ensure that you have adequate coverage for transporting students in your private vehicle. Some auto insurance carriers require you to have commercial coverage to transport students. Shop around for the best coverage and the best price.

Get the school district's automobile insurance policy in writing. Make sure to understand these policies and procedures thoroughly to avoid unpleasant surprises. If you are involved in an automobile accident while transporting a student, you must know what your insurance responsibilities are as well as those of the district. Many school districts expect your private insurance carrier to bear the brunt of the financial burden. The district insurance may then cover any remaining financial responsibility.

Although the paperwork and precautions may be complicated, off-campus O&M instruction is one of the most rewarding and enjoyable aspects of our profession. Maintaining a focus on safety will keep it so.

RECERTIFICATION

If you are an O&M or dually certified professional working in the public schools you must posses a valid teaching credential in your state. Each state usually has its own recertification process. If you are not familiar with the recertification process in your state, contact the credentialing office at the university where you attended your teacher preparation program or your state's department of education (their web sites may also contain this information).

If you are a certified O&M specialist (COMS) you are responsible for renewing your certification every five years. COMS certifications are handled by the Academy for Certifying Vision Rehabilitation and Education Professionals (ACVREP). For more information about renewal requirements, contact AER or ACVREP (see Appendix B).

Some of your continuing education hours may be applied toward multiple certifications (that is, your teaching credential and your COMS certification). Double-check specific requirements for each certification, however. Make the most of your continuing education hours.

RESOURCES

Whether you are an itinerant O&M specialist or dually certified professional with a great built-in support system or isolated in your job, many, easily accessible resources are available at your fingertips. A few are listed here; there are many more in Appendixes A, B, and D.

Professional Resources

- *Journal of Visual Impairment & Blindness* published by the American Foundation for the Blind
- newsletters from professional organizations such as those listed in Appendix B
- textbooks and professional materials, such as *Foundations of Orientation and Mobility* (Blasch et al., 1997), *Orientation and Mobility Techniques: A Guide for the Practitioner* (Hill & Ponder, 1976), *Orientation and Mobility: Techniques for Independence* (LaGrow & Weessies, 1994), *Teaching O&M in the Schools* (Knott, 2002), and *Imagining the Possibilities* (Fazzi & Petersmeyer, 2001)
- electronic discussion lists (internet listservs)
- Internet
- co-workers
- professional conferences
- professionals in related fields

Make the most of the resources at hand, accept help when it is offered, and do not be embarrassed to ask for help.

SUMMING UP

A great sense of pride and fulfillment comes with being an itinerant O&M specialist or dually certified professional. This profession can be truly rewarding. Remember to keep obstacles in perspective; they are obstacles, not barriers. Use your best skills to negotiate them. Adopting the following principles will help to ensure your success as an itinerant O&M specialist:

Principles for Success

- Don't be afraid to be creative.
- Trial and error is a way of life.

- Be flexible and adaptable.
- Make the most of the resources at hand.
- O&M is fun!

REFERENCES

Blasch, B. B., Wiener, W. R., & Welsh, R. L. (Eds.). (1997). *Foundations of orientation and mobility* (2nd ed.). New York: AFB Press.

Fazzi, D. L., & Petersmeyer, B. A. (2001). *Imagining the possibilities: Creative approaches to orientation and mobility instruction for persons who are visually impaired.* New York: AFB Press.

Hill, E., & Ponder P. (1976). *Orientation and mobility techniques: A guide for the practitioner.* New York: AFB Press.

Knott, N. I. (2002). *Teaching orientation and mobility in the schools: An instructor's companion.* New York: AFB Press.

LaGrow, S., & Weessies, M. (1999). *Orientation and mobility: Techniques for independence.* Palmerston North, New Zaland: Dunmore Press.

Pogrund, R., Healy, G., Jones, K., Levack, N., Martin-Curry, S., Martinez, C., Marz, J., Roberson-Smith, B., & Vrba, A. (1995). *TAPS: Teaching age appropriate skills—An orientation and mobility curriculum for students with visual impairments.* Austin: Texas School for the Blind and Visually Impaired.

CHAPTER

A Rural Perspective

Jane Stewart Redmon

Rural itinerant programs for students with visual impairments are similar to urban and suburban programs, except for the many miles teachers travel between schools, the sometimes more frequent use of teaching assistants or paraeducators, and the program options available to the students being served. Although federal and state regulations may require a full range of program options for students with visual impairments, in practice usually the only options available to students in rural areas are a state residential school and an itinerant program. The rural itinerant teacher often must drive hundreds of miles to see one student and then turn around and drive back at the end of the day.

Nevertheless, rural programs can be rewarding for many reasons. First, rural communities are generally close-knit, and the people tend to care about the people in their communities. When approached tactfully, schools, workplaces, and churches and other religious institutions are glad to help further the skills of a student with disabilities. The schools are often a major source of pride for the communities. Frequently, they are the major meeting places in the community for adults and for afterschool activities for students. Establishing good relationships with the principal and key teachers will truly help to further the acceptance of your student.

Second, rural people are likely to care about you—the itinerant teacher. Classroom teachers and parents will be thrilled to see that someone knows how to help educate a student with visual impairments so that he or she can continue living at home. They can be there to help you in many ways. For example, a number of years ago, before the widespread use of computers, one itinerant teacher convinced a local bridge club to hand-enlarge textbooks for a certain visually impaired student. The women put their cards away and met all summer long to complete those textbooks—and not one of them was related to the student. The textbook was handwritten in ½-inch letters. Later, the same teacher taught several of the women to braille. She now has a great source of volunteer braillists for her students.

The use of technology has greatly improved the professional lives of itinerant teachers for students with visual impairments. The use of cell phones, pagers and text pagers, global positioning systems (GPS), and personal computers (including e-mail, instant messaging, electronic discussion lists, etc.) has made communication between schools and professionals easier and helped with the organization of documents.

All the information in this book is important to the rural itinerant teacher. You, like your counterparts in the city and the suburbs, will have to adhere to the regulations of the IDEA, create IEPs, write lesson plans, keep progress notes, order materials, and so on. This chapter offers a few additional ideas to help you be effective in a rural setting.

DEALING WITH ISOLATION

Teachers' Isolation

When you are an itinerant teacher in a rural area, you are usually the only teacher of students with visual impairments for miles—probably counties. You are expected to know everything about students with visual impairments, from those who are gifted to those who are also profoundly retarded, and from braille readers to readers of print. There is often no one for you to talk with about the problems and joys you encounter.

You will therefore find it helpful to keep in touch with other teachers of students with visual impairments. If you have Internet access, at home or at school, the easiest way to keep in touch is via e-mail or instant messaging, or both. Electronic discussion lists are a great way to keep up with what is currently on the minds of itinerant teachers, and a quick way of promoting discussion of questions or concerns you might have.

If you do not have Internet access, become pen pals via postal mail with neighboring itinerant teachers. Start an informal newsletter with them. Just jot down ideas and notes—nothing formal, or you will find it becomes a chore—and start a continuing letter. If you are a first-year teacher, keep in touch with the other teachers with whom you graduated; you will generally feel more comfortable with them than with the neighboring teachers who are probably strangers to you. Whomever you write to, however, remember to keep your students' names and other identifying information confidential.

In states with a state coordinator or supervisor of vision services or a central state office for ordering instructional materials for students with visual impairment (often known as the IMC), or both, make contact with the offices (contact the State Office of Education to locate these offices). Make sure you are on their e-mail or postal mailing lists and communicate with the personnel in these offices to keep updated on events in the state, such as workshops offered by state schools for students with visual impairment to help bring teachers together and provide in-service training.

Join professional organizations. When joining AER, make sure to join Division 16, Itinerant Personnel Division (see Appendix B). This division provides extensive information for itinerant teachers; they also organize workshop sessions and enjoyable evening gatherings at international conferences. Attend state and regional conferences annually. Most administrators and supervisors of itinerant programs understand the issue of professional isolation and are willing to let you attend conferences; some require you to attend them.

Discuss with your supervisor or director your need to solve problems with other teachers of students with visual impairments. Get permission to organize a regional meeting of teachers of students with visual impairments. Keep it simple and include rural itinerant teachers like yourself—maybe five to eight teachers at a time. Since directors are more likely to approve a meeting with an agenda, write a simple one that might include review of information from recent conferences, discussion of tricks of the trade, technology specific to students with visual impairments and a case discussion time to brainstorm specific concerns. Again, remember to keep your students' names and other identifying information confidential.

Expand your concept of teaching students with visual impairments. Learn from teachers in other disciplines, such as those who teach students with hearing, learning, and multiple impairments. You will learn a lot, and learning from other teachers is a good way to teach them about students with visual impairments.

Isolation of Students and Parents

The feelings of aloneness experienced by students with visual impairments and their parents also need to be considered. Frequently these feelings are more difficult to handle than your own. Administrators may often understand the need for the teacher to have contact with other teachers but may not recognize the need for the student to be with other students or the parents to be with other parents. Again, try a newsletter. Have the students and parents write it, and you coordinate it. Incorporate the writing of articles into IEP objectives for handwriting, keyboarding, and so on. The articles can be about things that a student who happens to be visually impaired may do, as well as awards received, other honors, and interesting events. Parents can write similar articles about their activities, and provide questions and answers about resources, self-help concerns, support groups, and the like.

Encourage both parents and students to use the Internet. Since not all families may have computers, encourage them to use those available at public agencies, such as libraries. Provide information about appropriate web sites and electronic discussion lists; a wealth of information and connections is available. With written permission, give parents the e-mail addresses of other parents and do the same for the students. Both groups may need some encouragement to get started but they can develop supportive, lasting friendships.

In addition, try to arrange for pen pals among your students and act as mail clerk for those who are not using e-mail. Students enjoy receiving letters from other students. Match up students with similar interests and those who could help each other with skills, such as by pairing a student with good braille skills with a student who is less experienced with braille.

Summer camps are a great way for students to start a friendship with other students with visual impairments. State schools often have special summer programs for public school students. Service organizations such as the Lions also provide summer camp opportunities to many age groups.

Organize study trips for your students and have the trips be a regular part of the year's planning. Write IEP objectives to include field trips with other students with visual impairments. Often the O&M instructor will have good ideas of activities to enhance skills, practice (or teach) social skills, and have fun. Try simple ideas such as a trip to a Christmas tree farm, going bowling followed by a picnic in a park, or riding a city bus a short distance to a museum. Make sure you have activities that encourage the students to interact with each other.

Exchange days can also alleviate feelings of isolation. Have one student visit another's school for a day or part of a day. It is a great learning experience for the student and can be an even better experience for the student's sighted classmates. Arranging exchange days between students who are pen pals can foster a deeper relationship.

TRAVEL TIME

Using Travel Time Productively

Driving can be a good time to think through lesson plans, IEP objectives, presentations for parents' groups, conversations with parents, and so on, provided that you can also keep your mind on the road. Keep a tape recorder or digital recorder in your car for your use; one that is voice-activated is especially useful. Record notes while you are driving. You can also review students' tapes, but for safety reasons do not try to write notes or lessons while driving. Some people eat their lunch in the car and then use their lunchtime to take a walk to restore their energy. This can be hazardous; if you are inclined to eat while driving, do not become overly involved with the food instead of the road.

Finally, remember that driving is meant to get you from one place to another.

A lot of driving is expected in your job. If you cannot safely drive and record, listen, or eat at the same time, don't. Just drive.

Getting Good Directions

For a person who has never lived in a rural environment, interpreting directions may be the biggest challenge. To an urban person, some of the vocabulary rural people use may sound foreign. Terms like "the four lane," "the blacktop," "the old man's farmhouse," "a ways," and "a piece" may be common. You may learn that "the four lane" is the interstate highway, "the blacktop" is any "out of town" asphalt road, and "the old man's farmhouse" is a field where a farmhouse used to stand—20 years ago. "A ways" and "a piece" are vague terms, although you may learn through experience that "a ways" is a shorter distance then "a piece."

Another trick is to figure out how blacktops are named. A road's name is often determined by the name of the town to which you are heading, and one road can have two names. For example, in Joppa the road would be called the Metropolis road. In Metropolis, the same road would be called the Joppa road.

Directions obtained from a local person may be filled with landmarks that relate to an event that occurred long ago or bear the name of a person who is dead. "Turn left at the Johnsons' farm" sounds harmless, but the Johnsons may have been the original owners and the Smiths now have their name on the mailbox. Try instead to get specific information about the distance to be traveled; the position, color, and size of the landmark; and so forth. Many rural people also seem to like using compass directions. Therefore, put a compass in your car.

Purchase a detailed county road map, which is available for most counties. You can use the Internet to get directions from your favorite route planner program (MapQuest, Expedia, and the like). Remember, however, that Internet-derived information is not always correct, so use these directions cautiously. Integrate all the information you have to give you the safest route to your destination. GPS is very helpful, if it is affordable and available. Local fire departments, police departments, or post offices are excellent sources of directions if you are disoriented. The best way to get good, useful directions is to phone your destination—the school, home, or business—before you leave your office.

MAINTAINING YOUR CAR

Your car is your office, your faculty room, and your best friend. In many rural itinerant programs, you will be in your car more than half your workday. Your car needs special care to keep you happy.

Choose a car that you will be comfortable in, that gets excellent gas mileage, and that you like. Keep it in good repair. Complete your scheduled maintenance checks. Check the oil regularly. If you do not know much about cars, find a friendly mechanic to teach you the basics. Learn to change a tire. If you consider joining an organization like the American Automobile Association, make sure its services extend to your area.

Finally, and most important, as a rural driver, carry some special equipment in your car in case of an emergency. Most important is a cell phone and its charger. Make sure you have important phone numbers in the phone's directory, such as office and school numbers. Carry a local or regional phone book in the car to find emergency numbers. Disaster packs containing essential items for survival are available from discount or auto stores. Other items you might want to keep on hand include at least one gallon of water (some for you and some for the car), blankets, a small shovel, flares, high-energy snacks, and (the most frequently used items) a pair of casual pants and comfortable shoes for those days when you are all dressed up and you need to change a flat tire en route.

ABSENCES AND UNSCHEDULED SCHOOL CLOSINGS

The most frustrating experience in a rural program is to drive for hours only to discover that your student is absent. The best way to avoid this situation is to let everyone—from the room teacher, principal, secretaries, and janitors to parents and students—know your schedule. Having a cell phone and giving the number to all these people is the simplest way for you to receive important information in a timely manner. Otherwise, provide the telephone numbers where you can be reached throughout the day. Give each of these persons copies of your weekly schedule, which should include the time, school, town, telephone number, and contact person for each of the places where you will be. In this way there is no question about where they can call in case of an absence. In bold print at the top of this schedule put your name, position, office telephone number, and cell phone or pager numbers, if appropriate. If your office has a toll-free number, post it on the top of your schedule. In bold type write something like "When calling about a student being absent or a schedule change, do not leave a voice message. Talk to a HUMAN who can get the message to me ASAP!" Messages left on an answering machine or through voice mail may take hours to retrieve; by that time you may have already arrived at the school. When a person has remembered to call you about a student's absence, be sure to thank them by telephone, e-mail, or regular mail, to show your appreciation.

Some parents will always let you know when their children will be out of school. Give some of them your home telephone number so they can call you early in the morning if their child is going to be absent. (But be cautious about giving your home number out—this information can be abused.)

For a chronically absent student, other arrangements may be made. One is that you call the home early in the morning on the days you are to see the student, just to make sure that he or she will be in school. This can save you from making many useless trips and the district will find it cheaper to reimburse you for those calls than to pay mileage for futile travel. You can also ask parents or responsible students to call your home or office collect in case of absence or snow days. Letting them call you collect means that the district assumes the expense of the call (if that arrangement has been authorized). Once again, encourage them to avoid leaving voice mail and talk to a real person who will get the message to you.

If you are not informed when a student is absent, you can still use your time at the school wisely: to meet with teachers or other school staff, observe your student's classroom, check out classrooms and teachers for next year, or investigate possible areas for O&M lessons. You can also catch up on reports on your laptop, tackle some of the stacks of paperwork you have been putting off, or read professional materials that you keep in your car for instances just like this.

It can be difficult for a teacher who travels through many counties to keep up with unscheduled school closings for snow and other types of poor weather, heating or cooling problems, and so on. The weather may be clear in your area and unsettled just a few miles away; although your office may not be closed, one of your schools may be. Therefore, close contact with the school principals is important. Many schools have created telephone chains to inform personnel of closings. Become part of that chain in every school where you have a student. Some schools inform students and staff about closings via e-mail. Make sure that your schools have your e-mail address for such emergencies—and make sure you check your e-mail before you leave in the morning.

Another problem arises when you get stuck at a school because of bad weather and cannot get to your home that evening. Be prepared in advance. Check your employer's policy on reimbursing you for staying at hotels or motels in such cases. Many rural communities do not have hotels you would want to stay overnight in, so you may want to become a buddy with someone in the area in case you need to spend the night. Always carry a few emergency items in case you get stranded: a change of warm clothing, a toothbrush, necessary medications, and so on.

CONSIDERING PROGRAM OPTIONS

As stated earlier in this chapter, in rural areas, there are generally only two program options for educating a visually impaired student: an itinerant program and a state school. When determining a student's placement, it is essential to consider the student's needs. Itinerant programs do not meet the needs of all visually impaired students, and the IEP team must weigh all alternatives carefully.

One option is that your program and the program from a neighboring area could jointly open a resource room between your two areas. Another is to arrange an open door policy with the state school, so that a student can attend the school for a specified amount of time to learn specific skills and then return to his or her local school.

All itinerant teachers (including teachers of students with visual impairments) need to be realistic about what they can accomplish in an itinerant program. Furthermore, teachers in rural itinerant programs need to use a team approach and communicate frequently with all the people who work with a student. When you are with a student only for a limited amount of time, other team members must know about and be able to reinforce the skills you are teaching. This might be accomplished by having regular team meetings, e-mailing team members regarding the student's progress, or keeping a written log in the classroom regarding progress (make sure you read other team members' entries as well as entering your own comments).

WORKING WITH ASSISTANTS AND PARAEDUCATORS

You may find a greater use of teacher assistants or paraeducators in rural programs for students with visual impairments than in urban areas. Depending on how your area is funded, these assistants may be hired through the special education office or through the districts in which the students attend school. These assistants may be stationary (that is, assigned to one classroom at one school) or itinerant.

The primary job of a paraeducator is usually to prepare materials, not to instruct the students (see Chapter 4 for more information on working with paraeducators). In general, teaching assistants who work with students with visual impairments will need to be trained to read and to write braille, to prepare large-print materials, or to prepare both braille and large-print materials. It is usually the itinerant teacher's responsibility to provide the training. Although on-the-job training can be effective, it may be more efficient to meet with the teaching assistants at a special time during the week, once or twice a week for an hour or more, until training is completed. Training in how to prepare large-print materials will be considerably shorter than training related to braille. Include information about other compensatory skills during the training so that the assistants are aware of the scope of the students' needs. Skills training can be done through a correspondence course as well as at a central location. The Hadley School for the Blind (see Appendix B) has a variety of such courses.

The responsibilities of paraeducators vary from one district to another. To make sure you have knowledgeable assistants, you can arrange for a one-day in-service meeting annually that the assistants must attend, in which you discuss program concerns and individual problems and their solutions, as well as responsibilities and differences in the curricula of the various districts. Speakers and workshops can address topics pertinent to the current needs of the assistants. Although the in-service program can provide helpful information to the paraeducators, regular contact and observation throughout the school year are necessary to ensure that the assistants' work is appropriate to meet the needs of the student.

Assistants can be among the best assets for an itinerant teacher. They are generally persons from the local area who have wide contacts. Treat them as the professionals they are.

WHO'S MY BOSS?

Many rural itinerant programs are regionally based, encompassing several special education cooperatives or districts. Within this structure, you may have many bosses. This can be confusing for itinerant teachers. You may be dealing with one director of special education at a regional level and another at the district level. You may work with a vision supervisor, a state supervisor, and principals of schools who all think that you are theirs. Therefore, deal with each person in a professional manner, but also remember who hired you and pays your salary. This is the person to whom you are ultimately responsible.

Providing services to students with visual impairments in rural areas presents some interesting challenges not generally experienced by teachers in urban areas. By utilizing tight organization and technological tools, these challenges can be overcome and your students will benefit from your special efforts.

CHAPTER

Assistive Technology

James Carreon

Assistive technology refers in general to equipment and devices that help students with disabilities complete tasks that they could not ordinarily complete or would have difficulty completing without the use of that equipment or device. A physically disabled student who has difficulty holding onto a pencil might use a rubber pencil holder; a student with low vision might use a magnifier to read a document; and a student who is blind might use synthetic speech to work on a computer. All these devices are assistive technology. The most important principle regarding students and technology is to identify the particular student's needs and then find the appropriate assistive technology to meet that need.

The new technologies available today allow blind and visually impaired students to access more information more easily than has been possible at any other time in history. By allowing students who are blind or visually impaired to gain access to information available in print and by enabling them to find an entire universe of information over the Internet, assistive technology has revolutionized the school experiences of these students and provided them with an array of employment and professional opportunities.

Perhaps the most useful pieces of assistive technology for most students who are blind or visually impaired are a computer with a screen reader, which uses synthetic speech to read aloud the text displayed on the computer screen, and a screen magnification program to enlarge display on the computer monitor. Most students will benefit from the use of numerous other technology tools, such as video magnifiers (also known as closed-circuit television systems, or CCTVs), optical devices, braillewriters, slates and styli, and both tape and digital recordings of printed information. With these tools, students can create a document, share it with classmates, and send it around the world via e-mail, as well as accomplish a wide range of educational, employment and personal tasks.

Because assistive technology can play a significant, if not pivotal, role in a student's learning and success in school, it is essential that the teacher of students with visual impairments address the issue of appropriate technology for a student. From assessing the student's needs and determining the right tools to meet them, recommending equipment and securing it, obtaining necessary training for the student, and storing devices that have been purchased, the teacher's role with regard to assistive technology is crucial.

TECHNOLOGY ASSESSMENT

A technology assessment is required by IDEA in some form for every student receiving services from the teacher of students with visual impairments. This evaluation includes determining the need for the use of equipment such as a video magnifier and reading-writing stands, as well as computer equipment. Formal assessment protocols may be available from sources such as a university or through a representative from the technology center at the state school for visually impaired students. Some school districts have devised their own assessment protocols. The state department of rehabilitation may provide funding for the assessment. If the teacher of visually impaired students does not conduct the assessment, he or she needs to make appropriate arrangements for it to be undertaken and completed.

EQUIPMENT NEEDS

Computers in programs for students with visual impairments may too often be hand-me-downs from the school district's computer labs. Because it must support specialized software, a computer for a blind or visually impaired student needs to be powerful enough to run the standard application software in addition to the assistive technology used by the student. It is important to start with an adequate computer and an accessible operating system.

OPERATING SYSTEMS

The operating system of the computer supports all the functions the computer performs. The systems most widely used in the schools currently are Apple Macintosh and Microsoft Windows operating systems. The majority of students with visual impairments use the Windows operating system on their computers. With this system most tasks can be accomplished with simple keyboard commands. In addition, many companies are creating programs designed for people who are blind or visually impaired that facilitate working in the Windows operating system.

The Macintosh operating system often lacks basic keyboard commands to accomplish simple tasks, requiring the user to employ a mouse or other pointing device. Using such a visual interface can be challenging for students who are blind or visually impaired. In addition, few companies are creating software that allows access through synthesized speech, braille, or screen magnification to programs using the Macintosh operating system. For these reasons the Windows system may be a better choice for most visually impaired students. However, if your school uses Macintosh computers running System X or higher, your students may be able to do most basic tasks, such as word processing, without difficulty. Newer Macintosh operating systems are being released with more accessibility options.

Equipment Purchases

Presenting a set of specifications for selecting a computer might seem easy. In light of the frequently posited rule of thumb that the processing power of computers doubles every 18 months or sooner, however, such specifications would be out of date very quickly, as would any information giving specific descriptions of technology equipment or devices. Therefore, this chapter will offer general information that can be applied to a variety of situations and equipment.

To start becoming informed about what equipment to purchase, look at what your school or district's computer lab is using. Talk to technology teachers and ask for recommendations. Obtaining information from the web sites of national computer makers is also an effective way of determining appropriate equipment to buy.

Although gathering this general information will be helpful, it is important to consult with experts in assistive technology for people with visual impairments to ensure that the system to be purchased is an integrated system of compatible components and will perform the tasks for which it is being obtained. Technology centers at state schools for students with visual impairments often have outreach programs to assist with the selection of the right computer and software to meet students' needs. The state department of rehabilitation, nearest Lighthouse for the Blind, or Lions center may also be informative. The organization Closing the Gap, which focuses on computer technology for people with special needs, provides information resources through its extensive web site (www.closingthegap.com), bimonthly newspaper, and annual resource directory in addition to its annual conference. The Center on Disabilities at California State University at Northridge (CSUN at www.csun.edu/cal) also holds a widely attended annual conference featuring all aspects of assertive technology. In addition, *AccessWorld: Technology and People with Visual Impairments*, published by the American Foundation for the Blind, evaluates and rates products used by people who are visually impaired, and the *AFB Directory of Services for Blind and*

Visually Impaired Persons in the United States and Canada is a comprehensive resource for information about local sources of assistance (both are available on AFB's web site, www.afb.org; see Appendix B for information about sources).

Purchasing decisions usually need to take into account students' needs for the next three years. The following list outlines equipment needed at a site where there are students who read in braille, students who read large print, a sighted paraeducator to help with braille production, and an itinerant teacher. Each of the necessary components listed here is discussed in the following sections.

Basic Equipment Needed

- windows-based computer with a 19- to 21-inch monitor
- laser printer
- color inkjet printer
- braille embosser
- braille translation software
- scanner with optical character recognition software
- screen-reading software
- screen magnification software
- video magnifier (CCTV)
- braille notetaking device or accessible personal digital assistant (PDA) with braille display

Computers

When purchasing a computer there are three major components to consider: processing speed, random access memory (RAM), and hard drive space. The processing speed of the computer is determined by the central processing unit and is rated in gigahertz. Any computer running at less than 1 gigahertz should be scheduled for replacement. Conversely, any new computer should run significantly faster than 1 gigahertz today.

RAM and hard drive space are often confused. As a general rule, you cannot have too much of either. RAM is temporary storage. This is where programs and information are located when the computer is running. Hard drive space is your permanent electronic storage cabinet. All programs are installed onto the hard drive. All of your documents can be saved onto your hard drive as well. When a document is being created, it is temporarily stored in the computer's RAM. If you turn off the computer before you save the document onto the hard drive, the document is lost. Information stored in RAM is erased when the power is turned off. For this reason work should be saved to the computer's hard drive or to another permanent storage device such as a memory card before turning off the computer. As of this writing, a computer should have at least 256 megabytes of RAM and at least a 20-gigabyte hard drive.

Monitors

Bigger is not always better when referring to the size of a monitor. A 17- or 19-inch monitor is usually sufficient for the needs of most students. Although a larger monitor may help some students, a student with a field loss would have difficulty locating the cursor or text when using a larger monitor. Although a larger monitor provides an enlarged image, it also increases the distance between the students' eyes and the information they are trying to view. This factor becomes extremely important and has a pronounced effect for smaller individuals using 25-inch and larger monitors.

Flat-screen monitors produce less glare than typical curved monitors. Traditional cathode ray tube (CRT) monitors generally are less expensive and have a better resolution than the newer thin-screen liquid crystal diode (LCD) monitors (such as those usually found on laptops). If desk space is available, a 19-inch monitor is adequate in most cases.

Printers

The two most widely available types of printers are inkjet and laser printers. Each has its advantages. An inkjet printer is initially less expensive to purchase but more expensive to run on a per page basis. It can produce both color and black ink documents.

A laser printer is initially more expensive to purchase, but cheaper on a per page basis. It is faster than the inkjet printer and generally produces a better-quality document. Color laser printers have recently become much more available and affordable, and the benefit to students with low vision of having full-color graphs, maps, and pictures in large print is well worth the price. If you will be printing documents for students in large print, the faster speed of the laser printer typically makes it a better long-term buy than the inkjet printer.

The critical issue when considering the purchase of a printer is whether it is compatible with any braille notetaker, PDA, or similar device used by the students. Not all printers are compatible with these devices. Check with the manufacturer of these devices to be certain that the equipment is compatible with the printer you want to purchase. In addition, check that a printer connects through the appropriate, compatible port for any computer, PDA, or other device your students will be using. Buying a printer that produces color documents and accepts 11-×-17-inch paper as well as 8½-×-11-inch paper will enable your transcriber or paraeducator to print enlargements of scanned textbook sections in which color plays a crucial role.

Braille Embossers

An embosser is essential for students who read braille. It may be the most expensive single piece of equipment being considered for purchase; a good-quality embosser today costs several thousand dollars. There are less expensive models, but if high-quality production of braille is important, don't skimp on this item. The quality of production is not the only consideration, however. An important factor to consider when deciding on a braille embosser is the quantity of braille that you anticipate producing. Less expensive models may be fine if you have only one student reading braille. However, they may not provide you with solid, long-term performance if you have to do much more than provide reading materials for that single student.

There are several key issues to understand when selecting an embosser. As already indicated, perhaps the most important is the quality of the braille produced. Not all embossers are equal. If possible, have students compare the output from several different embossers when determining which you will purchase.

Next, consider the speed rating for each embosser. Some embossers are rated as slow as 10 characters per second (cps) while others are rated at 80 to 100 cps. Interpoint embossers are capable of producing braille on both sides of a page, accounting for their faster speeds. All interpoint embossers can also be programmed to produce braille on only one side of the paper.

Finally, make sure the embosser can use several sizes of paper, from 8½ × 11 inches to 11 × 17 inches. Most use tractor-feed paper, but some can use single sheets with friction feed.

Braille Translation Software

Braille translation software is essential to make full and effective use of an embosser. This kind of software can take word-processing files, text files, HTML files from the Internet, and various other files and create documents in contracted braille. It can also take a complex math document created by using specialized software such as a math editor and translate it into a Nemeth braille document. Braille translation software is a fundamental component of assistive technology for blind students. However, a braille translation software program does not eliminate the need for a knowledgeable braille transcriber in the preparation of high-quality braille materials; this is especially important for the transcription of mathematical materials.

Scanners and Software

Scanning and optical character recognition (OCR) software is useful if you want to scan textbooks and worksheets to create braille documents from them. Start with a good quality flatbed scanner. If you do a lot of scanning, you may want to consider one with an automatic document feeder. This will allow you to place a small stack of documents in the scanner and scan them automatically. The latest scanners connect to a computer through the universal serial bus port and are generally faster and easier to set up than scanners connecting through a parallel port.

Buying a scanner that has a color component will enable a transcriber or paraeducator to scan important textbook information that is in color. The information can then be enlarged, printed, and included in a large-print copy of the text.

Two types of OCR software programs should be considered for use with a scanner. The first is software designed specifically for the user who is blind. Its main function is to scan in a paper document, recognize the text, and read it aloud. The drawback to this type of software is that there may be limited control over what is scanned into the computer. If you have a page with a map, chart, or picture, it is possible that this element will be scanned along with all of the text, thus introducing recognition errors. The two most widely used scanning and reading software programs as of this writing have their own software speech synthesizer, talking dictionary, and the ability to convert a document to text for producing large-print text or for translation into braille.

The other type of OCR program is designed for users who are sighted. This type of program entails the use of a mouse to select areas of a page to scan into the computer. In this way, areas of the page that will not scan in correctly can be eliminated, thus saving editing time.

Screen-Reading Software

Screen-reading software is the heart and soul of a computer for a user who chooses to access the computer's display through speech output. This software allows students to work on a computer by using synthesized speech to read aloud the information displayed on the screen. Students can hear each letter or word as they type it. When a menu or dialogue box opens, important information is read out loud to the user. A good screen reader also has the ability to read text from a web site.

Before students use a screen reader, they need to know the Windows operating system and the keys needed to navigate through each program. For example, when the Window key, found between the Alt key and Ctrl key, is pressed it will open the Start menu. Inside a program such as Microsoft Word, pressing the Alt key will move the focus to the Menu bar at the top of the screen. Pressing the underlined letter of the menu will then open that menu: F for the File menu, E for the Edit menu, and so forth. These keyboard commands are built into the Windows operating system and are not part of the screen reader program. A quick reference list of these commands is provided here (see "Keyboard Commands Quick Reference"). It is recommended that teachers learn and practice these keyboard commands in order to teach them to their students.

Keyboard Commands Quick Reference

This is not an exhaustive keyboard command reference sheet. It contains the most commonly used keyboard commands used in Windows. If a student uses a screen reader, there will be additional keyboard commands specific to that screen reader.

- Alt-key moves the focus to the menu bar.
- Tab-key moves the focus to the next option in a dialogue box.
- Shift-tab moves the focus to the previous option in a dialogue box.
- Up and down arrows move the focus up or down a menu list or line of text.
- Left or right arrows move the focus left or right on a menu or left or right one character.
- Space bar key is used to check or uncheck a check box in a dialogue box or on a web page.
- Ctrl key stops synthetic speech temporarily (clears the buffer).
- Home key moves the cursor to the beginning of a line of text.
- End key moves the cursor to the end of a line of text.
- Ctrl-Home moves the cursor to the beginning of your document or web page.
- Ctrl-End moves the cursor to the end of your document or web page.
- Shift key with any movement command will highlight text (e.g., Shift-Home highlights text from the cursor to the beginning of a line).
- Alt-Tab moves to the next open application.
- Alt-Shift-Tab moves to the previous application used.
- Ctrl-a highlights all text in the document.
- Ctrl-s saves the current document.
- Ctrl-x cuts highlighted text and puts it on the Windows Clipboard.
- Ctrl-c copies highlighted text and puts it on the Windows Clipboard.
- Ctrl-v pastes text from the Windows Clipboard at the cursor location.
- Ctrl-z undoes the last keystroke (can be repeated up to the last save).
- Ctrl-b boldfaces highlighted text.
- Ctrl-u underlines highlighted text.
- Ctrl-i italicizes highlighted text.
- Ctrl-[increases the font size of highlighted text.
- Ctrl-] decreases the font size of highlighted text.
- Ctrl-e centers line of text.
- Ctrl-L left justifies line of text.
- Ctrl-r right justifies line of text.
- Ctrl-2 double-spaces highlighted text.

- Alt-Tab moves the focus to the next open application.
- Alt-Shift-Tab moves the focus to the previous application used.
- Context-sensitive menu key (third key to the right of the space bar) lists suggested spellings for misspelled words when the cursor is on the misspelled word.

Source: Adapted from James Carreon and Joan Anderson, *Basic Computer Curriculum Guide* (Fremont: California School for the Blind Technology Program).

Screen Magnification Programs

Screen magnification programs allow students with low vision to see an enlarged view of the computer screen. However, by enlarging what is on the screen, the user will see less of it; that is, have a smaller field of view. Thus, with too much enlargement there is a diminishing benefit to the student. When using screen magnification, it is very important for the student to know and use the keyboard commands built into the Windows operating system. Too often a student will leave nose prints on the computer screen while looking for the cursor to click on a menu. In that case, a new technology assessment may be in order to provide the equipment and training needed to improve the student's efficient use of the computer.

The most widely available screen magnification programs today allow the user to change the magnification level and modify contrast on the screen by changing from a positive image to a negative image of the screen with simple keyboard commands. These programs also provide enhanced cursors and special navigation commands.

Video Magnifiers

Video magnifiers (CCTVs) are designed to assist students with low vision in reading print. A document containing text or graphics, or an object itself, is placed under the unit's camera and magnified for projection onto the monitor. Color or black and white units are available, as are stand-alone models and units that can share the monitor with a computer screen.

In addition, mobile video magnifiers can be attached to a laptop computer or to head-mounted display that place a tiny screen directly in front of the eye, giving the user a virtual view of the image equivalent to that produced by a 17-inch monitor. Some of these devices have cameras with the ability to flip up to view a distant object and flip down to focus on a paper document. The only way to choose the video magnifier that is right for a student or a resource classroom is to sit in front of it and try it out. This can be done at conferences, by visiting other programs for visually impaired students, or by meeting with a vendor. Arrange to

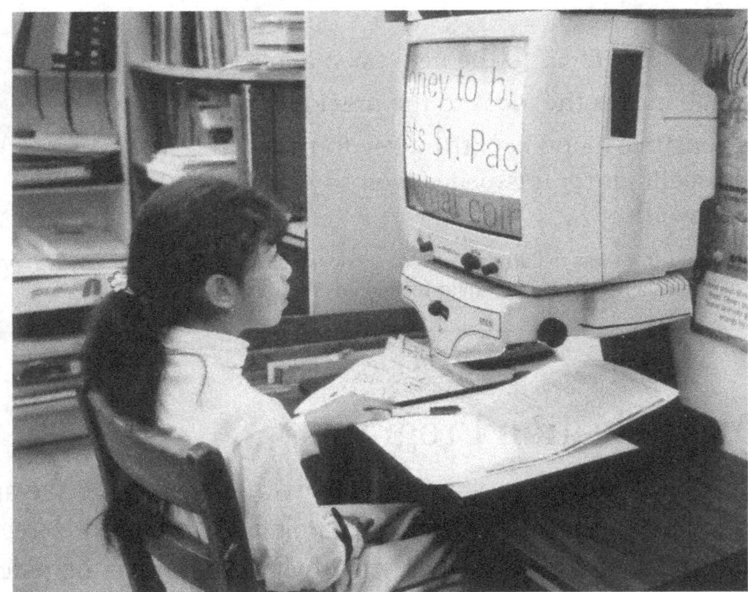

Video magnifiers are one form of technology that can help students access their classroom assignments.

Chad Batka/American Foundation for the Blind

take the student who will be using the video magnifier with you to try it out; sometimes a student will have a preference that never occurred to the teacher.

Notetaking Devices

Braille notetaking devices and accessible PDAs are invaluable for some students with low vision and for both the new and the advanced braille reader. The notetakers are similar to laptop computers in the functions they can perform, except that they have no screen. Students input text through a six-key braille keyboard or a standard QWERTY keyboard. The information entered is stored electronically in the device's RAM or flash memory card.

All notetakers have voice output, and some have a refreshable braille display that enables students to read documents in braille with or without speech. These devices also all have the ability to send documents to a disc drive, printer, or embosser and can exchange files with a computer through a compatible memory card.

Accessible PDAs generally have less functionality than the notetakers, but allow the user to keep track of appointments, telephone numbers, and simple notes. Some accessible PDAs are now built into cellular telephones. These devices are changing rapidly, and more powerful accessible PDAs will be available soon.

DUPLICATION OF TECHNOLOGY

Because technology provides students with critical access to information that might otherwise be unavailable to them, it is extremely important that equipment purchased for their use at school also be available to them at home. In addition to their homework, students may not be able to complete all of their classwork school assignments during the school day and may need to finish it at home. Nevertheless, complete duplication of equipment is not always necessary or possible. For example, a student might use a video magnifier at school but use large-print books with a reading stand at home. Acceptable alternatives exist, based on the student's needs and circumstances.

In general, braille notetaking devices do not need to be duplicated, since they are relatively light and can be easily transported between school and home. These devices should travel with students because they will need information put into the notetaker during the school day in order to complete their work at home.

Other practical considerations may also come into play. For example, given the special equipment and materials students need to carry, expecting them to add laptops to their overstuffed backpacks may be too much for some, if not many, students. An accessible notetaker that is lightweight, has a sustained battery life, allows braille input, and has a refreshable braille display may be more efficient for the student who reads braille.

School administrators who balk at buying duplicate equipment and software for students may need an explanation of their specific needs. Being assertive on behalf of the student's needs; mentioning the Americans with Disabilities Act (ADA), which states that no one with a disability can be penalized because of that disability; and referring to the regulations outlined in IDEA may also be important. Alternative sources of funding are reviewed later in this chapter.

When placing devices in students' homes, have students and their parents or guardians sign forms indicating that they are responsible for returning the equipment in reasonable shape when they are no longer needed or the students graduate or leave the school district (see Figure 9.1 for a sample form). Parents concerned about this responsibility can be reminded to check their homeowner's or apartment insurance for coverage of devices in their possession.

TRAINING

There is too much technology and too many frequent changes for any one person to keep up with all of it—which brings up the important item of training. When people purchase equipment, they seldom purchase training for the student or teacher. The resulting lack of familiarity and absence of technical support can mean that equipment may sit in its box for weeks before the teacher finally finds the time to experiment with it. It should be noted that assistive technology services provided for in IDEA include training for the student, educators working with the student, and even parents when necessary.

Sources of training include state schools, departments of education and rehabilitation, and instructional materials centers; technical assistance units; and assistive technology consultants. Manufacturers and distributors of assistive technology products may provide basic training as well as information about ad-

FIGURE 9.1

Receipt of Assistive Equipment Form

Date 9/14/05

Re Charles Fujita

Certain electronic devices have been purchased to enable Charles to complete schoolwork at home. In signing this form you are:

- acknowledging receipt of and responsibility for these items
- promising to return them in working shape given reasonable wear and tear
- promising to contact Ms. Olmstead if problems occur with the equipment
- promising to return the equipment to the school district upon Charles's graduation or transfer to another school district.

The following device(s) has been loaned for use at both home and school:

Braille notetaking device #577XL539875

The following devices have been delivered to Charles's home for his use:

Computer #VLS558832685
19-inch monitor #52WRT568799780
Laser printer #23HLX4599
Screen-reading software version 05
Scanner #3456987VDG543

Jean Olmstead

Jean Olmstead
Itinerant teacher of students with visual impairments
320-4500
jeo@xxx.edu

Our signatures below indicate our agreement to the conditions stated above.

Charles Fujita
Student's signature

Beth Fujita
Parent or guardian signature

9/14/05
Date

Assistive devices need to be available for students in their homes as well as at school. This student works at home on equipment provided by his school district.

Jean E. Olmstead

ditional training resources. Other programs for visually impaired students may offer opportunities for sharing expertise or training time. Some professional organizations, such as the Council for Exceptional Children and the Association for Education and Rehabilitation of the Blind and Visually Impaired (AER) (see Appendix B), also offer some training.

You may find that once your students know the basics, they will quickly surpass you in their knowledge of the equipment and software. That is to be expected. The students will use the devices every day, and you may use them only occasionally or when a student needs help with them. However, it may be necessary to obtain some training for students, who will not always understand the usefulness of some of the more advanced options available in their software and hardware. It is the teacher's responsibility to help students understand when these advanced features can assist them. Although an instructor may not know how to operate all the advanced features, being able to help a student understand them and learn to use them is important.

For these reasons, when you have a student who needs training, it is often very effective to arrange for a student who is already familiar with the equipment or software to provide the training. Peer training is often more effective, and both students can benefit from such an arrangement.

FUNDING SOURCES

If a school district is unable to allocate money for needed assistive technology devices, assistance may be available from alternative sources. Some states have special programs that fund resources for students with a low-incidence disability. Equipment may also be available from your state instructional materials center. Appeals to local service organizations such as the Lions clubs are other possibilities, as is writing grants to sources that provide funds for education. Knowledgeable sources at your state's school for visually impaired students and department of education may have information about funding sources. The Internet can also be a tremendous resource (try searching for "assistive technology grants + schools"). Although the cost of this equipment can be high, the cost of illiteracy is much higher.

USING THE EQUIPMENT

The equipment has been purchased. You, the students, the transcriber, and paraeducator have received appropriate training. Either before or after the training, a location on site for the devices must be found. The equipment should be placed in a room that is secure but to which the students have easy access. Computer equipment may be placed in the school's computer laboratory to allow students access to the Internet. In elementary schools it may be possible to place the equipment in the classrooms, making it more accessible to students.

Deliver duplicate devices to the students' home. While doing so, make sure that the students and their parents or guardians sign forms indicating their responsibility for the equipment.

Students

Using a computer to complete assignments and research topics provides students with a significant savings in time dedicated to homework. For research, students will find a wealth of information on the Internet. They can also visit web sites or join electronic discussion groups dedicated to topics related to visual impairments. They will be able to communicate easily with friends and family members via e-mail.

When doing assignments, students with low vision can type in large print for easy reviewing, then reduce the font size and print out their paper to hand in. Likewise, blind students can review their work on their computer using speech output or, if they are braille users, on a braille notetaking device before printing it out.

Teachers

Accessing documents on the computer also saves teachers time. Store your reports, assessments, letters, and IEP information in electronic files. In addition, when transferring a student to a different teacher of students with visual impairments or O&M instructor, that person will be glad to receive computer copies of the student's records.

Become conversant with a program for designing templates for forms. Using forms makes finding information easier and can simplify one's professional life. In addition, if you write your goals and objectives for students on the computer, it takes little time to copy and paste them into a checklist for easy data collection about your students' progress.

The Internet can be used for researching the latest information on visual conditions and assistive devices and for joining electronic discussion groups. Choose carefully which electronic discussion groups you join. If you belong to too many, the e-mail can be overwhelming. Groups with a large number of members tend to have strings of mail about both philosophical and practical issues. Smaller groups, such as ones serving members mainly in one state, seem to have correspondence about more practical issues such as locating copies of books in large print or braille. In some cases, when state officials and staff from the state instructional materials center participate in or monitor the smaller lists, they can be a forum for dialogue that can result in changes in policy. For example, one discussion group solved the issue of copies of standardized tests in braille and large print that were delivered late to schools. This tardiness sorely inconvenienced the students: it was addressed when it came to light through e-mail interchanges. The BLIST: The Comprehensive Index of Blindness-Related E-Mailing Lists (http://www.hicom.net/~oedipus/blist.html) offers a starting point for teachers. (Although it has not been updated recently, many of the numerous lists are still active.) Another good source is the Oregon Commission for the Blind Technology Center at www.cfb.state.or.us/techlinks=email.htm.

Transcribers and Paraeducators

Using a computer represents a major change from relying on a braillewriter and large-print typewriter to reproduce materials. Pairing the computer with a scanner, embosser, and color printer drastically reduces the time needed to transcribe materials.

A good scanner can be used not only to scan text to be converted to braille quickly but also to enlarge materials, avoiding the time and paper used in making generations of enlargements on a copier. With a color scanner and printer, the transcriber can reproduce important information in color, enlarge it, print it, and include it in large-print books. Providing information in color in large-print texts means that students who are blind or visually impaired finally have easy access to the same materials as their sighted peers. Providing large-print texts in an 8½-×-11–inch format is also possible using special equipment, which allows the convenient use of regular sized notebooks and file folders. The use of technology means that materials can also be produced in the student's preferred font and point size and that materials for different purposes can be produced in different point sizes as needed.

A transcriber or paraeducator needs to have Internet access. Teachers at other sites can then create worksheets on computers and e-mail them to the transcriber, who can then either enlarge them or convert them to braille for a student via a translation program. Transcribers can also use electronic discussion groups to locate needed materials in braille or large print. Some of these materials may be borrowed from other districts; some may be downloaded directly from the Internet. In some instances the transcriber is the team member who monitors the school district's discussion group, if there is one, and relays pertinent information to the teachers in the program.

KEYBOARDING SKILLS

Keyboarding, or typing by touch, is one of the most important basic skills that students who are blind or visually impaired can learn. With this skill they can create documents, send e-mail, and surf the Internet. Voice-recognition programs are improving and may play a more important role in people's lives and work in the future. However, nothing will replace the ability to write one's thoughts independently and directly through the use of a keyboard.

It is also important to teach the use of the special keys needed for keyboard navigation as well as for shortcuts, as described earlier. These keys include the Alt key, Ctrl key, Tab, the so-called six-pack keys (Insert, Delete, Home, End, Page Up and Page Down), and the numeric keypad. Some individuals find it easier to learn to navigate using the arrow keys and navigation keys embedded in the numeric keypad. Without a thorough understanding of the special keyboard commands, keyboard navigation for a person who is visually impaired will not be possible or efficient.

For elementary school students, a Macintosh computer with a simple talking word processor may be acceptable for learning keyboarding skills. By the time the student reaches the fourth grade, however, the Windows operating system with a complete screen reader or screen magnification program is the preferred medium, as discussed earlier.

ADDITIONAL HELPFUL DEVICES

Visiting office supply stores, perusing product catalogs, attending conferences, and reading technology updates are good ways to learn about devices that may be helpful to your students. One is a monitor stand with a movable arm that clamps onto the desk. Using it with the monitor enables a student with low vision to move the monitor closer for more effective viewing.

Another is a copyholder that can be attached to the top of the computer; it has a flexible arm ending in a clip. Students with low vision can clip on a page and move it as close to their eyes as is needed. Using a copyholder can encourage the use of touch typing. Other adjustable copyholders can be clamped to the desk.

Many other types of useful technology, such as talking dictionaries and calculators, tape recorders, digital talking book players, and electronic braillewriters such as the Mountbatten brailler, can be used to great benefit by students. Although assistive technology presents fast-changing challenges to teachers and their students, it has opened up a whole universe of educational possibilities.

CHAPTER

10

Organization: The Key to Efficiency and Effectiveness

A teacher can sometimes feel overwhelmed when dealing with the myriad details of information and materials that teaching in an itinerant program involves. Superimposing these considerations on those relating to instructional strategies and the needs of your students can be challenging. Devise a method for organizing the details and deciding on the materials to take with you daily as you travel. This chapter outlines essential information and materials you will need.

ORGANIZATION OF INFORMATION AND MATERIALS

A basic theme of this book is that as an itinerant teacher, you will find that your professional life will run more smoothly if you are organized. Having good organizational skills can be important when you are faced with a multitude of details. The process of getting organized may seem like a big time investment initially, but it can save time and reduce stress and frustration in the long run.

Each teacher can tolerate a certain level of organization before the act of organizing itself becomes too onerous. The following information is fairly detailed. Use the suggestions you find helpful; avoid using too many for your individual tolerance.

Faith Dunham-Sims contributed to the information in this chapter.

Calendars and Planners

Implement some type of organizational system or combination of systems. One option is a calendar planner. Your local office supply store will have many to choose from. Mail order companies that specialize in organizational materials for professionals offer daylong seminars on how to use their products. You might want to experiment with different types of organizational systems or with an electronic organizer to see what works best for you. Try to get some sort of system in place as soon as possible, however, before the details you need to keep track of become unmanageable.

Organization specialists recommend that you work from only one calendar, day planner, or teacher planner. Having multiple planners or calendars can lead to more work, more frustration, and less efficiency. If you eventually find that the system you adopted isn't quite right for your style, don't hesitate to change to a different one. Some teachers change organizational strategies every few years as their need to make lists of tasks changes or decreases.

Organizational Principles

Once you have an organizational system in place, set priorities for your tasks by becoming an expert list maker. You might keep daily, weekly, and even monthly lists of tasks; this is where a well-chosen planner or calendar earns its keep. Here are a few tips to keep in mind when prioritizing your tasks.

Tips for Efficiency

- *Do the simple things right away.* If a task takes just a few minutes, do it immediately. For example, take a few minutes to read the memo in your in-box so that you can get it out of your box and route it to the next person in a timely manner.
- *Make time to go through your task list daily.* Whether you are someone who likes to plan for the weeks ahead or just the next few days, once your planning and prioritizing are done, revisit your list routinely. Use it as a tool to monitor your priorities and keep you on task.
- *Cross off completed tasks.* The sense of accomplishment this provides is a boost.

Another way of improving organization is to make optimal use of the computer. If you feel that you are not computer literate or skilled enough, enlist the help of a friend or colleague to get you started with a few basics or advise you on sources that can help you to acquire broader skills. Basic computer classes are available at community colleges or through adult education programs as well as through many organizations and computer training companies. The computer is a great tool to help establish and maintain organization. The following are suggestions for using the computer to make your job easier, save time, and keep you organized.

- *Become familiar with a spreadsheet or similar program.* This will enable you to create professional-looking charts, diagrams, spreadsheets, graphics, and other visual aids. Once you learn a few basic rules about these programs, you can create countless formats.

Efficiency Through Technology

- *Experiment with templates.* A template is a document created on the computer that you can use again and again. It is a shell or basic format. Simply copy the template each time you want to use it and fill in the information. It is like making a photocopy of an uncompleted form. You can use word processing programs or other programs to create templates. A few examples of great uses for templates include the following:
  - —letters
  - —lesson plan sheets
  - —report formats
  - —charts
  - —assessment protocols
  - —data collection sheets

Appendix E includes many examples of forms that can be set up as templates that you might find useful as an itinerant teacher. Feel free to copy and use these forms, or let them be a starting point to create your own format designs.

Pertinent Information and Supplies

Certain information is essential for you. Gather and compile it at the beginning of the year; arrange it in a folder, file, or binder or in some other way; and use it as an invaluable resource that you can refer to throughout the school year. Generally, the information, supplies, and equipment listed in this section are important to have in your car; some generic items may be stored at school sites.

For Each Student

Information recorded for each student should include

Basic Student Information

- first, middle, and last names
- birth date
- address
- telephone number

- parents' names, telephone numbers, and e-mail addresses at work
- names and telephone numbers of persons to contact in an emergency
- name and telephone number of the student's physician
- data from the latest eye report

A one-page list of this information for all your students is a handy reference. At the beginning of every school year, each parent or guardian is usually asked to submit an emergency card with updated information. The card is a good source for most of the items on this list.

For Each School

Information kept on file for each school that you go to should include

Basic School Information

- address and pertinent telephone numbers
- bell schedule
- map
- names of additional personnel who work with the students, such as aides, speech and language therapists, occupational therapists, and O&M instructors, and the times they are scheduled to see the students

For each secondary school, also include

- the master schedule
- room-use chart
- each student's class schedule with teachers' names and room numbers and counselor's name

You may find it useful to have all your students' schedules and the bell schedules for each school on one page. If you reduce the copies of the schedules, you can arrange them all on a page or two for quick reference.

For the District

Information kept about the school district should include

Basic School District Information

- the school calendar
- directory of schools
- map of the school district
- mileage chart
- mileage and attendance forms (which should be completed each day, since it is easy to forget where you were a few days ago)

- schedules for psychologists, nurses, standardized testing, other itinerant teachers, and related services

Forms

These can include lists of materials that have been checked or loaned out, observation forms, and grade forms (see Figures 10.1, 10.2, and 10.3). It's wise to keep these forms in your car, even if you choose not to carry them into each site. They are more conveniently completed on site rather than at your office.

Basic Materials

Some materials you will need to have with you every day. Sometimes you can keep a cache of supplies in every school; other materials will be stored in the trunk of your car.

Stationery Supplies

At a minimum, you will need to have

Basic Supplies

- paper (notebook paper, different styles of bold-line paper, lined carbonless copy paper, bold-line graph paper, and braille paper)
- computer disks and paper
- correction fluid
- black felt-tip pens with fine, medium, and bold points
- pencils (number 2 for test answer sheets and number 1 for younger children)
- erasers
- ruler
- scissors
- chalk
- stapler
- self-stick note pads
- stopwatch

Leave as many of these supplies as possible in a drawer in each of your work areas so that you do not have to carry them from site to site. It is advisable to label the drawers clearly to indicate that the supplies belong to the program for visually impaired students.

FIGURE 10.1

Materials on Loan

Student Stephen Young Year 2005-06

School Hillcrest

	Materials Loaned	Location	Date	Return Date	Transferred To	Date
1.	Medium reading stand #6	home	9/05			
2.	Typing mat #12	home	9/05			
3.						
4.	Math in Our World–6 vols.	Rm. 21	8/05			
5.	Macmillan English–3 vols.	"	"			
6.	Spelling Words & Skills–1 vol.	"	"			
7.	Series R-levels 18, 19, 20, 21					
8.	22, 23, 24 and worksheets	"	"		Rm. 17	10/05
9.	HBJ Science–2 vols.	"	"			
10.	Health & Growth–1 vol.	"	"			
11.	Regions–2 vols.	"	"	10/05		
12.	Medium reading stand #43	"	"			
13.	School district–4 vols.	"	10/05			
14.	Video magnifier #3 (green screen)	"	11/05			
15.						
16.						
17.						
18.	Computer #78ZX453	speech room	10/05			
19.	Monitor #BY794	"	"			
20.	Printer #94625	"	"			
21.	Talking Typer, disc #3	"	"			
22.	Talking Typer, manual #2	"	"			
23.						
24.	Student desk #1	"	"			

FIGURE 10.2

Observation Summary

Student Diane Kolachayevsky Observer Jean Olmstead

Setting Classroom/playground Date 10/28/05

Time	Observations	Comments
Classroom 9:00	Sitting in circle. Raises hand to name a letter at 15'-18' Says "S" for "X" [Letter about 4" tall]	Check letter recognition
9:10	Coloring worksheet at 3"-4". Difficult staying in line	
	Continually stamps feet	
	Chin on page	
	Frequently makes soft sound with lips	
	Cuts along dotted line with paper at 3"	Coordination problems?
	Aide assists by holding paper as she cuts	Hand motion awkward-assess cutting skills
	Has trouble following lines	
Playground 9:30	Running	1. In circle: move closer to board and teacher and assess vision again.
	Slides down slide 2 times	
	Nearly collides with another girl; seems startled	2. Darken worksheets.
	Bell rings. Diane walks to line	3. Verbalize anything demonstrated visually.
	Keeps changing place in line	4. Extra support from aide good.

FIGURE 10.3

Grade Summary

Student Paul Wong Year 2004-05/2005-06

School Spenser

Period	Subject	Teacher	Room	Grade* 1st Q	2nd Q	1st Sem	3rd Q	4th Q	2nd Sem	Final
1	Eng. 1	Ms. Monteiro	213	A[1]	C	B[3,4,6]	D[3]	C[1,3]	D	C
2	Alg. 1	Ms. Spivack	225	C	C	C	B	C[3,4]	C	C
3	P.E.	Mr. Jones	Gym	D[3,7]	F	F[5]	F[3,4,6]	D[3,6]	D	D
5	Comp. Sci.	Mr. Daniels	336	D[6]	F	F[6,8,9]				
6	Wld. Hist.	Ms. Peters	114	C[6,8]	D	D[1,6,8]	F[4,6,8,9]	C[2,4,6]	D	D
7	Electronics	Mr. O'Brien	35	C[6]	D	D[2,3,5,7]				
5	Computer	Ms. Lee	242				F[4,6]	C[1,3]	D	D
7	Economics	Mr. Watson	211				D[4]	D[4]	D	D
1	P.E.	Mr. Jones	Gym	C[3,4]	D[3,4,7]	D				
2	Eng. 2	Ms. Martini	217	B[4]	C[4,5]	B	B[1,4]	D[2,4,5]	C	C
3	Am. Govt.	Ms. Brown	26	C	D[3,5]	C	B	C	C	C
5	Computer	Ms. Lee	242	D[2,5]	C	C	C	B	C	C
6	Radio	Ms. Allen	112	B	A	B	C	B	B	B
7	Alg. 2	Ms. Jenkins	227	D[2,3]	C	D	B	C	C	D
1	Comp. Sci.	Mr. Daniels	336				C	B[1]	B	B

Explanation of Comments

X–Excellent progress
G–Good attitude/conduct
1–Showing some improvement
2–Achievement is not up to apparent ability
3–Absences/tardiness affecting schoolwork
4–Books/materials are not brought to class
5–Assignments are incomplete or unsatisfactory
6–Oral participation needed
7–Inattentive/wastes time/does not follow directions
8–Conduct in class is not satisfactory
9–(To parents) Please contact teacher through counselor

*Note: the numbers next to some of the grades on this form refer to the Explanation of Comments at the bottom of the form. Readers who adapt this form for their own use may wish to substitute an explanation code from forms used in their districts.

Calendar or Planner

As mentioned earlier in this chapter some sort of calendar or planner is essential to keep track of details on a day-to-day basis. When you get the district calendar, transfer important information to your own calendar so that you can see at a glance the dates of special programs or other events that affect scheduling or gathering data. For example, knowing when report cards are distributed lets you check your students' grades at the appropriate times.

Laptop Computer

A laptop is a wonderful tool for itinerant teachers. In addition to using it to store necessary files, you can work on it at a site when a student is unavailable and there is no time to drive to another school before your next student. You can also teach keyboarding on the laptop. Most are set up to allow for different users of the computer to have their own account with separate log-in and password. When each student enters his or her account, the accessibility settings will be appropriate for the student's visual needs. Be sure that the log-in codes follow a simple consistent scheme, such as each person using the first three letters of his or her name.

School-Related E-Mail Address

Using e-mail is a viable way to keep in touch with school personnel, your students, and their families. School staff can e-mail class materials for adaptation. Make sure that your laptop as well as the desktop at your office can access your e-mail.

Business Cards

Business cards are appropriate to give to eye care specialists, vendors, and other professionals, as well as to school personnel and students' families or guardians.

Notepaper

You can save time by creating notepaper for writing to pertinent people. Copying your business card or including your name, title, phone number, and e-mail address will save you the effort involved in writing the same information for each note (see the sample in Figure 10.4). Generally a half sheet, $8\frac{1}{2} \times 5\frac{1}{2}$ inches, will accommodate most notes. Using carbonless copy paper will provide a copy for both you and the recipient. Also, printing the note on colored paper, such as yellow, may enable the recipient to find it more easily on a cluttered desk.

Additional Forms

Collect a few copies of every form you may possibly need. Store them in the trunk of your car so that they will be available whenever you need them.

FIGURE 10.4

From the car of

JEAN OLMSTEAD

Itinerant Teacher of Students with Visual Impairments
Orientation & Mobility Specialist
Phone: x144 or 320.4500
E-mail: jeo@xxx.edu

11/4/05

Re: Ann Sawyer

Dear Ms. Smith,

The second semester is approaching. I need to speak with you about the materials you'll be using in your class so we can start enlarging them for Ann. I can meet with you at the beginning of period 3 in your classroom, 126, on Thursday, 11/11/05. Please e-mail me or call my office to confirm or reschedule the meeting.

Thanks,

Jean

ORGANIZATION OF THE PROGRAM

In a district with several itinerant teachers, a well-organized itinerant program will enhance the effectiveness of each teacher. Basic components include regular staff meetings, appropriate materials, adequate office space and staff, and forms to facilitate organization.

Staff Meetings

Itinerant teachers can be like the proverbial ships that pass in the night. They often feel isolated from each other. Therefore, in any program with more than one teacher, weekly staff meetings are advisable. As a group, teachers can arrange these meetings; sometimes your supervisor might be involved with the planning. At the beginning of the school year, meet as a group and determine which day and time the meetings will be held so that you can all avoid scheduling students at that time.

These weekly meetings (preferably held at the end of the day) provide teachers with the opportunity to support each other, hear guest speakers, order materials, discuss referrals to the program, plan study trips and in-service programs, and write reports and letters. Regular meetings can provide a more cohesive, effective delivery of services for the students.

Program Materials

One of the keys to the success of an itinerant program is the availability of an extensive range of supplies, materials, and equipment that are needed to serve a variety of students from birth to age 21, in general and special education classes, and with mild to severe visual and other impairments. It can take a long time for a new program to acquire all the supplies in adequate amounts. As noted earlier, some of these supplies you will be carrying around with you every day, while others remain at your work sites.

Carrying bulky, heavy pieces of equipment from place to place can produce stress, strain, and discomfort. A program should have enough of these items, such as reading-writing stands and electronic devices, so that they can be left at each of the sites where they are used.

It is impossible to list here all the supplies needed by a program, but some of the more important items are listed here. More extensive information about computerized equipment can be found in Chapter 9.

Basic Program Equipment and Supplies

- *Computerized equipment.* Computerized devices should be available to students, itinerant teachers, and transcribers to use. These include computer systems with adaptations, electronic braille notetaking devices, laptop computers, scanners with color capabilities, and printers that print in color and on both 8½-×-11 and 11-×-17-inch paper. The needs of the individuals using the equipment will determine which types should be purchased. Computer systems used at sites by the students should be duplicated at home for their use.

- *Video magnifiers.* Having various types of video magnifiers (CCTVs) with different options will allow students to use the ones that best enhance their individual visual functioning. The number of devices needed is determined by the visual needs of the students. Students who need electronic magnifiers at school should also have access to them in their homes.

- *Braillers.* If there are not enough electronic braille notetakers for the students who need them, there should be one brailler in each classroom where one is needed, one machine in your workroom, and one for the home of each student who uses a brailler.
- *Enlarging copier.* A copier with enlarging capabilities is invaluable for providing materials in the optimal print size for visually impaired students. If funding allows, purchasing a color copier will enable a program assistant, paraeducator, or transcriber to enlarge parts of texts in which color provides pertinent information.
- *Alternate media devices.* Each program should have sufficient equipment for providing access to texts, including enough battery-run, four-audiotape track recorders and CD players for use by teachers, students, and support staff. Keep an eye out for new technology such as e-books and e-book readers.
- *Reading-writing stands.* Having 60 stands for a program that serves 40 students is not excessive. It is not unusual for a student to use at least three stands: one in the classroom, one in the room where you work with the student, and one at home. Having different types and sizes lets students experiment to determine which works best for them.
- *Low vision devices.* Accumulate a wide range of monoculars and handheld and stand magnifiers, some with lights. Students with low vision can benefit from being able to experiment with different types of magnifying aids. They will find this experience helpful when attending a low vision examination at which a device is prescribed. It's important to remember that on a regular basis students should *only* be using magnifying devices as prescribed by an eye care specialist.
- *Lamps.* Having different types of lamps allows students to determine which provides the best illumination for them.
- *Rubber pads.* Use pads under braillers to reduce noise and under reading-writing stands to counteract sliding.
- *Stopwatches.* Have at least one stopwatch for each itinerant teacher if needed to time keyboarding, reading, and standardized tests.
- *Novels and reference books.* A wide range of books should be purchased in large print or braille, on tape, and, when available, on disk.
- *Paper.* Order a wide range of different types of paper for both braille and print users. If a particular type of bold-line paper is not available, create it

yourself and make extras on your copier. You can also create and order lined carbonless copy paper for notetakers or other purposes as needed.

- *Felt-tip pens.* Felt-tip pens with fine, medium, and bold points can be ordered by the gross to be used by itinerant teachers and distributed to students and their classroom teachers.
- *Correction fluid.* Students who use felt-tip pens can make corrections with correction fluid.
- *Pencils.* Younger elementary school children may choose to use number 1 pencils with softer lead rather than pens.

In addition to these items, the program should have materials available pertaining to the development of concepts, communication skills, vocational skills and awareness, living skills, motor skills, listening skills, O&M skills, pertinent assessment tools, academic skills, recreation and leisure activities, visual functioning, and impairment and other areas as needed. Being aware of and utilizing materials available in the schools and resource centers reduces the amount you will need to purchase. Suggested professional reference materials are listed in Appendix D. Sources of catalogs to guide you in ordering supplies and equipment are included in Appendix B.

You may find that you need equipment that is no longer available for purchase or is unavailable in a desired size. District carpenters and shop teachers may be able to make these items for you.

To reduce loss, keep careful records when taking nonconsumable items from your office. One option is to establish a binder in the office to record the items checked out, with a page for each teacher to list items kept in his or her car or otherwise used for more than one student. Set up an alphabetical list with a page for each student listing the items checked out to that individual. For example, Suzy Jones would have a page filed under *J* listing the brailler, cane, and other items in her sole possession. Items returned to the office should be crossed off the appropriate list. When carefully maintained, the binder will provide succinct information about the items that need to be returned to the office at the end of the school year.

Office and Staff

A room in a centrally located building in your district is desirable for an office. Telephones, a desk for each teacher, filing cabinets, a copier, computer equipment, Internet connections, a table for meetings, and storage space for materials should be provided.

To expedite locating materials, you can categorize them according to their content and store them according to their categories. It is much easier to find materials for working on listening skills, for instance, if they are all in one location. A system for classifying materials is presented in Appendix C. When new nonconsumable items are delivered, use a permanent marker to identify each one with the appropriate classification number. In addition, number each item according to the total quantity available; the first light box received would then be marked #1, the second #2, and so forth.

The office may be staffed by a secretary or a transcriber who has the time and is willing to assume additional responsibilities. An efficient, competent worker will take care of many details, freeing the itinerant teacher to spend more time with students. Duties for this staff member include the following:

Office Staff Duties

- Preparing or locating sources for materials in braille or large print or on tape or a disk.
- Maintaining equipment in good repair.
- Keeping a continuing tally of federal quota and district-program budgets and typing orders.
- Ordering basic supplies as needed.
- Assisting the itinerant teachers to organize materials in a logical manner.
- Maintaining a current inventory of materials and equipment.
- Maintaining a cross-checked system for distributing materials.
- Monitoring electronic discussion lists and relaying important messages to the teachers.
- Answering the telephone.
- Maintaining files of special policies, requirements, procedures, and forms used by your district.
- Relaying messages to itinerant teachers in the field.
- Contacting schools when the itinerant teachers are absent. Pertinent information on an itinerant teacher's absence form (for a sample, see Figure 10.5) enables the secretary to notify the appropriate personnel at each site.

Forms

Some forms are helpful for keeping a program of four or five itinerant teachers organized. You can use the samples offered throughout this book and collected in Appendix E or create ones that are more useful for your specific purposes. Using forms standardizes information and makes it easier to find; however, having too many forms can defeat your purpose. The forms described here are generally stored at the program's office and completed there.

To organize data on students, you may wish to have a binder for each stu-

FIGURE 10.5

Notification of Itinerant Teacher's Absence

Please fill in the name of the teacher/office to be notified when you are absent.

Teacher Jean Olmstead Year 2005-06

Student	*School*	*Person/Office to Notify*
Roger Higgins	Mountain View	Ask secretary to notify teacher (Mr. Smith).
Michael Bell Catherine Aaron Nancy Keller Dan Perry	Park	Ask counselor's clerk at x3000 to send a note to the students' classes.
Bruce Lowell	Belmont	Ask secretary to tell teacher (Ms. Bennett).
Shirley Chapman	Doyle	Call teacher (Mr. Jerry) on classroom phone, x5000.
Gayle Harper David Moore Ray Jordan	Green Valley	Ask secretary to tell teachers: Ms. Hall, Mr. Wong, Ms. Collins.

dent. Dividers can be used to create sections for vision reports and data, IEPs, correspondence and memos, observations, anecdotal records, educational profiles, medical information, work samples, and O&M.

Forms are helpful for many reasons. Having information such as test results recorded on forms can assist you in analyzing and comparing data (see the sample form in Figure 10.6). Also, it can be disheartening to wade through anecdotal records to determine which materials a previous itinerant teacher used with a student. However, the information is readily available if you use a checklist similar to the one presented in Figure 10.7. A summary of continuing data about a student can be recorded on a 5-×-8–inch card for easy reference (see Figure 10.8).

When a student is referred to your program from a school served by an itinerant teacher, it is helpful to have that teacher process the referral. Referrals from other schools can be assigned to teachers on a rotating basis. It is a good idea to keep a record of referrals to the program (for a sample form, see Figure 10.9).

If a referral is closed or not accepted to the program, keep the information you collected in the back of a file cabinet. Students are often rereferred, so it is helpful to have records of your initial screenings.

Creating forms and devising organizational strategies takes time, perseverance, and willingness to work as a group. In the long term, however, you will find that services will be provided to students more easily, loss of materials and equipment can be held to a minimum, and you'll be able to locate important information more readily when it's organized and standardized on forms.

FIGURE 10.6

Academic Tests Summary

Student: Elisa Diego — Date of Birth: 6/10/96

Test: California Achievement Test (CAT) — Date: 5/14/03

Scores: (percentage/stanine)
Reading 33/4
Vocabulary 43/5
Math 65/6

Comments:
- large-print copy
- time and a half - didn't need it
- marked answers on test booklet
- aide marked answer sheet

Test: CAT — Date: 5/22/04

Scores: (percentage/stanine)
Reading 60/6
Vocabulary 50/5
Math 51/5

Comments:
- same as above
- resisted using LP copy

Test: CAT — Date: 5/18/05

Scores: (percentage/stanine)
Reading 58/5
Vocabulary 47/5
Math 26/4
Spelling 70/6

Comments:
- conditions same as 5/03
- needed extra time for math
- check re: extra help for math

FIGURE 10.7

Student Checklist

M: Mastered area/skill
C: Continue instruction or use
E: Exposed to area/skill

Name Tom Yee

Teacher's Initials	F.D.	F.D.	J.O.
School Year	2002 to 2003	2003 to 2004	2004 to 2005
Information about Visual Impairment			
Myopia, nystagmus	E,C	E,C	E,C
Visual acuity and significance		E,C	E,C
Model of eye		E,C	E,C
Vision Assessments			
Near vision	✓	✓	✓
Intermediate vision	✓		✓
Stereopsis/binocularity	✓		✓
Color	✓		
Tracking	✓	✓	
Cover/uncover	✓		✓
Reading speed—regular print			✓
Reading speed—large print			✓
Distance vision			✓
Optical Aids			
Amber slip-ins	E	E	
Reading stand (small/large) and pad	M,C	M,C	M,C
No. 1 pencils, felt-tip pen	C	C	C
Bold-line paper	M,C	M,C	M,C
Amber filter for dittos		E	C
Sunshade			C

Note: The categories and key used in this form can be adapted or changed for the reader's use.

(continued)

FIGURE 10.7 (continued)

Teacher's Initials	F.D.	F.D.	J.O.
School Year	*2002 to 2003*	*2003 to 2004*	*2004 to 2005*
Instructional Materials			
Reading			
Mathematics			
Finger math	C	C	C
Telling time	C	C	
Addition, subtraction flashcards	C	M	
+, – Quizmo	C	M	
Moving Up in Time			C

(continued)

FIGURE 10.7 (continued)

Teacher's Initials	F.D.	F.D.	J.O.
School Year	2002 to 2003	2003 to 2004	2004 to 2005
Language/Spelling			
Moving up in Grammar		C	C
Capitalization & Punctuation			
Alphabetizing exercises		C	C
Punctuation exercises			C
Handwriting			
Peter Possum (upper and lower-case manuscript)	C	M	C (knows all lower case & B, J, M, N)
New Links to Cursive			
Keyboarding Manual			
Talking Typer			thru Lesson 3
Computers			
Macintosh in class	✓	✓	
Macintosh in lab			✓

(continued)

FIGURE 10.7 (continued)

Teacher's Initials	F.D.	F.D.	J.O.
School Year	2002 to 2003	2003 to 2004	2004 to 2005
Career Education			
Summer School	E	E	E
Living Skills			
Department store math	E,C	E,C	M
Money Bingo	E,C	E,C	M
Money Dominoes		E,C	M
Judy Clock		E,C	E,C
Auditory Skills			
Library books	C		
Listen & Learn		C	C
Simon			C
Games			
Hangman—spelling words	C	C	C
Miscellaneous			
California Achievement Test enlarged 154%—marked answers on copy	C	C	C
Copying from chalkboard		C	C

FIGURE 10.8

Student Data Card

Name Ray Figuera Parent(s) Name Helen & Roberto Figuera

Date of Birth 1/1/88 Address 10 Main Street, Westview 00003 Student I.D. # 00032

Home telephone 321-4567 Emergency telephone 777-1122 Work telephone Mother 765-4321 Father 234-2340

Year	Itinerant Teacher	School of Attendance	School of Residence	Gr.	Special Class	Reading Level	BL/ LV	Media Used	Bus	Other
1995-96	Jackson	Dickson	Jennings	2	Yes	1	BL	LP	Yes	
1996-97	Jackson	"	"	3	"		"	"	"	
1997-98	Jackson	"	"	4	"	3.2	"	"	"	
1998-99	Gonzalez	"	"	5	"	4	"	"	"	
1999-00	Jones	"	"	6	"	5	"	"	"	
2000-01	Jones	Central	Central	7	No	6	LV	"	No	
2001-02	Olmstead	"	"	8	"		"	"	"	
2002-03	Olmstead	Fredericks	Wicks	9	"		"	"	"	
2003-04	Davis	"	"	10	"		"	"	"	
2004-05	Davis	Spenser	"	11	"		"	"	"	
2005-06	Davis	"	"	12	"		"	"	"	

Gr. = Grade BL = Legally blind LV = Low vision LP = Large print BR = Braille

FIGURE 10.8 (continued)

Student Data Card (side 2)

RFBD # 2222222 NLS 10/84 Rehab. 6/90 Transit I.D. No SS # 333-33-3333

Hospital ______ Physician Constantinos Medical # 2820386

Eye Condition Albinism, nystagmus Entered Program 10/95

Vision Reports 9/95, 12/00, 2/02
9/03, 2/05

Acuity: 10/80; 10/80 w/cor.
R-20/200; L 20/70

Psychological Evaluation 1988

Passed Proficiency ✓

Graduated 6/90

or Left Program ______

Low Vision Exam Dr. Meyerov

O&M Received 00-01,
01-02, 02-03, 03-04,
04-05

Other Handicaps Learning impairment, diagnosed as mild (6/94)

Comments Prim Hand Code 31-vi
Monocular prescribed & purchased 3/00

RFBD = Recording for the Blind & Dyslexic NLS = National Library Service Rehab. = Department of Rehabilitation SS = Social Security O&M = Orientation & Mobility

FIGURE 10.9

Program Referrals

Date	Name	Referred By	Investigating Teacher	School	Date of IEP or Closing		Reason for Closing
10/03	Caitlin O'Reilly	School Study Team	Mary	Jennings	5/04		
11/03	Ellen Pittman	"	Barbara	Green		4/5/04	DNQ (didn't qualify)
11/03	Piotr Petrovich	"	Don	Central	1/11/04		
12/03	Jacob Nemovsky	Ms. Greene	Barbara	Jennings			
1/22/04	Jean O'Grady	Mr. Jones	Mary	Southport		2/15/04	DNQ
2/28/04	Helena Gomez	Mrs. Wong	Barbara	Walker		3/26/04	Moved out of district
3/2/04	Joseph Chan	Paul Diaz	Don	Summit	5/9/04		
3/12/04	Nick Sullivan	Parents	Mary	Nichols			

CHAPTER 11

The Three Rs: Relationships, Responsibilities, and Rights in Schools

Your student's progress and participation in school activities can be enhanced by your relationship with the faculty and staff. The better the rapport, the more the school staff will support and cooperate with you to provide an effective program for students with visual impairments.

RELATIONSHIPS AND RESPONSIBILITIES

Be Visible

At the start of the year, make an appointment with the appropriate administrator in each school to discuss the needs of your students, your role, and whatever special arrangements you need (such as a workspace, mailbox, and provisions for using the school copier). Make sure you are introduced to or meet the teachers and support staff (secretaries, clerks, custodians, counselors, nurses, and so on), and maintain good relationships with them; they can provide crucial information and support.

Give copies of your schedule at each school (see Figure 11.1) to appropriate personnel (administrators, secretaries, counselors, the students' classroom teachers, the nurse, the psychologist, and so forth). If you write the schedule on a small piece of paper, secretaries who have older furniture with glass on their desks can slip it under the glass.

FIGURE 11.1

2005–06 Schedule—Grant

Jean Olmstead
Itinerant Teacher of Students with Visual Impairments
Office phone: 320-4500
jeo@xxx.edu

Day	*Student*	*Time*	*Room*
Mondays	Suzy Chavez	10:10–10:40	Classroom or library
Tuesdays	Suzy Chavez	8:30–9:00	Speech/vision room
Wednesdays	Joan Freeman	9:00–9:30	Classroom or library
	William Watkins	9:40–10:10	Classroom or library
	Don Fong	10:10–10:40	Classroom or library
Thursdays	Suzy Chavez	8:30–9:00	Speech/vision room
	Joan Freeman	9:00–9:30	Classroom or library
Fridays	William Watkins	8:30–9:15	Speech/vision room
	Don Fong	9:40–10:25	Classroom or library

The first faculty meeting of the year is usually when new teachers are introduced. You may wish to be introduced then too.

Adapt

Evaluate and fit into the atmosphere of each school; each is different. Some schools are more structured than are others. In some schools, you may need to go through a lengthy process to do something special; others may have a more laissez-faire attitude. The more you fit in, the more you will be accepted.

Classroom teachers often have their own special chairs in faculty rooms. Wise itinerant teachers make sure they are not offending these teachers by sitting in their favorite chairs. Sometimes you may find it difficult to get a problem solved at a school. A friendly, reliable teacher may be willing to share some insights about how to resolve a difficulty at that particular site.

Be Sensitive and Realistic

In an itinerant program all worksheets cannot be adapted and all learning situations cannot be ideal for visually impaired students. Your students are in general education classrooms because they can adjust and adapt to such situations and be responsible for requesting assistance when they need it.

Keep in mind all the demands placed on classroom teachers. Whenever a traveling teacher comes to a school, there is more work for the administrators, faculty members, and staff. Be gracious in acknowledging their extra efforts. Repay them with favors when possible. Treats for the faculty room will be appreciated.

If it is permitted in your district, one way to help the classroom teacher is to use reverse mainstreaming by including some of his or her students when you work with your student. For example, if your student needs to work on making change, you may choose to have him or her play an appropriate game with some classmates who need help with that skill. Doing so will not only help the classroom teacher but may also benefit your student academically and socially.

Finally, follow the rules. In a hurried day of traveling from school to school, it is sometimes tempting to circumvent some rules, such as signing in when you arrive and signing out when you leave. Allow adequate time to follow the procedures of your district and those of each school.

YOUR RIGHTS IN SCHOOLS

As you have responsibilities in schools, such as following rules and procedures, so should the school district have responsibilities regarding your working conditions. Administrators have an obligation to provide you with the basic accommodations that other teachers receive: an appropriate room, furniture suited to instructional needs, keys, a mailbox, and a safe place to store equipment. Your time at each site is limited; having to move equipment around and look for a room to work in on a frequent basis robs you and your student of valuable time together. If necessary, the basic accommodations and rights outlined here should be bargained for in the contract between the school district and the teachers' representatives.

An Appropriate Room

Good lighting, privacy, consistent accessibility, space for necessary furniture, and a place to store materials and equipment safely are requisites for a room, as are heat and windows. Establishing your schedule relatively early in the year may ensure that you have an adequate work space in each school. Make sure that furniture is the appropriate size for the teacher as well as the student. The need for electrical outlets with surge protectors for computers and adaptive equipment should go without saying, but check to make sure these are adequate.

Sometimes you may try two or three rooms before you find an appropriate

FIGURE 11.2

Schedule for Room 320

Year 2005-06

To all personnel: Please indicate the day and time you regularly use this room.

Time	Monday	Tuesday	Wednesday	Thursday	Friday
8:00	*Grant Darwood Psychologist* ↓	*Olga Kirby Speech Therapist* ↓		*Olga Kirby Speech Therapist* ↓	*Grant Darwood Psychologist* ↓
9:00					
10:00					
11:00	J. Olmstead Vision Specialist		J. Olmstead Vision Specialist		J. Olmstead Vision Specialist
12:00					
1:00			*Emma Nystrom Vocational Education* ↓		
2:00					
3:00					

one. Often you will use a room that someone else uses at other times. Be diplomatic and tactful yet aggressive in your efforts to obtain a suitable space in which to work. Other itinerant or on-site personnel may use your assigned rooms for various purposes. Some schools may post room-use schedules. If not, you may tape to the door a form similar to that presented in Figure 11.2 to reduce conflicts.

Keys and Mailbox

Necessary keys should be easily accessible or lent to you for the school year. Be sure to get a restroom key if one is needed. If you have several school keys, you may choose to put them on a separate key ring from your car keys and take them into schools only when you need them.

Having a mailbox at each school served is essential to communicate easily with other teachers. Because your time is limited at each school, much of your contact with classroom teachers is carried out via notes regarding materials to be transcribed, class activities, and your students' participation.

A mailbox is also helpful for finding out what is going on in each school. Ask the office staff to put *all* notices for school personnel in your box. You will receive some extraneous materials but will also learn about field trips, special schedules, testing, school activities, or programs that may affect or interest your students.

Sometimes advance notice of changes in school or class schedules will not be put in your mailbox. Some schools, usually secondary ones, have master calendars in the office area; these usually list all the special activities and schedule changes. Ask to see it; checking it regularly (at least once a month) can enable you to keep abreast of changes that affect your schedule at the site.

Safe, Secure Storage

Leave necessary equipment at each school. Carrying bulky equipment to three or four schools per day quickly diminishes the joy of itinerant teaching. In an ideal situation, the equipment is stored in the room that only you use. In reality, more than one person probably uses the room, or equipment must be stored in another location. If the equipment is in another location, make sure it is close enough to your room so that you can carry it easily. When your materials are in rooms used by other personnel, be sure to label them clearly, for example:

Table for Visually Impaired Program
Please do not remove during school year 2005–06

Jean Olmstead

Itinerant Teacher of Students with Visual Impairments

320-4500
jeo@xxx.edu

Access to Copy Machines

When serving a site where a student with low vision requires enlarged print, ask for access to the copy machine so that you will be able to enlarge materials the same day you receive them. For this purpose, take 11-×-17-inch paper to the school. Make sure that other adults on the site understand how to enlarge materials properly and know where to obtain the larger size of paper. In some instances, your student, if responsible, may obtain permission to use the copier to enlarge materials.

Your Workday

The scope of an itinerant teacher's day is often ill-defined. Be clear with your supervisor about what your workday entails. One option is to work the hours of secondary school teachers, which usually gives the itinerant teacher the rights for defined conference and lunch periods. Occasionally, it is necessary to work before or after normal school hours on a regular basis. In such a situation the itinerant teacher should be compensated on a per diem basis or be allowed to come late or leave early to offset the extra time worked.

Preparation and Lunchtime

Travel time between schools does not constitute preparation time. Conference preparation periods should be available to you just as they are to other teachers so that you can make and receive telephone calls, write reports, and prepare for lessons with students.

Each teacher should be guaranteed the standard district-approved lunch period in addition to travel time; eating while driving does not lend itself to either safe driving practices or a healthy state of mind or body. You should have the right to schedule a lunch period for yourself at an appropriate time each day, even though you may find yourself enlarging a last-minute worksheet or proofreading during that time.

This chapter discusses two important topics: your relationships and responsibilities in schools and your rights in schools. You will find that by being visible, adapting to each school's atmosphere, and being sensitive and realistic, it is more likely that appropriate working conditions will be available to you whenever possible.

CHAPTER 12

Other Essentials

Itinerant teachers face a number of concerns and issues that classroom teachers do not. Many of these issues relate to the fact that traveling from school to school daily instead of working at only one site presents somewhat unusual complications.

ABSENCES

Absent Students

One of the most frustrating experiences an itinerant teacher will encounter is to dash madly into a school and breathlessly set up equipment only to discover that the student with visual impairments is absent. Inform parents of your schedule (see the sample in Figure 12.1), and ask them to call you or your office when their child is absent on your scheduled day. Some students, from ages 10 to 12 on, can be expected to call you themselves; teach them to use the telephone, and encourage them to take this responsibility. You may ask school personnel (a secretary, a teacher, or an attendance secretary) to call you when your student is absent, but notification by the student or parent is usually more reliable.

Absent Teachers

Itinerant teachers usually have substitutes only for long-term absences. When you schedule a student, inform the appropriate teacher that when you are ab-

Faith Dunham-Sims contributed to the section on Stress Management.

FIGURE 12.1

To Janice Rivera

Year 2005-06

I have listed below the days and times I will be working with you this year. Please call or e-mail my office to let me know when you are absent on one of those days.

Mondays: 8:30-9:00
Wednesdays: 11:10-11:40
Thursdays: 8:30-9:00

Thank you,

Jean Olmstead

Jean Olmstead
Itinerant teacher of students with visual impairments
320-4500
jeo@xxx.edu

Dear Ms. Olmstead,

I have read your schedule of days and times to work with *Janice*.

I will help *Janice* remember to call or e-mail you if she is absent on a day when you come to work with her.

Rosa Rivera
Parent's signature

9/24/05
Date

sent, the student will come to or remain in class. In some instances (usually in elementary schools), the student waits for you to get him or her from class; all you have to do is let the teacher know, via the site secretary, that you will not be there that day.

In secondary schools, in which the student comes to you for a full period, an appropriate staff member can notify the student of your absence by sending a note to him or her during the first-period class. If you are to see a secondary school student during the first period, call the student at home early in the morning to tell him or her to go to his or her regular first-period class.

You may work with some secondary school students for a full period at the same time every day. At the beginning of the school year, you should arrange for a place such as the library where these students can work during the period if you are absent.

Sometimes special events necessitate a change in schedule. Notify the principal and teacher involved before your absence with a form similar to the one in Figure 12.2.

When a classroom teacher is absent, the substitute would be more effective if he or she had some information about the visually impaired student's participation in activities. The form presented in Figure 12.3 is set up to be signed by the classroom teacher and left with his or her lesson plans.

FIGURE 12.2

To Mr. Menzies

Date 5/25/05

Because of a scheduling conflict, I will be unable to be at your school at the following time(s):

10:00 a.m., Thursday, May 28

Ellen Newhall will come to PE instead

Jean Olmstead

Jean Olmstead
Itinerant teacher of students with visual impairments
320-4500
jeo@xxx.edu

FIGURE 12.3

Date *10/5/05*

To my substitute:

Please be aware that *Steve Sanchez* is in my *4th* period class.

Steve is a student with visual impairments and reads *in braille*.

Please remember that

1. Anything you write on the board will need to be verbalized.
2. During fire drills or disaster drills, you will need to take extra care to make sure this student is safe. I have made the following special arrangements to ensure his safety:

   Fire drills/evacuations: Tom Jordan, Phil Cross, or Viven Hong will assist Steve.

3. Other: *Steve's handouts are with the other students'. If Steve needs extra assistance, he will let you know. He is a capable student.*

Should you have other questions or concerns, talk with *Mr. Johnson, our counselor* here at the school, or contact the teacher of students with visual impairments, *Jean Olmstead* at *320-4500* or *jeo@xxx.edu*.

Sincerely,

Janet Grimes

Teacher, Language Arts

ADDITIONAL STRATEGIC ITEMS

Extended Year (Summer School)

A summer school class for students with visual impairments has several important benefits. The students can work on skills, such as motor development, cooking, and cleaning, which are sometimes difficult to teach on an itinerant basis during the school year. They can also participate in group discussions regarding visual impairments and adaptive devices and techniques.

You may be involved in recommending that a summer school class be established and suggesting which students on your caseload would benefit from attending the class. It is helpful to prepare for the teacher of the class a list of skills on which each student should concentrate.

Students' Lockers

By keeping a record of students' locker combinations, you can help students if they have problems opening their lockers. Special click or magnetic locks are available for those who have difficulty opening combination locks. Utilizing a lock with a key is another option.

Some schools are reducing hallway lighting to conserve electricity, which makes it more difficult for some visually impaired students to see the numbers on their locks. A staff member on site can change a student's locker to one in a more well-lit area or even to one closer to eye level. Using penlights for extra lighting may help some students to open their lockers more easily.

Location of Offices and Teachers

Finding the main office at a new school may be confusing if the building has several doors or there are several buildings in the complex. The door or building closest to the school's flagpole is usually close to the main office. If you are looking for a staff person who is not in his or her assigned location, check with the main office for the person's whereabouts. Some schools post pictures of faculty and staff members or have yearbooks available in the faculty room or office, which you can ask to see to identify a staff member you need to find for the first time.

Food and Weather

Eating cottage cheese warmed to 110 degrees from being in a hot car all morning is unhealthy. Insulated bags with ice packs are readily available and are a wonderful boon for the traveling teacher. It will be easier to carry the lunch bag into a school with the rest of your materials if the bag has a shoulder strap.

In rainy weather, a poncho may be sufficient protection. It generally covers all the paraphernalia toted around and, unlike an umbrella, does not add to the number of items to be carried.

YOUR CAR AND RELATED ISSUES

If you have a choice of vehicles, the most useful kind has four doors and safe storage in the trunk or under the hatchback. Be prepared to carry a lot of materials and papers in your car. Organizing your gear will reduce your frustrations. Cloth tote bags and plastic crates or containers are useful for organizing materials you cannot leave on site.

Safety

Being aware of some issues may ensure your safety.

Safety Tips

- Take a partner to home visits in questionable neighborhoods. Don't make home visits if there are family problems that may endanger your safety.
- If you have access to a cell phone, make sure it is positioned where you can see and reach it easily and that you are familiar with operating it. Use a hands-free phone with maximized sound quality. Use speed dialing. Be sure to program numbers for local police and fire departments.
- Enroll with an emergency road service and maintain your car regularly. Keep your doors locked, windows up, and your sunroof closed when parking at a site. Park in well-lighted areas. Glance into the back of your car before you get into it.
- Plan your trip ahead; avoid looking lost as you study a map en route.
- In a minor accident, have the other driver follow you to a safe, well-populated area.
- Keep your car keys separate from other keys and have them ready while walking to your car.
- Drive safe routes to sites even if they may not be the shortest.
- Make sure someone at work or home is expecting you and knows whom to call if you are late.
- Carry personal emergency information with you.

Logistics

Keep software in a cooler or other insulated container so that it will not overheat in hot weather, and carry it in plastic bags or holders in case of rain. In hot weather, a shield for the front windshield may reduce the build up of heat in your car. Also available is a solar car ventilator that keeps the interior temperature the same as the exterior by recycling the inside air periodically.

If your car can be locked without using a key, you may choose to carry a spare key with you or have one in a magnetic container hidden under your car, in case you inadvertently lock your keys in your car.

On dark, rainy, or foggy days you may drive with your headlights on for safety reasons. Develop a strategy for ensuring that your headlights are off when you park. For example, you can make it a habit to check your headlight switch every time you remove your keys from the ignition.

If your mileage reimbursement for any given year is less than the standard rate allowed by the federal government, you may deduct a percentage of your automobile expenses and depreciation on your income tax return. To do so, keep good records of your car-related expenditures, total mileage, and mileage used for professional purposes.

Parking and Commuting

Parking at some schools, particularly secondary schools, can be difficult. Some schools may assign a numbered space to you; others may require a sticker to park in the faculty lot. You may request a special parking space close to the entrance because of the heavy materials you unload and the time constraints inherent in being itinerant.

Overall, itinerant teachers often spend a good part of their workdays in their cars. You may find it advisable if you can to live close to the school district or area in which you teach to minimize the amount of time you spend driving.

STRESS MANAGEMENT

Whether you are a seasoned professional or just starting your career, it is wise to establish and maintain a reasonable pace for yourself. It may be easy to think you have no control over your job. However, you *are* in control of how you perceive and react to potential stressful issues. Anything can cause you stress if you let it. You must respond to demands on your time, but the manner in which you respond can make the difference.

The following are tested and practical suggestions to help you manage existing stress and reduce the introduction of more stress into your life.

Evaluating Tasks

If you think an added chore is stressful or overwhelming, it will be. Before you simply react to a situation, take time to evaluate it. How are you going to deal with this? Do you have alternatives? Can you get help? Then develop your plan of attack. As a list maker, write everything down, do a task analysis, and prioritize the tasks. Then see how this all fits into your existing schedule and "To Do" list. With some careful preparation it may not be as bad as you think or as bad as it could be if you were to panic without planning.

Occasionally you may have no choice about performing a particular task, even after you've talked seriously to your supervisor about its impact on your job performance. Sometimes the best thing you can do is to try to accept that disruption is necessary. Your blood pressure will certainly be steadier if you just complete the chore and return to your normal routine, instead of letting it add stress to your life.

Inherent Stress Factors

Be aware of stress factors inherent in the job. The majority of people who become teachers innately value being helpers. They undertake the role in order to help (teach) children to become independent contributors to society. Therefore, stress can occur when a student resists being helped or does not follow up on lessons you have tried to teach. For example, when students resist using their low vision devices or adapted materials independently, we can feel frustrated and stressed.

As students mature, they need to become advocates for themselves. If they resist taking that responsibility, teachers can be torn between rescuing them and letting them fail. Despite our need to be helpful, students need to fail sometimes so they will experience the consequences and perhaps be more assertive in the future. After graduation we will not be there to help. You may be disappointed if students aren't using appropriate materials (such as a monocular) or being self-advocates. One way to deflect this disappointment is to tell the student, "When you are a mature adult, you'll remember what you've learned and will use the monocular when it will provide you with information you need." Planting this seed can give you the hope that your sage advice will be used at some time, even if not now.

Familiarity with Students

Working one-to-one with students is a unique privilege, but at times it can foster too much familiarity. A certain level of involvement with students is healthy. Be involved enough to provide appropriate, creative interventions, but resist becoming involved to the point at which you try to deal with global issues for which there may be no solutions. One sign of overinvolvement is the feeling that you should take a student from a deprived living situation into your own home. Appropriate professional detachment is a necessary part of stress reduction for itinerant teachers. This detachment will lead you healthily to contact family service agencies designed to intervene and improve the student's living situation.

Tension with Co-Workers

Nothing adds to an already stressful situation more than tension among co-workers. If you are experiencing problems with your co-workers, you owe it to yourself and them to discuss problems as soon as possible. Do not allow an issue to fester. A tension-filled work environment is not pleasant and certainly is not conducive to efficient work or effective teaching.

Networking

If you are experiencing a work-related problem outside of your program's office, use your co-workers as a sounding board when trying to solve your dilemma. They may have tackled the same problem themselves, in which case their input could be very helpful. At the very least it is a sharing of ideas, which in itself is an opportunity to learn something new.

Saying No

One way to prevent adding more stress is by not taking on more than you can handle. Stress occurs when your mouth says yes and your gut says no. If you are already working at your limit, do not take on additional responsibilities, no matter how compelling they may be. This includes both at the office and at home. This does not mean that you can never take on the responsibility of being the union representative for your department or helping with the soccer team carpool. It just means that you will wait until you feel comfortable about adding it to your list of responsibilities. Added roles should be enjoyable and not perceived as chores.

Taking Time for Yourself

Perhaps the most important aspect of stress management is to make sure that you are taking time for yourself. You are more effective with your students when you feel calm, capable, and energetic. If you do not take care of yourself, it's unlikely you will be able to serve your students (or your family) optimally. A wide range of literature about handling stress is available. Read about techniques that you might find helpful. Sometimes just wearing your watch on the other wrist or taking a different route to a site can divert you from feeling that you are in a rut and lessen feelings of stress.

There are many ways to reduce stress and improve your health. Those specific to the role of the itinerant teacher include the following:

Stress-Reduction Techniques

- Your car may be used as a private therapy room while driving to your next site. You can vent frustration as needed or sing and laugh with joy.
- Meet regularly with other itinerant teachers to reduce feelings of isolation. These meetings will be more productive if each of you has a sense of humor and an appropriate perspective. It's helpful to be with people who are experiencing the same joys and frustrations. You can also communicate through e-mail and electronic message boards, as well as by attending workshops and conferences.
- Sometimes you may feel you don't have much autonomy on the job. However, you may have more than you suppose. Think about what activities inspire you and incorporate them in the students' IEPs. For some teachers, that might involve teaching students new games for leisure activities. For others, it may entail scheduling appropriate study trips that provide helpful information to the students as well as break up the monotony of following a regular schedule day after day. At least once a month, try to schedule an activity that leads you to say, "Yes! That's why I became a teacher."
- Consider adopting the motto "Dare to be average." It doesn't mean that you won't work hard or will care less about each student. It does suggest, however, that you are giving up the "miracle worker" image and that you don't try to find solutions to unsolvable situations. You can also volunteer less frequently. Best of all for your students, you may find that you don't rescue them as often as before. Adopting this motto may seem drastic. If you try it in a balanced way for a short period of time, however, you will no doubt find that the school district has not fallen apart and that your students are still operating at levels commensurate with their abilities.

CHAPTER

13

Tricks of the Trade

Teachers of students with visual impairments are often isolated from their peers. This isolation may lead us to think that others may have developed strategies for effectiveness that we have not yet discovered. The truth is that each of us has found some solutions as well as having some concerns for which we haven't found solutions. It's important for us to share our tricks so we can all benefit. Each of us will find validation for the ones we've already begun using; each of us will find some ideas that we hadn't yet thought of.

After the publication of the first edition of this book, workshops on itinerant teaching were held throughout the United States and Canada. Teachers at these workshops submitted their own ideas and suggestions for making the lives of itinerant teachers of visually impaired students easier and their work more effective. Many of the same suggestions were submitted by a number of writers in slightly different forms; some were one-of-a-kind gems. These responses and suggestions are pertinent to all the chapters of this edition of *Itinerant Teaching*. The best of these ideas are presented here, arranged by category, for easy reference.

ATTITUDE, ATTITUDE, ATTITUDE

"Build self-esteem in students. Listen to them carefully. Be polite."

"Have a 'can do' attitude. The abilities of multiply disabled students with whom I've worked usually meet or exceed expectations."

“Understand what learned helplessness is, and rethink your teaching strategies to counter helplessness. Give your students control over their outcomes.”

“Act the part of a guest in any classroom.”

COLLABORATION

Classroom Teachers, Colleagues, and Staff

“Put together an itinerant teacher handbook and share it with your peers.”

“At the beginning of the year, show classroom teachers enlarged copies of very poor quality worksheets to emphasize the importance of copies with good contrast to expedite enlarging.”

“Leave something in print with the classroom teachers describing their visually impaired students' needs. Include information that will be useful for the teachers if they are unable to reach you.”

“No matter how much an adaptation matters to a student, some classroom teachers will view whatever input you give as only a suggestion. You have to demonstrate for the teacher that a technique works.”

“Carry braille alphabet cards or bookmarks and poster board signature guides to hand out as prizes to teachers who ask good questions at in-service training sessions. The first questioner always gets one, so it tends to break the ice and helps the questions flow.”

“After I provide an in-service session, I give each teacher a one-page summary. It gives the name of the student's eye condition and a short explanation, a sample of type size needed, distance he or she can see, and low vision support needed.”

“Make use of outreach consultants from your state school for visually impaired students.”

“Borrow ideas from OTs, PTs, speech therapists, and adapted PE specialists.”

“Give information about what you do (including an overview of O&M) to principals and other personnel at your sites.”

Students and Classmates

“Conduct a braille workshop for classmates of the visually impaired student so they understand what braille is.”

“Set up notetaking classes for peers of your visually impaired student to train them to take notes from the board using NCR bold-line paper.”

“For a newspaper for visually impaired students, have each student columnist or author record the article on cassette, so that students have the entire auditory newspaper recorded by each author. This is good for socialization and saves time and paper using print or braille. Give the cassette to the editor or teacher in charge of the newsletter."

"Have students act as advocates for themselves by helping to arrange the time of an informational program and choose the topics and other activities, calling on you when needed."

"Don't include only teachers and parents in in-service sessions. Include peers and other students (not necessarily the whole school, but the same grade level at least)."

"Having the student participate makes a presentation very effective. There is more meaning with the combination of explanations from both teacher and student."

"When one of my students began to assume responsibility for contacting her teachers about her special needs, we compiled the following list of steps to follow:

1. Choose a time when the teacher can concentrate on what you're saying.
2. Make eye contact.
3. State or restate the situation. Explain your vision condition(s) or acuity and the problem: for example, some worksheets are too light.
4. Ask for what you need: for example, high-contrast copies of worksheets.
5. Suggest or ask how you can help the teacher: You'll make the copies if the teacher will give you a clear copy.
6. If the teacher can't provide the information or materials at the time, ask him or her to commit to a specific plan of action.
7. Thank the teacher for his or her cooperation."

Working with Families and the Community

"Have a meeting to introduce parents to one another, whether or not their children have the same special needs or diagnosis. Then they can begin to create their own support group."

"Send home a note after working with each student to let parents know what progress or change was made during the visit. This technique saves telephone calls. I always include my phone number, but get few calls."

"Invite capable blind or visually impaired adults to spend time with your students at least once a year."

"Teach parents the basics of the abacus so they can help their child with homework."

"Make time for one-to-one informal talks with parents or guardians in a neutral environment."

"Contact the local chapter (Aerie) of the Fraternal Order of Eagles or a similar local group. Their projects include one called Youthful Blind, which has been invaluable in helping us get equipment we couldn't get otherwise, such as a copy machine and a Braille Talk."

"Utilize community agencies, for example those serving people with visual impairments, to teach students those daily living skills required to function properly. Some agencies offer programs for kids. Tap local resources (especially during summer vacations and other nonteaching times)."

PROVIDING INSTRUCTION

"I do four half-day mini-workshops throughout the year on different subjects. I bring the students together and teach social skills, computer skills, use of low vision aids, and other topics."

"Determine students' color preferences to help with settings on CCTVs and computers."

"Fit vision stimulation activities in with what the student is doing. Over time, stimulation exercises in isolation do not appear to transfer."

"Chart behaviors and keep anecdotal records to document effectiveness."

"On Fridays get work from classroom teachers to be transcribed into braille or large print for the next week."

"Schedule an additional 15 minutes per lesson to talk with school personnel."

"Some classroom teachers are willing to write on a pad of easel paper with a felt-tip pen, rather than use the chalkboard. The visually impaired student can then have the page of notes or information."

"Braille 'cheat sheets' can be left in classes where students read in braille. Other people working with the students can refer to the sheets if the need arises."

Planning and IEPs

"Begin as early as possible on vocational, self-help, and O&M skills."

"All my high school students have a long-term goal for independent functioning. As each year passes, the short-term objectives grow, while direct intervention goals from the vision teacher decrease. Goals shift responsibility for obtaining adapted materials, advocacy, and managing unexpected problems during the school day from teacher to student."

"Explain the IEP process and have the students create their own goals. Allow them to present them at the meeting. If the students invest in the IEP, they will probably succeed in accomplishing beyond their goals."

"I have a check sheet for each student regarding his or her IEP goals. I give a copy to my supervisor intermittently so he'll know how hard I work."

Activities of Daily Living

"When teaching shoelace tying, attach one-half of a flat shoelace to one-half of a round shoelace. Put the lace in the shoe. You can then refer to the 'flat' lace and the 'round' lace during the teaching process."

"When cooking from a recipe, get out all the ingredients before beginning. Put each one away after it's been used. If anything is left over at the end, it's been omitted."

"Put containers on a tray with a lip to contain spills when pouring liquids for cooking or eating."

"When modeling hand-over-hand or hand-under-hand (coactive) eating, the spoon or fork should make contact with the plate or bottom of the bowl, so the student will have a better chance of getting food with every bite when independent. Use the nondominant hand on the edge of the bowl or plate as a guide."

"Peanut butter is easier to spread on bread that is frozen."

VISUAL ASSESSMENT

Tools

"Have a large bag for assessment materials for all ages and impairments. Include a 4-×-4-foot piece of black felt and one of white for assessing contrast, or paint a black cookie sheet white on one side."

"Useful supplies include the following:

- vision charts from Lighthouse for the Blind, especially house/umbrella/apple cards
- cake decorations spread on black cloth
- bright, shiny objects such as Christmas lights, tree garlands, and decorations
- small edibles

- preferential looking test
- flashlights and penlights with colored caps
- feather duster
- red, orange, green, yellow, and blue balls, 8 inches to 1 foot in diameter
- APH light box
- beads and pipe cleaners
- wind-up toys
- pinwheel
- bells
- finger puppets
- pictures and photographs of real objects
- switch with adapted toys
- spinning tops in various sizes
- pegs and pegboard
- bubble-blowing solution
- tape measure"

Techniques

"I generally refuse to conduct an assessment until the eye specialist's report is in to ensure that the student has the best possible correction."

"Read *all* medical reports to determine whether existing conditions affect visual functioning."

"Ask the parents and teachers what their main concerns are about the student's vision."

"Talk to anyone who has significant contact with the student (e.g., parents, foster parents, teachers, aides, sibling, peers) about the objects, people, and activities to which the student responds."

"Observe the student in activities and settings where he or she is actively involved."

"Look through the student's eyeglasses to understand how these affect visual functioning."

"Have someone familiar to the students (e.g., parent or aide) assist with the assessment."

"Play a videotape. It can help to focus the student's attention and provide functional data."

"Conduct assessments for near vision in the home with the parents or guardians present to foster understanding of the student's visual functioning."

"Take time to build rapport and a means of communication."

"Learn and use best positioning."

"With a nonverbal student, look for slight changes in the face or body that might indicate a visual response."

"Physically stimulate the student for 15 minutes prior to the assessment to increase the levels of response."

"Use at least two people for the assessment."

"Have the helper assist in positioning the student in the most comfortable position. The helper can also attract and keep the student's gaze."

"Assess visual functioning at least three times, average the data, and discuss the range of responses."

"Write the report with the parent in mind. Avoid or explain jargon."

ORIENTATION AND MOBILITY

"Use a cardboard core from wrapping paper as a first cane for some smaller students."

"Create a monthly 'emergency' with O&M students. Get stuck somewhere and have the students develop a plan for rescue *other* than calling 911."

"When students turn 16, they need written identification. This process can be used to create many O&M lessons for a student, involving calling the Department of Motor Vehicles to make an appointment, filling out the form, seeking assistance to get in the proper line for the picture, and other necessary activities."

COMPUTERS AND ASSISTIVE TECHNOLOGY

"Sometimes students will lose sight of the cursor on the computer screen. Have them roll the mouse around: a moving cursor is easier to spot than one that is stationary. If they still haven't spotted it, have them use the mouse to go to the top of the screen and highlight a section so they'll know where the cursor is."

“Use a larger cursor. This is an option in many screen-enlarging software programs, or you can download them for free."

“For students who are having trouble understanding the directions given by the speech synthesizer on the computer, I tape-record the directions as they are read. When the speech synthesizer is talking and I'm trying to explain the directions, I end up talking over the next set of directions. With tape-recorded directions, we can proceed through these at a slower pace, stopping and starting if necessary, so the students can understand one line before we proceed to the next. The next time the program is loaded, the students will understand the directions better."

“Keep software in a cooler to keep it from overheating."

“Use bright colored labels to color code software according to its use or the student who uses it."

“Keep types of software together: for example, word processing or games."

“Get to know the computer experts at a site; their expertise can be invaluable."

ORGANIZATION OF TIME AND MATERIALS

“When making your schedule, try to schedule the students closest to your home as your first and last students of the day, because you don't get paid for the time you travel before and after school."

“If you have two students in the same grade at the same school, try to arrange their schedules so that they have the same teachers (say, for English or history), even though they may not be with the teachers at the same time. This can considerably reduce the amount of time you spend consulting with the teachers and adapting materials."

“I ordered labels with my address to put on envelopes for teachers to return information to me; it saves on handwriting. You could also have a return address stamp made."

“Carry a set of index cards in a coupon holder with information on each child needed frequently (parent and school, addresses and phone numbers, eye condition, medication, acuity, etc.)."

“For each student, I keep a daily log sheet denoting what work was done, what teachers I spoke to, all parent contact, and any other notes. This helps with accountability and makes writing IEPs and progress reports easier."

“Use highlighters a lot."

“Carry a thin notebook with a page for each student on which you can write notes. When the page is filled, put the notes in file folders. Copy a lesson plan page with schedule, students, and times, and a space for writing in a plan for the time you are at a site. This saves on carrying folders in and out of sites."

“Use an individually indexed manila folder for each child to organize that child's personal information (such as IEP, lesson plans, ocular report, etc.). If you serve several students in a school, all the folders for that school can be kept in an expandable folder."

“On color-coded folders for students, put students' parents' names, telephone numbers, addresses, school information, etc. List teachers' free times if appropriate."

“Take extra folders to conferences so that you can organize handouts and information on the spot."

“Folders can be color-coded for various topics."

“Make a large folder (braille paper size) with pockets to help organize braille work."

“Use spiral-bound index cards to keep a handy listing of important names and telephone numbers for each school district."

“Dictate notes, correspondence, and reports into a small tape recorder in the car when not singing along with the radio."

“Listen to conference tapes in the car when driving between sites."

“Use different-colored self-stick note pads to mark important things."

“Carry a fanny pack; it leaves your hands free for other things."

“Keep a zippered pouch in your purse or briefcase to organize pens, pencils, scissors, glue sticks, and other items."

“Keep change for a telephone call or have a calling card. Carry telephone numbers with you."

“Always have paperwork to do in case a student is absent."

“Have something to read or do in the car if you get caught in a traffic jam."

EQUIPMENT AND SUPPLIES

“A hot glue gun makes fast tactile outlines, coloring and cutting projects, and smiley faces."

“Use bags of all kinds and sizes to hold different types of materials; use accordion files for pictures. Portable file cabinets with dividers and built-in trays are good for storage in your car's trunk."

A classic itinerant pose.

Jean E. Olmstead

"Small portable white dry-erase boards can be useful."

"Get a portable dolly to haul materials. There are occasions when time won't permit making numerous trips to the car. It also saves your back."

"Color-code book list requests when ordering next year's books."

"You may find that Hi-Marks tubes dry out too soon. They also can stain clothes. Elmer's Glue Colors are nontoxic, washable, and not permanent—great for making changes or correcting mistakes. The glue doesn't dry up before you use it all and it's less expensive and more versatile."

"A stuffed animal with a bell around its neck is a helpful audible reinforcement."

"Use cookie sheets with magnets to hold materials up in front of students."

"Use a stereocopier to make raised-line communication symbols."

"I use a laptop computer to practice letters and sounds with precocious preschoolers who have auditory and visual or motor skills impairments."

"Buy a 4-×-8-foot sheet of white board (sold for bathrooms) from a lumberyard. Install it in a classroom by placing it in the chalkboard tray and holding it in place with clips at the top. It can be moved each year as the students change classrooms."

"Use buff-colored paper for students with photophobia."

"I put smelly stickers in a small photo album. The students can quickly go through pages to choose their own stickers."

"The case with a zipper from the APH light box is great for carrying toys and other items. It keeps them all in one place and they don't fall all over."

"Clamping switches to reading stands is helpful for some students with multiple impairments."

"Put contrasting materials on switches when appropriate."

"Wear washable clothing; use only objects that can be disinfected."

AT THE SCHOOL

"Pay attention to your hunches. If you have a feeling that a student is absent, check with the school. Your hunch may be right and you may avoid an unnecessary trip."

"Remember students' birthdays and those of certain teachers."

"I establish a relationship with the resource specialist at each school so that I have a contact person and maybe a place to work in."

"Get to know the wood-working teacher at the high school, if there is one. He or she and the students can help make specialized furniture and equipment for you."

"Have every item at each site that you could possibly need. Most teachers are willing to give you a spot for your stuff in the classroom. If you're lucky, you may even get a room."

"If you enjoy baking, consider making a cake or other treat for each site once a year. Write a cheerful note in braille and large print and place it next to the cake."

"I have several elementary-age students with low vision with whom I consult on a monthly basis. I found it very difficult to be in touch with how they're doing. This year I volunteered in their classrooms (like a parent volunteer) once a week. I work with small reading groups, math groups, and others. I don't always have the students with visual impairments in my group, but sometimes I do. This has been very successful for me, because I see the students weekly in their classroom, working in the school environment; the teacher has regular contact with me, and I'm much more helpful to her; and the teacher will ask me to check on something with my student (such as whether or not a computer program or a board game is appropriate), which never happened when I popped in once a month."

"At a new school, always get a map of the school for yourself and enlarge it or put it in braille for the students."

"Make sure to get a calendar for the year at each school you work in, since holidays, staff development days, and parent-teacher conferences in each school don't always coincide, especially if you work in a county office of education rather than in one school district."

❝Be sure to stop by the office of each school as you arrive and leave. Lots of last-minute messages find you that way."

❝Eat lunch with staff as often as possible."

❝Wear your name tag."

❝Find resources. For example, at one school, half the fifth and sixth graders go to band while the other half have study hall. I utilized some of the latter group of students to help me to adapt and copy materials."

❝Attend the teachers' meeting before the school year starts; you can learn what's happening in the district."

❝Do whatever you can to make the classroom teacher's job easier. If you help, the teacher may be more willing to help you."

❝Many elementary classrooms have copies of manuscript or cursive alphabets above the chalkboards for students' reference. I make sure that my students have appropriate copies available for their use."

IN THE CAR

Organization and Supplies

❝Use color-coded baskets for different types of supplies."

❝Have snacks, water, and a blanket in the trunk."

❝Plan once a week to clean out, organize, and inventory what's in your car. Decide what to throw away or store elsewhere for the next week."

❝Use a station wagon so that you do not have to do so much bending over and lifting."

❝Buy a car with a large trunk, automatic transmission, coffee cup holder, and power door locks."

❝Use separate tote bags for each child or school so you can presort materials. Keep a basket in the car for materials shared between schools for easy access. Different colored folders for each student are also helpful."

❝A cabinet-drawer-sized file box kept in your car can work wonders."

❝Always carry some food that you can eat in the car, for example, PopTarts. I keep them in the back window so they are warm; if I'm really busy, I can eat on the road."

❝Carry disposable wipes."

“Keep a file box of all the forms you'll ever need and store it in your car trunk."

“A note pad with a suction cup that attaches to the dashboard is very handy for jotting down brief notes and recording mileage. Or tape a piece of paper to your car's dashboard and use it to jot down notes."

“Keep your mileage records on a clipboard under your car seat."

“Write your mileage down on the actual sheets you turn in for reimbursement. It saves tons of time."

“Keep an organizer on the passenger seat for food and other items."

“If you are in the early stages of pregnancy, keep a bucket in the car."

“Instead of sticking all the site parking stickers on my car windows, I put them on separate pieces of paper and put the appropriate paper on my dashboard when I'm at a school. This keeps my windows cleaner and helps to keep my car safer, because students can't see stickers from what may be rival schools."

“Keep a crate in your car with all (complete) student files so you have the information available but don't have to haul it in."

“For confidentiality reasons, don't carry files in your car unless you need them for a meeting. In that case, return the files to their storage place as quickly as possible."

“Keep a charger for your cell phone that plugs into the cigarette lighter of your car."

“With a cell phone and hands-free connection in the car, you can make calls that used to have to wait."

Safety

“If you can't afford a cellular phone, get one that only dials 911. It could save your neck."

“A citizen's band radio can be useful for long-distance traveling."

“Don't keep a loose clipboard on your car's dashboard. It can be a real safety hazard."

“Be careful of your back when getting things out of your trunk."

“Carry a car kit and know the basics for when your car breaks down. Keep a survival kit in your trunk with a blanket, food, flashlight and other items you'll need if you're stranded."

“Join AAA or a similar organization that will provide emergency road service. Carry a charge card in case of emergency."

“No matter what you do, do not speed while driving between schools. You may be late, but at least you'll arrive."

Traveling

“Don't forget to plan bathroom stops."

“Always know where every accessible or findable restroom is. Accessible may mean in unexpected places such as police stations, drugstores, or libraries, but avoid gas stations—usually too dirty."

“Find out where the public libraries are. You can use the restroom without having to buy anything, and if you have some extra time, you can do paperwork there."

“Get maps from area telephone books or city halls. Ask people at gas stations for directions. It's surprising that there are not usually signs or any indication of the location of a school that is off the main road in a small town."

“If you fly between sites, find a good travel agent who is responsive to your particular needs and desires."

MANAGING STRESS AND ISOLATION

“New itinerant teachers will not believe how much different their second year will feel, once people know them!"

“When I get really frustrated, I look at some funny postcards I've pinned on the wall; they give me a chuckle."

“Have weekly staff meetings, to blow off steam and discuss student concerns."

“Acquaint yourself with other itinerant teachers in areas surrounding yours to contact, share, and support each other. Perhaps you can meet for lunch once in a while. This reduces the isolation we often feel."

“Remember that you are not alone. There are a number of us with a multitude of experiences. We are all just a phone call away. Let's share our expertise."

TIPS FROM PARENTS

“As a teacher, please remember that as parents we cannot separate ourselves from the emotional ties we have with our children, for example, at IEP conferences. They are ours 24 hours a day. We don't go home."

“I would like to see itinerant teachers work with visually impaired students to present to the class what the teacher and child work on outside the classroom and maybe suggest to the class and teacher ways they can help in the learning and teaching process. Help sighted classmates who are not visually impaired to understand."

"Remember to advocate for the students and yourself. If you are a good advocate and good with kids, you will be listened to."

CHAPTER 14

Final Words of Wisdom

I hope you find the suggestions and information in this book helpful. I have provided a lot of information, but I certainly have not answered all the questions that arise for itinerant teachers. In fact, for some questions there are no absolute answers.

The strategies I have outlined are not the only ones to use. Many fine itinerant teachers do things differently, and their procedures are just as correct as the ones presented here. One wish I had as I first wrote this book is that a dialogue among itinerant teachers would grow and that we would meet more often at conferences and in small groups as well as being more willing to share our ideas in publications and newsletters. Because we are relatively isolated from our peers, we often feel that the itinerant teacher in the next county has the answers to the concerns that confound us. The truth is that each experienced teacher has some good strategies to share and some issues for which he or she is searching for solutions. My wish came to fruition with the establishment of Division 16 for Itinerant Personnel in AER. The division publishes a newsletter regularly and sponsors workshop sessions at conferences.

Another wish was that working conditions would improve for itinerant teachers as others realize the complexities of our role and recognize that many of the students served in itinerant programs require more extensive intervention than they are receiving. Overloading teachers with too many students at too many sites robs the students of the important assistance they need to attain competencies in critical areas. The members of Division 16 continue to address the issue of appropriate caseloads and working conditions and will appreciate your support and involvement.

I have offered suggestions for organizational structures, but flexibility is a key trait of any successful itinerant teacher. There are too many situations that we cannot control, and we need to be able to change at any given moment, as conditions demand change. Murphy's law states that if anything can go wrong, it will. As we deal with the challenges and demands of our jobs, it may sometimes seem as though Murphy was an optimist. My best suggestion is to avoid letting the changing conditions affect us adversely, meet them with equanimity and a sense of humor, strive for a realistic perspective of what is important, and keep them from detracting from the services we provide to students with visual impairments and from our sense of satisfaction in doing so.

APPENDIX

Sources of Materials, Equipment, and Services

Providing materials to meet the individual needs of your students is an important aspect of your job. You will find it helpful to be on many mailing lists to receive catalogs and information about products. The following is a sampling of companies and organizations from which you may obtain equipment and materials, as well as those that provide specific services that may be of use to you and your students. Brief descriptions of the products or services available are included.

Order materials as you need them, but do not wait until your supplies are depleted. Delivery of products can take up to two months after you send in a purchase requisition.

Ai Squared
130 Taconic Business Park Road
Manchester Center, VT 05255
(802) 362-3612
Fax: (802) 362-1670
sales@aisquared.com; support@aisquared.com
www.aisquared.com
Products to make computers accessible for people with low vision, including screen readers and ZoomText screen magnifiers.

American Action Fund for Blind Children and Adults
Kenneth Jernigan Library for Blind Children
18440 Oxnard Street
Tarzana, CA 91356

(818) 343-2022
www.actionfund.org

Lends braille and Twin Vision books to children, schools, and teachers.

American Optometric Association
243 North Lindbergh Boulevard
St. Louis, MO 63141
(314) 991-4100; (800) 365-2219
Fax: (314) 991-4101
www.aoanet.org

Pamphlets about vision and visual impairments, models of the eye.

American Printing House for the Blind
1839 Frankfort Avenue
Louisville, KY 40206-0085
(502) 895-2405; (800) 223-1839
Fax: (502) 899-2274
info@aph.org
www.aph.org

A wide variety of books in braille and large print, including braille music materials; educational materials and equipment for visually impaired students, including speech synthesizers and other computer equipment, educational software, and braille computer paper. The Louis Database of Accessible Materials for People who are Blind or Visually Impaired contains information about tens of thousands of titles of accessible materials, including braille, large print, sound recordings, and computer files.

American Red Cross National Headquarters
2025 E Street, NW
Washington, DC 20006
(202) 303-4498
www.redcross.org

Lifeguard, first aid, and CPR training. Maintains local chapters in most states.

American Thermoform Corporation
1758 Bracket Street
La Verne, CA 91750
(909) 593-6711; (800) 331-3676
Fax: (909) 593-8001
atc@atcbrleqp.com
www.atcbrleqp.com

Materials and equipment for reproducing materials in braille, including embossers, computer paper, and other related equipment.

Bernell Corporation
4016 North Home Street
Mishawaka, IN 46545
(574) 259-2070; (800) 348-2225

Fax: (574) 259-2102
amartin553@aol.com
www.bernell.com

Vision assessment supplies, magnification devices, and other optical low vision devices.

Bookshare.org
480 California Avenue, Suite 201
Palo Alto, CA 94306
(650) 475-5440
Fax: (650) 475-1066
info@bookshare.org
www.bookshare.org

Publications for people who have visual or other print disabilities. Books can be downloaded from the Internet in formats used with common braille or synthetic speech reading devices.

Dancing Dots
1754 Quarry Lane
Valley Forge, PA
(610) 783-6692
Fax: (610) 783-6732
info@dancingdots.com
www.dancingdots.com

A variety of products related to music and technology for people who are blind or visually impaired, including braille music courses.

Dolphin Computer Access
60 East Third Avenue, Suite 301
San Mateo, CA 94401
(650) 348-7401; (866) 797-5921
Fax: (650) 348-7403
info@dolphinusa.com
www.dolphinusa.com

Screen magnification, screen reader and braille translation software to make computer systems accessible to people with visual impairments.

Enabling Technologies
1601 Northeast Braille Place
Jensen Beach, FL 34957
(772) 225-3687; (800) 777-3687
Fax: (772) 225-3299
enabling@brailler.com
www.brailler.com

Braille embossers.

Enhanced Vision Systems
17911 Sampson Lane
Huntington Beach, CA 92647

(714) 374-1829; (888) 811-3161
Fax: (714) 374-1821
info@enhancedvision.com
www.enhancedvision.com

Video magnifiers for people with low vision.

Exceptional Teaching Aids
20102 Woodbine Avenue
Castro Valley, CA 94546
(510) 582-4859; (800) 549-6999
Fax: (510) 582-5911
ExTeaching@aol.com
www.exceptionalteaching.com

Educational materials and equipment for visually impaired students, including tutorial and other educational software, braille materials for reading readiness, math readiness, and math practice; and books on cassette.

Flaghouse
601 FlagHouse Drive
Hasbrouck Heights, NJ 07604-3116
(800) 793-7900
Fax: (800) 793-7922; (201) 288-7887
sales@flaghouse.com
www.flaghouse.com/ContactUs.asp

Special Populations catalog featuring adapted equipment for individuals with developmental and physical disabilities.

Freedom Scientific
11800 31st Court North
St. Petersburgh, FL 33716
(727) 803-8000; (800) 444-4443
Fax: (727) 803-8001
Info@FreedomScientific.com
www.freedomscientific.com/

Technology-based products and services for people with vision impairments and learning disabilities. Products include hardware products such as personal notetakers, braille embossers, braille displays and scanning and reading printed systems; screen reading, screen magnification, web access, scanning and reading, and WYNN literacy software; software and hardware accessories, cables, embosser supplies, and notetaker parts. Also offers on-site and off-site training seminars and tutorials on using specific software and applications with screen readers, Windows, and more.

Gopher Sport
220 24th Avenue, NW
Owatonna, MN 55060-0998
(800) 533-0446
Fax: (800) 451-4855

sales@gophersport.com
www.gophersport.com/Gopher/

Products for adapted physical education, health, athletics, recreation, and fitness.

GW Micro
725 Airport North Office Park
Fort Wayne, IN 46825
(260) 489-3671
Fax: (260) 489-2608
sales@gwmicro.com
www.gwmicro.com

Window-Eyes, software that converts components of the Windows operating system into synthesized speech.

Howe Press
Perkins School for the Blind
175 North Beacon Street
Watertown, MA 02172-2790
(617) 924-3490
Fax: (617) 926-2027
HowePress@Perkins.org
www.perkins.pvt.k12.ma.us/area.php?id=9

Materials and equipment for reproducing materials in braille, including Perkins braillers and accessories, brailling slates and accessories, handwriting and mathematical aids, braille paper, measuring devices, games, and drawing supplies.

Human Kinetics
P.O. Box 5076
Champaign, Illinois 61825-5076
(800) 747-4457
Fax: (217) 351-1549
info@hkusa.com
www.humankinetics.com/

Sports and fitness catalogs, books, videos, and software.

Independent Living Aids
200 Robbins Lane
Jericho, NY 11753
(516) 937-1848; (800) 537-2118
Fax: (516) 937-3906
can-do@independentliving.com
www.independentliving.com

A wide variety of devices for people who are visually impaired, hearing impaired, or physically impaired, including braille slates and writing aids, magnifiers, lamps, writing guides, games, cassette recorders, and measuring devices.

Innovative Rehabilitation Technology
725 Airport North Office Park
Fort Wayne, IN 46825
(260) 489-3671
Fax: (260) 489-2608
info@irti.net
www.irti.net

Talking products and devices, four-track cassette reading machines, recording machines, Arkenstone document readers, talking computers, screen reading software, talking synthesizers, CCTVs and recreational products by Sony and other major manufacturers.

Kaplan School Supply Corporation
1310 Lewisville Clemmons Road
Lewisville, NC 27023
(800) 334-2014
www.kaplanco.com

Learning materials for early childhood education.

Lakeshore
2695 East Domingo Street
Carson, CA 90810
(800) 421-5354
www.lakeshorelearning.com

Curriculum materials for infants, preschool, elementary school, and special education students.

Library Reproduction Service
14214 South Figueroa Street
Los Angeles, CA 90061-1034
(310) 354-2610; (800) 255-5002
Fax: (310) 354-2601
lrsprint@aol.com
www.lrs-largeprint.com

Large-print textbooks, laboratory manuals, study guides, tests, and reference and general reading materials.

Lighthouse International
111 East 59th Street
New York, NY 10022
(212) 821-9200; (800) 829-0500; (212) 821-9713 (TTY)
professionalcatalog@lighthouse.org
www.lighthouse.org/prodpub_procat.htm

Optical, adaptive, and vision testing products for vision-care and vision rehabilitation professionals, vision assessment supplies, and magnification aids; independent living products for visually impaired individuals; and educational and research publications.

LS&S Group
P.O. Box 673
Northbrook, IL 60065
(847) 498-9777; (800) 468-4789
Fax: (847) 498-1482
lssgrp@aol.com
www.lssgroup.com

A variety of products for independent living, including magnification aids.

MaxiAids
42 Executive Boulevard
Farmingdale, NY 11735
(631) 752-0738; (800) 522-6294
Fax: (631) 752-0689
sales@maxiaids.com
www.maxiaids.com

A variety of devices for people with visual or physical disabilities, including talking calculators, magnification screens for televisions, computer keypads with enlarged letters, and adapted physical education equipment.

National Association for Visually Handicapped
3201 Balboa Street
San Francisco, CA 94121
(415) 221-3201
Fax: (415) 221-8754
staffca@navh.org
www.navh.org

A variety of large-print books in such categories as literature, language, mathematics, reading, science, social studies, spelling, and leisure reading; pamphlets about visual impairments; and low vision devices.

National Library Service for the Blind and Physically Handicapped
Library of Congress
1291 Taylor Street, NW
Washington, DC 20542
(202) 707-5100 or (800) 424-8567; (202) 707-0744 (TDD/TTY)
Fax: (202) 707-0712
nls@loc.gov
www.loc.gov/nls

Free reading materials in braille and on recorded disks and cassettes to persons who are visually impaired and physically disabled who cannot utilize ordinary printed materials.

Optelec
321 Billerica Road
Chelmsford, MA 01824
(978) 392-0707; (800) 828-1056
Fax: (978) 692-6073

optelec@optelec.com
www.optelec.com

A variety of handheld and portable video magnifiers.

Opus Technologies
13333 Thunderhead Street
San Diego, CA 92129-2329
(858) 538-9401; (866) OPUSTEC (678-7832)
Fax: (858) 538-9401
opus@opustec.com
www.opustec.com/contact.html

Develops and sells software, print, and braille materials for learning and using braille, especially braille music.

Pulse Data Humanware
174 Mason Circle
Concord, CA 94520
(916) 652-7253; (800) 722-3393
Fax: (925) 681-4630
info@humanware.com
www.pulsedata.com

Speech and braille technology, a range of video magnifier solutions, screen reading Software, and speech synthesizers.

Quantum Technology Pty Ltd
5 South Street (P.O. Box 390)
Rydalmere NSW 2116
Australia
02 8844 9888 (International: +61 2 8844 9888)
Fax: 02 9684 4717 (International: +61 2 9684 4717)
info@quantech.com.au
www.quantech.com.au

Braillers, including the Mountbatten and Jot a Dot, and a variety of other products, including notetakers, screen readers, and screen magnification systems for people who are blind or have low vision.

Recording for the Blind & Dyslexic
20 Roszel Road
Princeton, NJ 08540
(609) 452-0606; (866) 732-3585
custserv@rfbd.org
www.rfbd.org

Books and other educational materials on tape, free on loan to people who cannot read standard print because of visual, physical, or perceptual impairments. Books in major fields of study recorded on request.

Scholastic, Inc.
P.O. Box 5710
Jefferson City, MO 65102

(800) 325-6149; (800) 392-2179 (in Missouri only)
www.scholastic.com

Educational software for preschool and elementary school students.

School Specialty
W6316 Design Drive
Greenville, Wisconsin 54942
(888) 388-3224
www.beckleycardy.com/index.jsp

A wide selection of office and educational supplies and materials. (Formerly Beckley-Cardy.)

Science Research Associates/McGraw Hill
220 East Danieldale Road
De Soto, TX 75115
(800) 201-7103 (product information); (888) 772-4543 (orders)
Fax: (972) 228-1982
www.sra4kids.com

Instructional and educational assessment materials.

Seedlings
P.O. Box 2395
Livonia, MI 48151-0395
(800) 777-8552
www.seedlings.org

A variety of print-braille books.

Sighted Electronics
69 Woodland Avenue
Westwood, NJ 07675
(201) 666-2221; (800) 666-4883
Fax: (201) 666-0159
sales@sighted.com
www.sighted.com

Braille notetakers, braille displays, braille keyboards, braille embossers, and a variety of braille and computer access software.

Smith-Kettlewell Eye Research Institute
2318 Fillmore Street
San Francisco, CA 94115
(415) 345-2000
Fax: (415) 345-8455
www.ski.org

Vocational and educational aids for people who are visually impaired.

Sportime
One Sportime Way
Atlanta, GA 30340

(800) 444-5700
customer.service@sportime.com
www.sportime.com/index.jsp

Catalog of rehabilitation equipment.

Telesensory Corporation
520 Almanor Avenue
Sunnyvale, CA 94085-3533
(408) 616-8700; (800) 804-8004
Fax: (408) 616-8719
info@telesensory.com
www.telesensory.com

A wide variety of technological equipment, computers, and computer-related products, including video magnifiers and scanners with speech output.

Texas School for the Blind and Visually Impaired
1100 West 45th Street
Austin, TX 78756-3494
(512) 454-8631
Fax: (512) 206-9452
www.tsbvi.edu

Professional publications, assessments, curricula, and videotapes.

ViewPlus Technologies
1853 SW Airport Avenue
Corvallis, Oregon 97333
(541) 754-4002
Fax: (541) 738-6505
www.viewplus.com

Braille embossers, software, and accessories.

Vision Associates
2109 US Highway 90 West Suite 170 #312
Lake City, FL 32055
(407) 352-1200
Fax: (386) 752-7839
www.visionkits.com

Vision assessment kits and materials, books, and infant development materials.

Wolverine Sports
School-Tech Inc.
745 State Circle Box 1941
Ann Arbor, MI 48106
(800) 521-2832
Fax: (734) 761-8711
service@school-tech.com
www.wolverinesports.com

Equipment and supplies for a variety of sports ranging from simple kids' games to all the major sports.

APPENDIX

Organizations Serving People Who Are Visually Impaired

A wide variety of organizations disseminate information that will be helpful to you, your students, and their families. In addition, many organizations on the national, state, and local levels also provide assistance and referrals, operate toll-free hotlines, and publish materials that are valuable resources for professionals and consumers. You may choose to join some of these organizations or to be on their mailing lists. Organizations that do not appear in the listing that follows may be included in the *Directory of Services for Blind and Visually Impaired Persons in the United States and Canada*, published by the American Foundation for the Blind (also available at www.afb.org), which also lists service and volunteer groups.

Academy for Certifying Vision Rehabilitation and Education Professionals
330 North Commerce Park Loop, Suite 200
Tucson, AZ 85745
(520) 887-6816
Fax: (520) 887-6826
info@acvrep.org
www.acvrep.org
A professional certifying body for vision rehabilitation and education professionals in three disciplines—orientation and mobility, rehabilitation teaching, and low vision therapy—in order to improve service delivery to persons with vision impairments.

American Association of the Deaf-Blind
814 Thayer Avenue
Silver Spring, MD 20910

(301) 588-8705
Fax: (301) 588-8705
info@aadb.org
www.aadb.org

A consumer organization that endeavors to enable deaf-blind persons to achieve their maximum potential through increased independence, productivity, and integration into the community. Is involved in advocacy activities, conducts service programs, acts as a referral service, maintains a library of materials on deaf-blindness, and holds a convention annually for deaf-blind persons and their families.

American Council of the Blind
1155 15th Street, NW
Suite 1004
Washington, DC 20005
(202) 467-5081; (800) 424-8666
Fax: (202) 467-5085
info@acb.org
www.acb.org

A consumer organization that acts as a national clearinghouse for information and has an affiliate group for parents. It also provides referrals, legal assistance, advocacy support, scholarships, and consultative and advisory services to individuals, organizations, and agencies.

American Council on Rural Special Education
ACRES National Headquarters
Kansas State University
2323 Anderson Avenue, Suite 226
Manhattan, KS 66502-2912
(785) 532-2737
Fax: (785) 532-7732
acres@ksu.edu
www.ksu.edu/acres

An organization specializing in services for exceptional students and their families living in rural areas. It distributes information, publishes a newsletter and a journal, and advocates for the rights of disabled persons.

American Foundation for the Blind
11 Penn Plaza, Suite 300
New York, NY 10001
(212) 502-7600; (800) 232-5463; (212) 502-7662 (TDD/TTY)
Fax: (212) 502-7777
afbinfo@afb.net
www.afb.org

A national organization serving as an information clearinghouse for people who are blind or visually impaired and their families, professionals, organizations, schools, and corporations. In addition to mounting program initiatives to improve services to visually impaired persons in such areas as aging, education, employment, literacy, and technology, conducting research, and advocating for services and legislation, AFB maintains the M. C. Migel Library and Information Center and the Helen Keller Archives; provides information and referral services; produces videos and publishes books, pamphlets, and videos on topics relating to blindness and visual impairment; publishes the AFB Directory of Services for Blind and Visually Impaired Persons in the United States and Canada*;* Journal of Visual Impairment & Blindness*; and* AccessWorld: Technology and People with Visual Impairments. *Maintains national program offices across the United States, and a Governmental Relations office in Washington, DC.*

American Printing House for the Blind
1839 Frankfort Avenue
P.O. Box 6085
Louisville, KY 40206
(502) 895-2405; (800) 223-1839
www.aph.org

The official supplier of textbooks and educational aids for visually impaired students under federal appropriations. Promotes the independence of blind and visually impaired persons by providing specialized materials, products, and services needed for education and life. Publishes braille, large-print, recorded, CD-ROM, and tactile graphic publications; manufactures a wide assortment of educational and daily living products; modifies and develops computer-access equipment and software; maintains an educational research and development program concerned with educational methods and educational aids; and provides a reference-catalog service for volunteer-produced textbooks in all media for students who are visually impaired and for information about other sources of related materials.

Association for Education and Rehabilitation of the Blind and Visually Impaired
1703 N. Beauregard Street, Suite 440
Alexandria, VA 22311
(703) 671-4500; (877) 492-2708
Fax: (703) 671-6391
aer@aerbvi.org
www.aerbvi.org

A professional membership organization that promotes all phases of education and work for blind and visually impaired persons on the local, regional, national, and international levels. Conducts conferences, provides continuing education programs, publishes newsletters and a journal, and operates a job exchange and reference information service. Includes several divisions in such areas as early childhood, elementary education, O&M, and one for itinerant personnel.

Challenge Aspen
P.O. Box M
Aspen, CO 81612
(970) 923-0578 (voice/TTY)
Fax: (970) 923-7338
possibilities@challengeaspen.com
www.challengeaspen.com

An organization offering recreational and cultural experiences, such as skiing, whitewater rafting, horseback riding, and fishing, for individuals who have mental or physical disabilities and their family and friends. Hosts a number of camps throughout the year, including a ski festival for people who are visually impaired and children's art and music camps. (Incorporates the former Blind Outdoor Leisure Development organization.)

Closing the Gap
526 Main Street
P.O. Box 68
Henderson, Minnesota 56044
(507) 248-3294
Fax: (507) 248-3810
info@closingthegap.com
www.closingthegap.com

An organization focusing on computer technology to enhance the lives of people with special needs through its bi-monthly newspaper, extensive web site, and annual international conference.

Council for Exceptional Children
Division for the Visually Handicapped
1110 North Glebe Road, Suite 300
Arlington, VA 22201-5704
(703) 620-3660; (888) 221-6830; (703) 264-9446 (TDD/TTY)
Fax: (703) 264-9494
service@cec.sped.org
www.cec.sped.org

A professional organization for teachers, school administrators, and others who are concerned with children who require special services. Publishes position papers as well as periodicals, books, and other materials on teaching exceptional children.

DB-LINK (The National Information Clearinghouse on Children Who Are Deaf-Blind)
345 North Monmouth Avenue
Monmouth, OR 97361
(800) 438-9376
www.tr.wou.edu/dblink

A federally funded clearinghouse that provides information and copies of written materials related to infants, children, and youths who have both visual and hearing impairments. It publishes the newsletter Deaf-Blind Perspectives.

Foundation Fighting Blindness
11435 Cronhill Drive
Owings Mills, MD 21117-2220
(410) 568-0150; (800) 683-5555; (800) 683-5551; (410) 363-7139 (TDD/TTY)
Fax: (410) 363-2393
mpalmer@blindness.org
www.blindness.org

An organization that conducts public education programs and supports research related to the cause, prevention, and treatment of retinitis pigmentosa. Maintains a network of affiliates across the country and conducts workshops as well as referral and donor programs.

Helen Keller National Center for Deaf-Blind Youths and Adults
111 Middle Neck Road
Sands Point, NY 11050-1299
(516) 944-8900 ext. 253; (516) 944-8637 (TDD/TTY)
Fax: (516) 944-7302
hkncinfo@aol.com
www.hknc.org

A national rehabilitation program serving youth and adults who are deaf-blind. Operates a residential and training facility and provides support services throughout the country through its system of field services.

Lighthouse International
111 East 59th Street
New York, NY 10022
(212) 821-9200; (800) 829-0500; (212) 821-9713 (TTY)
www.lighthouse.org

A national clearinghouse on vision impairment and vision rehabilitation. Provides vision rehabilitation services; conducts research and advocacy; trains professionals; engages in advocacy; and provides educational and professional products and adaptive devices through its catalogs.

Music Education Network for the Visually Impaired
c/o Southern California Conservatory of Music
Braille Music Division
8711 Sunland Boulevard
Sun Valley, CA 91352
(818) 767-6554
Fax: (818) 768-6242
www.superior-software.com/menvi/index.htm

An information network of parents and music educators of visually impaired students.

National Association for Parents of Children with Visual Impairments
P.O. Box 317
Watertown, MA 02471
(617) 972-7441; (800) 562-6265
Fax: (617) 972-7444
napvi@perkins.org
www.napvi.org

A membership association that supports state and local parents' groups and conducts advocacy workshops for parents of blind and visually impaired children. Operates a national clearinghouse for information and referrals and holds national and chapter conferences.

National Association for Visually Handicapped
22 West 21st Street
New York, NY 10010
(212) 889-3141
Fax: (212) 727-2931
staff@navh.org
www.navh.org

3201 Balboa Street
San Francisco, CA 94121
(415) 221-3201
Fax: (415) 221-8754
www.navh.org

An organization for people with visual impairments that acts as an information clearinghouse and referral center; offers counseling to persons with low vision, their families, and the professionals who work with them; produces and distributes large-print reading materials; and sells low vision devices.

National Association of State Directors of Special Education
1800 Diagonal Road, Suite 320
Alexandria, VA 22314
(703) 519-3800; (703) 519-7008 (TDD/TTY)
Fax: (703) 519-3808
nasdse@nasdse.org
www.nasdse.org

A membership organization of state directors of special education and other persons employed in state education agencies who direct, coordinate or supervise programs and services for the education of students with disabilities. Provides assistance to state education agencies in the delivery of quality education to children and youth with disabilities through training, technical assistance, research, and policy development; offers consultative services; publishes newsletters; and sponsors conferences.

National Braille Association
3 Townline Circle
Rochester, NY 14623-2513
(585) 427-8260
Fax: (585) 427-0263
nbaoffice@compuserve.com
www.nationalbraille.org

A national organization dedicated to providing continuing education to those who prepare braille and providing braille materials to persons who are visually impaired. Provides braille transcription and production services and consultation. Also maintains a depository of music materials in braille. Publishes manuals and guidelines for the production of braille and publishes a quarterly Bulletin.

National Coalition on Deaf-Blindness
175 North Beacon Street
Watertown, MA 02472

(617) 972-7347
Fax: (617) 923-8076

A coalition of groups that advocates on behalf of the interests of deaf-blind persons and provides information to consumers and professionals.

National Federation of the Blind
1800 Johnson Street
Baltimore, MD 21230-4998
(410) 659-9314
Fax: (410) 685-5653
nfb@nfb.org
www.nfb.org

A consumer organization that maintains affiliates in all states and the District of Columbia and works to improve the social and economic opportunities of blind and visually impaired persons. Evaluates programs and provides assistance in establishing new ones, funds scholarships for blind persons, and conducts a public education program.

National Library Service for the Blind and Physically Handicapped
Library of Congress
1291 Taylor Street, NW
Washington, DC 20542
(202) 707-5100; (800) 424-8567; (202) 707-0744 (TDD/TTY)
Fax: (202) 707-0712
nls@loc.gov
www.loc.gov/nls

A national program to distribute free reading materials in braille, on recorded discs and cassettes, and in Web-Braille to blind and visually impaired persons who cannot use printed materials. In addition, the service operates a reference section providing information on reading materials for disabled persons, offers braille transcription and proofreading courses, and maintains a music collection and music services for blind persons.

National Organization for Albinism and Hypopigmentation
P.O. Box 959
East Hampstead, NH 03826-0959
(603) 887-2310; (800) 473-2310
Fax: (603) 887-2310
info@albinism.org
www.albinism.org

A consumer organization that provides information on albinism, publishes a newsletter, and sponsors conferences.

National Resource Center for Blind Musicians
Music and Arts Center for Humanity
600 University Avenue
Bridgeport, CT 06601
(203) 366-3300

Fax: (203) 368-2847
info@blindmusicstudent.org
www.blindmusicstudent.org

A national center providing information and referral services for visually impaired students of all ages, their parents and teachers; offers learning opportunities for blind students headed to college; maintains a network of visually impaired musicians willing to share their expertise in braille music, technology and coping strategies; and provides teacher training. Holds the Summer Institute for Blind College-bound Musicians, a residential program that brings together students from several states and countries, who are studying music at the college level.

Office of Special Education and Rehabilitative Services
U.S. Department of Education
330 C Street, SW, Room 3006
Washington, DC 20202
(202) 205-5465
www.ed.gov/offices/OSERS

The federal agency with oversight responsibility for special education services.

Prevent Blindness America
500 East Remington Road, Suite 200
Schaumburg, IL 60173
(847) 843-2020; (800) 331-2020
Fax: (847) 843-8458
info@preventblindness.org
www.preventblindness.org

An organization conducting a program of public and professional education, research, and industrial and community services to prevent blindness. Services include screening, vision testing, and disseminating information on low vision devices and clinics. Has a network of state affiliates.

Recording for the Blind & Dyslexic
20 Roszel Road
Princeton, NJ 08540
(609) 452-0606; (866) 732-3585
custserv@rfbd.org
www.rfbd.org

A nonprofit volunteer organization serving people who cannot effectively read standard print because of visual impairment, dyslexia, or other physical disability. Lends audio or digital recorded textbooks and other educational materials at no charge. Recording is done in a network of studios across the country.

TASH
29 West Susquehanna Avenue, Suite 210
Baltimore, MD 21204
(410) 828-8274; (800) 482-8274; (410) 828-1306 (TDD/TTY)
Fax: (410) 828-6706

info@tash.org
www.tash.org

An advocacy organization for people with disabilities, their family members, other advocates, and professionals striving for equality, diversity, social justice, and inclusion. Advocates for educational services for disabled persons, disseminates information, publishes a newsletter and a journal, and acts as an advocate for the rights of people with disabilities. Holds an annual conference, and publishes Research and Practice for Persons with Severe Disabilities, TASH Connections, *and other publications.*

The ARC of the United States
1010 Wayne Avenue, Suite 650
Silver Spring, MD 20910
(301) 565-3842
Fax: (301) 565-5342
info@thearc.org
www.thearc.org

A national organization devoted to promoting and improving supports and services for people with mental retardation and related developmental disabilities and their families. Works on local, state, and national levels to promote services, public understanding, and legislation and foster research and education on behalf of all children and adults with cognitive, intellectual, and developmental disabilities.

United States Association of Blind Athletes
33 N. Institute Street
Colorado Springs, CO 80903
(719) 630-0422
Fax: (719) 630-0616
www.usaba.org

A national membership organization for blind athletes working to increase the number and quality of grassroots, competitive, and world-class athletic opportunities for people who are blind or visually impaired by providing athlete and coach identification and support, program and event management, and national and international representation.

Texas School for the Blind and Visually Impaired
1100 West 45th Street
Austin, TX 78756
(512) 454-8631; (512) 206-9451 (TDD)
Fax: (512) 206-9450
www.tsbvi.edu

The web site of the Texas School for the Blind and Visually Impaired offers a tremendous variety of information and resources for professionals, parents, and others associated with programs for people who are blind or visually impaired.

APPENDIX

Classification System for Materials

The following is a comprehensive numerical system for organizing the materials of a program for visually impaired students, including books and other publications, equipment, low vision, devices, assessments, toys, and so forth. You may choose to simplify or adapt this system or use it as is. If your program already has many materials, categorizing them can be a major task, but it can be well worth the effort to be able to keep materials organized and available with 15 itinerant teachers coming and going!

Keeping a record of each item in an electronic database enables your program to not only maintain an inventory of the program's resources but also to keep track of where they are at any given moment. Stickers containing bar codes can be used to assign each item a number corresponding to its database entry. As part of an effective organization strategy, the materials should be grouped in your office according to category so they can be located easily.

The database entry for each item can contain such information as the following:

- bar code number
- borrower's last name
- date checked out
- student's name

This expanded and adapted version of the original classification system from the first edition of *Itinerant Teaching* was provided by Theresa Postello from the San Mateo County Office of Education, Integrated Visually Impaired Services, San Mateo, California.

- type of item
- list of previous borrowers
- borrowers' comments

Entries for books and publications would also include the following information:

- large-print, braille, or print
- district's catalog number
- title
- author
- publisher
- copyright date
- grade level
- how many volumes in set
- ISBN number

Once bar code stickers are affixed to all the items, borrowed items can easily be checked out and in using a scanning wand. A list of borrowed items can be generated by teacher's name, student's name, or date borrowed, a very helpful feature for tracking items that need to be returned at the end of the year. As new books, materials, toys, equipment, assessments, are purchased, they are bar coded and entered into the database, and are ready to be checked out.

Classification System for Materials

000 Professional Library

- 001 Teaching techniques and theory
- 002 Learning activities
- 003 References (medical, low vision, ophthalmology, Journal of Visual Impairment and Blindness)
- 004 Resources for visually impaired persons
- 005 Awareness of disabilities
- 006 Mainstreaming/P.L. 94-142
- 007 Assessment
- 008 IEP writing
- 009 Catalogs
  - 009.1 Braille
  - 009.2 Tapes
  - 009.3 Large Print
  - 009.4 Educational material
  - 009.5 Office supplies
  - 009.6 Science
  - 009.7 Adaptive devices and equipment
  - 009.8 Computer access technology

- 010 Orientation & Mobility
- 011 Inservice material
- 012 Recreational
- 013 Video tapes

100 Mathematics
- 110 Math readiness
- 120 Basic skills
  - 121 Addition
  - 122 Subtraction
  - 123 Multiplication
  - 124 Division
  - 125 Fractions
  - 126 Problem solving
  - 127 Multiple skills
  - 128 Geometry
  - 129 Algebra and Trigonometry
- 130 Practical mathematics
  - 131 Time, calendars
  - 132 Measurement
  - 133 Money
- 140 Manipulatives
- 150 Math Series—Publisher—Grade

200 Social Studies
- 210 Economics
- 220 Geography
- 230 History
  - 231 American History and Government
  - 232 World History and Government

300 Science/Nature (also see Kits 2400)
- 310 Biology
- 320 Chemistry
- 330 Earth Science
- 340 Life Science
- 350 Physical Science
- 360 Physics

400 Health and Safety
- 410 Drug education
- 420 Eye education
- 430 First Aid
- 440 Home economics
  - 441 Cookbooks
  - 442 Nutrition
  - 443 Sewing
- 450 Sex education
  - 451 Anatomically correct dolls

500 Reading

- 510 Readiness
  - 511 Categorizing, classification
  - 512 Colors and shapes
  - 513 Letter recognition
  - 514 Opposites
  - 515 Rhyming
  - 516 Sequencing
  - 517 Visual discrimination
  - 518 Concept development
- 520 Auditory decoding
  - 521 Consonants
    - 521.1 Initial
    - 521.2 Final
  - 522 Vowels
    - 522.1 Short
    - 522.2 Long
  - 523 Blends and diagraphs
  - 524 General phonics
- 530 Comprehension
  - 531 Following directions
- 540 Special Skills Series
- 550 Structural analysis
  - 551 Syllabification
  - 552 Alphabetizing
  - 553 Affixes
  - 554 Compound words
  - 555 Sight vocabulary
- 560 Study skills
  - 561 Library skills
  - 562 Dictionary skills
- 570 General reading/print
  - 571 Reading series
  - 572 Literature
  - 573 Leisure reading
  - 574 Reference
- 580 General reading/Braille
  - 581 Reading readiness
  - 582 Instruction
  - 583 Reading series
  - 584 Literature texts
  - 585 Poetry
  - 586 Leisure reading

600 Communication Skills (also see Kits 2400)

- 610 Language development
  - 611 Vocabulary development
- 620 Written language
  - 621 Creative writing

622 Grammar
623 Handwriting
623.1 Manuscript
623.2 Cursive
624 Spelling
630 Non-oral language
640 Listening skills
650 Drama

700 Foreign Language
710 French
720 German
730 Spanish

800 Vocational Skills (also see Kits 2400)
810 Elementary
820 Secondary
830 Survival skills
831 Driver's Education
832 Daily living
833 Behavior

900 Self-Concept

1000 Assessment
1005 Vision
1006 Eye charts
1007 Functional vision
1010 Auditory perception
1011 Auditory discrimination
1012 Receptive language
1015 Visual perception
1020 Educational assessments
1021 District and state tests
1022 Mathematics
1023 Reading
1024 General aptitude test
1025 General psychological test
1030 Motor skills
1031 Visual/Fine
1032 Gross
1040 Preschool/readiness
1045 Behavior/social scales
1050 Communication/oral language
1055 Developmental checklists
1060 Orientation and mobility assessment

1100 Perceptual/Sensory Motor Skills (also see Kits 2400)
1110 Fine motor

1120 Gross motor
1130 Orientation in space
1131 Body awareness
1132 Spatial relations
1133 Directionality
1134 Laterality
1140 Visual memory
1141 Visual memory
1142 Visual motor
1143 Visual figure ground
1144 Visual discrimination
1145 Tracking
1146 Vision stimulation/efficiency
1150 Auditory perception
1151 Auditory memory
1152 Auditory motor
1153 Auditory figure ground
1154 Auditory discrimination

1200 References
1210 Dictionaries
1220 Encyclopedia

1300 Orientation and Mobility (also see Kits 2400)
1310 Curriculum
1320 Mapping materials
1321 Globes
1330 Mobility aids
1331 Cane
1332 Tip
1333 Compass
1334 Mowat sensor
1335 Rocker board
1336 Chang kit

1400 Music

1500 Visual Aids
1510 Magnifiers
1520 Monoculars
1530 Bookstands
1540 Lamps
1550 CCTV
1560 Miscellaneous

1600 Typing/Keyboarding

1700 Games
1710 Math games

1720 Recreation
1730 Spelling games
1740 Word games

1800 Braille Games/Toys

1900 Preschool Toys

2000 Tactile Discrimination

2100 Computer Software

2200 Tapes

2300 Developmental Learning Materials (DLM)

2400 Instructional Kits
- 2410 Career information (CI-TAB) Kits
- 2420 Peabody Language Kits
- 2430 Perceptual/Sensory Motor Kits
- 2440 Science (SAVI) Kits
- 2450 Sensory Kits
- 2460 Tactile Graphics Kits
- 2470 Visual Efficiency Development Kits

2500 Academic Equipment
- 2510 Communication
  - 2511 Typewriter
- 2520 Math
  - 2521 Abacus
  - 2522 Scientific calculator
  - 2523 Sharp talking calculator
  - 2524 Speech Plus
- 2530 Reading
  - 2531 Portable Line Scanner
  - 2532 Optacon

2600 Auditory Equipment
- 2610 Franklin Language Master
- 2620 Handicassette
- 2630 Headset
- 2640 Phone amplifier
- 2650 Phonograph
- 2660 Portable Sound Source II
- 2670 Tape player

2700 Braille Equipment
- 2710 APH Pocket Brailler
- 2720 Braille 'N' Speak

2730 Embosser
2740 Perkins Brailler
2750 Slate & Stylus

2800 Computer Equipment
2810 Adaptive devices
2811 Echo speech synthesizer
2812 Intellikeys
2813 Muppet Keyboard
2814 Power Pad
2815 Touch Window
2816 Unicorn board
2820 Hardware
2821 Apple monitor
2822 Disk drive
2823 Printer
2824 Scanner
2825 Speaker

2900 Office Equipment
2910 Book binder
2920 Photocopier
2930 Thermaform
2940 Transparency maker

3000 Tactile Equipment
3010 Tactile graphics kit
3020 Tactile Image Enhancer (TIE)

3100 Video Equipment
3110 Camcorder
3120 TV
3130 Sony black & white monitor
3140 Polaroid camera

3200 Vision Stimulation Equipment
3210 Light box

APPENDIX

Reference Library

All teachers, whether they are itinerant, work in a resource room, or have their own classroom of children, need a library of information on visual impairments, the learning needs of students who are blind or visually impaired, the education of blind and visually impaired students, and related issues. The books and other resources listed here represent a sample of essential texts and manuals for teachers. Professional journals and newsletters are included in this listing as well and are important sources of growing and changing knowledge and information. Electronic publications, discussion groups, and bulletin boards, although subject to frequent changes, are another important source of information, and just a few examples have been listed here. Be sure to also check the web sites of the organizations listed in Appendix B for more online information and additional discussion groups.

BOOKS AND PAMPHLETS

AFB Directory of Services for Blind and Visually Impaired Persons in the United States and Canada (27th ed.). (2005). New York: AFB Press.

Barraga, N.C., & Erin, J.N. (2001). *Visual impairments and learning* (4th ed.). Austin, TX: PRO-Ed.

Blasch, B.B., Wiener, W.R., & Welsh, R.L. (Eds.). (1997). *Foundations of orientation and mobility* (2nd ed.). New York: AFB Press.

Cassin, B., Solomon, S., & Rubin, M. (Eds.) (2001). *Dictionary of eye terminology* (4th ed.). Gainesville, FL: Triad Publishing.

Chen, D. (Ed.). (1999). *Essential elements in early intervention: Visual impairment and multiple disabilities.* New York: AFB Press.

Chen, D., & Dote-Kwan, J. (Eds.). (1995). *Starting points: Instructional practices for young children whose multiple disabilities include visual impairment.* Los Angeles: Blind Children's Center.

Corn, A. L., & Koenig, A. J. (Eds.). (1996). *Foundations of low vision: Clinical and functional perspectives.* New York: AFB Press.

D'Andrea, F. M., & Farrenkopf, C. (Eds.). (2000). *Looking to learn: Promoting literacy for students with low vision.* New York: AFB Press.

Downing, J. (Ed.). (1996). *Including students with severe and multiple disabilities in typical classrooms: Practical strategies for teachers.* Baltimore: Paul H. Brookes.

Edman, P. K. (1992). *Tactile graphics.* New York: American Foundation for the Blind.

Fazzi, D. L., & Petersmeyer, B. A. (2001). *Imagining the possibilities: Creative approaches to orientation and mobility instruction for persons who are visually impaired.* New York: AFB Press.

Ferrell, K. A. (1985). *Reach out and teach: Meeting the training needs of parents of visually and multiply handicapped young children.* New York: American Foundation for the Blind.

Harley, R. K., Truan, M. B., & Sandford, L. D. (1997). *Communication skills for visually impaired learners: Braille, print, and listening skills for students who are visually impaired* (2nd ed.). Springfield, IL: Charles C. Thomas.

Heydt, K., Allon, M., Edwards, S., Clark, M. J., Cushman, C. (2004). *Perkins activity and resource guide: A handbook for teachers and parents of students with visual and multiple disabilities* (2nd ed.). Watertown, MA: Perkins School for the Blind.

Hill, E., & Ponder, P. (1976). *Orientation and mobility techniques: A guide for the practitioner.* New York: AFB Press.

Holbroook, M. C., & Koenig, A. J. (Eds.). (2000). *Foundations of education* (2nd ed.). Volume I. *History and theory of teaching children and youths with visual impairments.* New York: AFB Press.

Hudson, L. J. (1997). *Classroom collaboration.* Watertown, MA: Perkins School for the Blind.

Huebner, K., Prickett, J., Welch, T., & Joffee, E. (Eds.). (1995). *Hand in hand: Essentials of communication and orientation and mobility for young children who are deaf-blind.* New York: AFB Press.

Jacobson, W. (1993). *The art and science of teaching orientation and mobility to persons with visual impairments.* New York: American Foundation for the Blind.

Knott, N. I. (2002). *Teaching orientation and mobility in the schools: An instructor's companion.* New York: AFB Press.

Koenig, A. J., & Holbrook, M. C. (Eds.). (1995). *Learning media assessment of students with visual impairments: A resource guide for teachers* (2nd ed.). Austin, TX: Texas School for the Blind and Visually Impaired.

Koenig, A. J., & Holbrook, M. C. (Eds.). (2000). *Foundations of education* (2nd ed.). Volume II: *Instructional strategies for teaching children and youths with visual impairments.* New York: AFB Press.

LaGrow, S. & Weessies, M. (1999). *Orientation and mobility: Techniques for independence.* Palmerston North, New Zealand: Dunmore Press.

Levack, N. (1994). *Low vision: A resource guide with adaptations for students with visual impairments* (2nd ed.). Austin: Texas School for the Blind and Visually Impaired.

Lewis, S., & Allman, C. B. (2000). *Seeing eye to eye: An administrator's guide to students with low vision.* New York: AFB Press.

Lieberman, J. L., & Cowart, J. F. (1996). *Games for people with sensory impairments: Strategies for including individuals of all ages.* Champaign, IL: Human Kinetics.

Longuil, C. (1991). *Oh, I see* [videotape]. New York: American Foundation for the Blind.

Lueck, A. H. (Ed.). (2004). *Functional vision: A practitioner's guide to evaluation and intervention.* New York: AFB Press.

Mangold, S. S. (1982). *A teacher's guide to the special educational needs of blind and visually handicapped children.* New York: American Foundation for the Blind.

Miller, C., & Levack, N. (1997). *Paraprofessional's handbook for working with students who are visually impaired.* Austin: Texas School for the Blind and Visually Impaired.

Olson, M. R., with Mangold, S. S. (1981). *Guidelines and games for teaching efficient braille reading.* New York: American Foundation for the Blind.

Pogrund, R. L., & Fazzi, D. L., Eds. (2002). *Early focus: Working with young children who are blind or visually impaired and their families* (2nd ed.). New York: AFB Press.

Pogrund, R., Healy, G., Jones, K., Levack, N., Martin-Curry, S., Martinez, C., Marz, J., Roberson-Smith, B., & Vrba, A. (1995). *TAPS: Teaching age appropriate skills—An orientation and mobility curriculum for students with visual impairments.* Austin: Texas School for the Blind and Visually Impaired.

Pugh, G. S., & Erin, J. (Eds.). (1999). *Blind and visually impaired students: Educational service guidelines.* Watertown, MA: Perkins School for the Blind in cooperation with the National Association of State Directors of Special Education.

Sacks, S. Z., & Silberman, R. K. (Eds.). (1998). *Educating students who have visual impairments with other disabilities.* Baltimore: Paul H. Brookes.

Sacks, S. Z., & Wolffe, K. E. (2000). *Focused On: Social Skills* [videotapes, 5 volumes]. New York: AFB Press.

Smith, M., & Levack, N. (1996). *Teaching students with visual and multiple impairments: A resource guide.* Austin: Texas School for the Blind and Visually Impaired.

Swenson, A. M. (1998). *Beginning with braille: Firsthand experiences with a balanced approach to literacy.* New York: AFB Press.

What do you do when you see a blind person? [videotape]. (2000). New York: AFB Press.

When you have a visually impaired student in your classroom: A guide for paraeducators. (2004). New York: AFB Press.

When you have a visually impaired student in your classroom: A guide for teachers. (2002). New York: AFB Press.

When you have a visually impaired student with multiple disabilities in your classroom. (2004). New York: AFB Press.

Wormsley, D. P. (2000). *Braille literacy curriculum.* Philadelphia, PA: Towers Press.

Wormsley, D. P. (2004). *Braille literacy: A functional approach.* New York: AFB Press.

Wormsley, D. P., & D'Andrea, F. M. (1997). *Instructional strategies for braille literacy.* New York: AFB Press.

JOURNALS AND NEWSLETTERS

Awareness
National Association for Parents of Children with Visual Impairments
P.O. Box 317
Watertown, MA 02471
(617) 972-7441; (800) 562-6265
Fax: (617) 972-7444
napvi@perkins.org
www.napvi.org

Closing the Gap
526 Main Street
P.O. Box 68
Henderson, MN 56044
(507) 248-3294
Fax: (507) 248-3810
info@closingthegap.com
www.closingthegap.com

Deaf-Blind Perspectives
345 N Monmouth Avenue

Monmouth, OR 97361
(800) 438-9376; (800) 854-7013 (TTY)
Fax: (503) 838-8150
dbp@wou.edu
www.tr.wou.edu/tr/dbp/

DOTS for Braille Literacy
AFB National Literacy Center
100 Peachtree Street, Suite 620
Atlanta, GA 30303
(404) 525-2303; (404) 659-6957
literacy@afb.net
www.afb.org

D.V.I. Quarterly
Division on Visual Impairments of the Council for Exceptional Children
brltrans@optonline.net
www.ed.arizona.edu/dvi/welcome.htm

Journal of Visual Impairment & Blindness
AFB Press
American Foundation for the Blind
11 Penn Plaza, Suite 300
New York, NY 10001

The National Newspatch: Quarterly Newsletter for Educators of Visually Impaired Preschoolers
Oregon School for the Blind
700 Church Street, SE
Salem, OR 97310

RE:view
Association for Education and Rehabilitation of the Blind and Visually Impaired
Published by Heldref Publications
1319 18th Street, NW
Washington, DC 20036-1802
www.heldref.org

See/Hear: A Quarterly Newsletter for Families and Professionals on Visual Impairments and Deafblindness
Texas School for the Blind and Visually Impaired Outreach Program
1100 West 45th Street
Austin, TX 78756
(512) 206-9103

Teaching Exceptional Children
Council for Exceptional Children
1110 North Glebe Road, Suite 300
Arlington, VA 22201-5704

(888) CEC-SPED; (703) 620-3660; (703) 264-9446 (TTY)
Fax: (703) 264-9494
service@cec.sped.org
www.cec.sped.org; www.ed.arizona.edu/dvi/welcome.htm

Young Exceptional Children
Division for Early Childhood of the Council for Exceptional Children
634 Eddy Avenue
Missoula, MT 59812-6696
(406) 243-5898
dec@selway.umt.edu

ELECTRONIC PUBLICATIONS, WEB SITES, AND MAILING LISTS

AER Online: Forums and Mailing Lists
Association for Education and Rehabilitation of the Blind and Visually Impaired
http://aerbvi.org/modules.php?name=Forums
http://lists.aerbvi.org/mailman/listinfo

AFB-Hosted Electronic Discussion Groups
www.afb.org/Section.asp?documentID=2252

CEC SmartBrief
Council for Exceptional Children
www.smartbrief.com/cec

National Center on Low-Incidence Disabilities
www.nclid.unco.edu/newnclid

New York Institute on Special Education
www.nyise.org/blind.htm

See/Hear: A Quarterly Newsletter for Families and Professionals on Visual Impairments and Deafblindness
Texas School for the Blind and Visually Impaired
www.tsbvi.edu/Outreach/seehear/index.htm

VisionConnection
www.visionconnection.org

APPENDIX

E

Sample Forms

Caseload Profile for Visual Impairment Program Staff

Teacher ____________________

Date __________

Number of schools served _____

Working day ________________

Available weekly minutes ________

Minus preparation/conference minutes ________

Minus lunchtime minutes ________

Remainder available ________

Total minutes per week per IEPs ______

Total minutes transition time per week ______

Total committed minutes per week ______

Student Name	*School/Grade*	*Direct Service Minutes*	*Monitoring/ Consultation Minutes*	*Vision Status (Acuity) and Other Disabilities*	*Total Weekly Minutes per IEP*	*Comments*	*Braille (Yes/ No)*	O&M *(Yes/ No)*
1.								
2.								
3.								
4.								
5.								
6.								
7.								
8.								
9.								
10.								

Book Order for September ______

Please return this form to ____________________________ by ___________ so books for your student who is visually impaired can be obtained for the start of school.

Please put this form in my mailbox or send it to me at _________________________ via e-mail or school mail.

Thanks.
Sincerely,

Student ____

Teacher of Visually Impaired Students ____

School ____ Grade ______________

Large Print _______ Braille _______

Title ____________________________________ Level/Edition ___________ ISBN _______________________

Author ______________________ Publisher ____________________________ Copyright date _____________

Office Use Only

Source	*Date Ordered*	*Date Received*

Title ____________________________________ Level/Edition ___________ ISBN _______________________

Author ______________________ Publisher ____________________________ Copyright date _____________

Office Use Only

Source	*Date Ordered*	*Date Received*

Title ____________________________________ Level/Edition ___________ ISBN _______________________

Author ______________________ Publisher ____________________________ Copyright date _____________

Office Use Only

Source	*Date Ordered*	*Date Received*

Schedule ____________________

Time	*Monday*	*Tuesday*	*Wednesday*	*Thursday*	*Friday*	*Notes*
8:00						
8:30						
9:00						
9:30						
10:00						
10:30						
11:00						
11:30						
12:00						
12:30						
1:00						
1:30						
2:00						
2:30						
3:00						
3:30						

Note: Dotted lines separate different activities at the same site.

To ____________________________

Please complete this questionnaire and put it in my mailbox by ______________________.

Thank you,

1. Texts to be used in class:

Title and Edition	*Author*	*Publisher*	*Copyright Date*	*ISBN No.*	*Dates Used*

2. I use ☐ no ☐ some ☐ many worksheets.

3. ☐ Yes ☐ No My worksheets sometimes involve print smaller than the size used here.

4. ☐ Yes ☐ No I use the chalkboards, whiteboards, overhead projector, films, or PowerPoint presentations at least three times a week.

5. ☐ Yes ☐ No I would like to learn how to enlarge worksheets using the office copier.

6. The best time to confer with me is

   Day of week ______________________

   Time/period ______________________

   Location ______________________

Referral Intake Form

Student's name ______________________________ Date of birth __________

Grade __________ Social Security no. ________________

School ______________ Referred by ____________ Telephone no. __________

Year __________ Counselor/teacher ________________ Room no. __________

Aide __________ Nurse __________ Investigating teacher __________

Parents'/guardians' names ______________________________

Address ______________________________ Telephone no. __________

Mother's work phone ______________ Father's work phone ______________

Physician ______________ Eye care specialist ______________

Address ______________ Address ______________

Telephone no. ______________ Telephone no. ______________

Low vision clinic ______________________________

Address ______________ Telephone no. ______________

Date of last eye exam ______________ Eye report requested on ______________

Visual condition ______________________________

Visual acuity

Uncorrected	Corrected	Field
O.D. __________	O.D. __________	O.D. __________
O.S. __________	O.S. __________	O.S. __________
O.U. __________	O.U. __________	O.U. __________

Information from parents/guardians, school personnel, doctors, cumulative and health folders (specify source and date)

Status of Functional Vision Assessment

Name ______________________________ Year ____________

	Assess	Done
Condition/Appearance		
Glasses		
Health		
Visual abnormalities		
Muscle imbalance		
Basic Responses		
Abnormal visual behavior		
Reaction to light		
Blink		
Pupillary response		
Eye preference/dominance		
Attending to environment		
Fixation and Localization		
Eye contact		
Patterns		
Horizontal		
Vertical		
Circular		
Oblique		
Toward/away		
Scanning		
Fields		
Peripheral		
Central		
Stereopsis/Binocularity		
Depth perception		
Suppression		
Color Vision		
Match/Holmgren		
Name		
Ishihara		
Mobility		
Balance/posture/gait		
Independence		
Settings		
Routes/reversals		
Follow directions		
Depth perception		
Travel aids		

	Assess	Done
Acuity		
With correction		
Distance		
Intermediate		
Near		
Without correction		
Distance		
Intermediate		
Near		
School setting		
Distance		
Intermediate		
Near		
Reading		
Print size		
Angle and distance		
Level		
Length of attending		
Visual Discrimination		
Size		
Shape		
Outlines		
Classification		
Picture details		
Visual Perception		
Figure/ground		
Form constancy		
Shape		
Size		
Position		
Visual Motor		
Fine eye/hand		
Writing		
Gross eye/foot		
Illumination		
Indoors		
Outdoors		
Time of day		
Photophobia/glare		
Light adaptation		
Night vision		

Assessed Needs Checklist

Student ______________________________ Birthdate ________________

Assessed by ______________________ Assessment dates __________________

This student has an assessed need for the following services, methods, media, materials, and equipment, in order to access core and/or alternative curriculum, and to meet unique needs as addressed in IEP goals.

V.I. program option for least restrictive environment: __ Itinerant __ Resource room __ Special day class for visually impaired students __ Special school

Services: __ Teacher of the visually impaired __ O&M specialist __ Transcriber __ Notetaker __ Describer __ Reader __ Paraeducator __ Assistive technology service

Literacy medium (P-primary, S-secondary): __ Braille __ Print (best size: ___ point) __ Nonreader

Learning medium (P-primary, S-secondary): __ Tactile __ Auditory __ Visual

Instructional strategies: __ One-on-one __ Small group __ Concrete experiences

Instructional materials: __ Manipulatives __ Models __ Real objects __ Raised-line drawings __ Accessible books __ Recordings __ Switches __ Reading/writing aids __ Organizational aids

Specialized paper: __ Raised-line __ Dark-line __ NCR __ Braille __ Tactile imaging __ Slate __ Computer __ Nonglare __ Hi-contrast __ Low-contrast __ Colored

Specialized instructional materials for: __ Concept development __ Sensory development __ Academics __ Communication __ Visual efficiency __ Listening skills __ Technology __ Leisure skills __ Orientation & Mobility __ Physical education __ Social development __ Functional curriculum __ Daily living __ Vocational skills __ Music/art

Low-vision and visual efficiency aids: __ Rx lenses __ Magnifiers __ Monocular/telescope __ Binoculars __ Special lights & lighting __ Light box __ Desktop easel __ Tilt desk __ Marking pens

Travel aids: __ Long white cane __ Electronic travel aid __ Sunglasses __ Visor/hat __ Maps __ Compass

Equipment and access technology: ___Braillewriter __ Video magnifier
__ Computer (__laptop __ desktop) __ Monitor __ Printer __ Talking software
__ Screen access software/hardware __ Braille translation software/hardware
__ Braille display __ Braille input device __ Braille embosser __ Scanner __ OCR
__ Braille notetaker __ External disk drive __ Talking book player __ CD playback device
__ Tape recorder/player (__ regular __ adapted __ 4-track __ voice-activated __ switch-activated)
__ Calculator (__ regular __ large print __ voice output __ scientific) __ Electronic references
__ Other: ____

____

____

____

____

____

____

Adapted with permission from the Oakland, California, Unified School District.

To ______________________________

Re ______________________________

Date ______________________________

Please return this questionnaire to me by ______________________________

Thank you,

1. Please evaluate ______________________________ participation in your class.

2. Have you noticed ______________________________ having any problems seeing materials, such as texts, worksheets, or board work? Yes ____ No ____
   Please specify:

3. Would you like me to contact you personally regarding ____________________? Yes ____ No ____
   If yes, what is a good time for me to contact you?

4. Other comments:

Paraeducator's Tasks

Listed below are a number of tasks that a paraeducator may perform. If you are a paraeducator, mark with a "p" those activities that you would be comfortable doing. If you are a teacher, use another form and mark with a "t" those areas in which you intend to make use of a paraeducator. Compare and discuss your lists.

Adaptation of materials

____ 1. Adapt materials to large print.

____ 2. Adapt materials to braille.

____ 3. Tape record written work.

____ 4. Make tactile drawings.

Orientation & Mobility

____ 5. Use human (sighted) guide technique when walking with student.

____ 6. Follow student quietly on familiar routes.

____ 7. Allow student to get confused on familiar routes and give the student time to correct the mistake.

____ 8. Be alert and warn student of any danger en route.

Support

____ 9. Allow student to make mistakes on class assignments.

____ 10. Let the student ask the teacher or peers questions about class work or activities.

____ 11. Maintain a distance from the student unless working directly with him or her.

____ 12. Let the student pick up dropped objects.

____ 13. If the student is working with a group of peers, withdraw to a distance when possible.

____ 14. Stay at a distance when the student is eating lunch.

____ 15. When a student has mastered a task, such as putting on a coat, allow him or her to complete the task independently even if it seems to take too long.

____ 16. When in doubt, do nothing; intervene only when necessary.

Classroom activities

____ 17. Reinforce concepts already presented by teacher in small groups or with individual students.

____ 18. Listen to students read.

____ 19. Read to students.

(continued)

Paraeducator's Tasks (continued)

___ 20. Supervise small groups of students in independent or group work.

___ 21. Modify written materials (i.e., rewrite at an easier level).

___ 22. Help students work on assignments and projects.

___ 23. Assist physically disabled students.

Behavior management support

___ 24. Provide or supervise earned reinforcement.

___ 25. Supervise time-outs.

___ 26. Be a resource for students who are experiencing stress.

___ 27. Monitor progress on behavior contracts.

___ 28. Provide positive feedback and encouragement.

Diagnostic support

___ 29. Correct and grade assigned activities.

___ 30. Observe and record academic behavior and progress.

___ 31. Observe and record social behaviors.

___ 32. Administer informal assessments.

Classroom organization

___ 33. Make instructional games.

___ 34. Develop and manage learning centers.

___ 35. Prepare displays.

___ 36. Locate instructional materials.

Clerical support

___ 37. Type or use the computer as directed.

___ 38. Duplicate materials.

___ 39. Record grades.

Orientation & Mobility-Specific Skills

Student ______________________ Grade ______________________

School year ______________________ School ______________________

Classroom number ______________________ Teacher ______________________

Itinerant teacher ______________________ O&M specialist ______________________

Telephone ______________________ Telephone ______________________

E-mail ______________________ E-mail ______________________

The above student has completed instruction toward the following orientation & mobility goals in order to promote self-sufficiency and independent travel. School personnel should allow the student to travel independently in the following settings:

The following goals are being taught during this school year. School personnel should reinforce and monitor the student's use of these techniques and routes.

The student needs to be monitored and supervised in the following settings and routes.

Natural Environment Interview

Child's name ______________________ Parents' name ______________________

Interviewer ______________________ Date of interview ______________________

Children have opportunities to learn in a variety of community and family settings. Please list or check places where your family goes and what your family does. The list will provide information that will help us help you see learning opportunities for your child.

Include things as routine as car or bus rides, window shopping, department or grocery stores, and walking around your neighborhood. Remember occasional things such as swimming, visiting friends, malls, outdoor playgrounds, petting zoos, restaurants, relatives' homes. Include special trips such as to theme parks, Halloween carnivals, reunions, picnics, the beach, and so on.

Family Life

____ **Routines**

- ____ Bathing ____ Driving ______________________
- ____ Cooking ____ Eating ______________________
- ____ ____________ ____ ____________ ______________________

____ **Entertainment activities**

- ____ TV ____ Looking at books ______________________
- ____ Videos ____ Local children's theater ______________________
- ____ Movies ____ Sports ______________________

____ **Socialization activities**

- ____ Play groups ____ Mother's groups ______________________
- ____ Family gatherings ____ ____________ ______________________

____ **Gardening**

____ **Family rituals or celebrations** ______________________

____ **Physical play** ______________________

Community Life

____ **Family outings** ______________________

____ **Children's attractions** ______________________

____ **Church/religious groups** ______________________

____ **Community events** ______________________

____ **Early childhood programs (describe)** ______________________

Home Visit Record

Child's name ______________________ Date of visit ______________________________

People present ____

Comments from last visit

Materials brought

Child's response

Parent's concerns

Suggestions

Teacher follow-up

Parent follow-up

Source: Developed by Kathy Fields, Rose Stamm, Nancy Dolphin, Julie Nesnansky, Cinda Wert Rapp, Sandra Hagood, Kyle McKune-Santos, Frances Delacio. *Itinerant Teaching: Tricks of the Trade for Teachers of Students with Visual Impairments*, by Jean E. Olmstead,

Meetings 20___ - 20___ School Year

August	September	October	November	December
January	**February**	**March**	**April**	**May**

Early Intervention History

Child's name ______________________ Date of birth __________

Service coordinator's name ______________________

Previous services/programs? ______ If so, where and dates of IFSP __________

Referral date to our program ______________________

Last IFSP? ______________________ Date __________

Service coordinator ______________________

Date of initial IFSP to our program ______________________

Services provided ______________________

Periodic review date ______________________

Changes to IFSP? ______________________

Annual IFSP date ______________________

Services provided ______________________

Periodic review date ______________________

Changes to IFSP? ______________________

Annual IFSP date ______________________

Services provided ______________________

Periodic review date ______________________

Changes to IFSP? ______________________

Transition plan meeting ______________________

Final IFSP date ______________ IEP date ______________

Notes ______________________

____

____

____

Lesson Plan

Student name________________________ Date/time ________________________

Route/environment ________________________ Materials needed ________________________

- ✓ +	*Lesson Objectives*	*Evaluation of Student's Performance*

Next lesson:

Lesson Plan

Student name________________________ Date/time ________________________

Route/environment ________________________ Materials needed ________________________

- ✓ +	*Lesson Objectives*	*Evaluation of Student's Performance*

Next lesson:

Itinerant Teaching: Tricks of the Trade for Teachers of Students with Visual Impairments, by Jean E. Olmstead, copyright © 2005, AFB Press. All rights reserved. This page may be copied for educational use only.

Receipt of Assistive Equipment Form

Date ______________________________

Re ________________________________

Certain electronic devices have been purchased to enable ______________________________ to complete schoolwork at home. In signing this form you are:

- acknowledging receipt of and responsibility for these items
- promising to return them in working shape given reasonable wear and tear
- promising to contact ______________________________ if problems occur with the equipment
- promising to return the equipment to the school district upon ______________________________'s graduation or transfer to another school district.

The following device(s) has been loaned for use at both home and school:

The following devices have been delivered to ______________________________'s home for his use:

Our signatures below indicate our agreement to the conditions stated above.

____
Student's signature

____
Parent or guardian signature

____
Date

Materials on Loan

Student ______________________________ Year ______________

School ____

	Materials Loaned	Location	Date	Return Date	Transferred To	Date
1.						
2.						
3.						
4.						
5.						
6.						
7.						
8.						
9.						
10.						
11.						
12.						
13.						
14.						
15.						
16.						
17.						
18.						
19.						
20.						
21.						
22.						
23.						
24.						

Observation Summary

Student ______________________ Observer ______________________

Setting ______________________________________ Date ____________

Time	*Observations*	*Comments*

Grade Summary

Student ______________________________ Year ______________

School ____

Period	Subject	Teacher	Room	Grade*						
				1st Q	2nd Q	1st Sem	3rd Q	4th Q	2nd Sem	Final

Explanation of Comments

X–Excellent progress
G–Good attitude/conduct
1–Showing some improvement
2–Achievement is not up to apparent ability
3–Absences/tardiness affecting schoolwork
4–Books/materials are not brought to class
5–Assignments are incomplete or unsatisfactory
6–Oral participation needed
7–Inattentive/wastes time/does not follow directions
8–Conduct in class is not satisfactory
9–(To parents) Please contact teacher through counselor

*Note: the numbers next to some of the grades on this form refer to the Explanation of Comments at the bottom of the form. Readers who adapt this form for their own use may wish to substitute an explanation code from forms used in their districts.

Notification of Itinerant Teacher's Absence

Please fill in the name of the teacher/ office to be notified when you are absent.

Teacher ____ Year _______________

Student	*School*	*Person/Office to Notify*

Academic Tests Summary

Student ______________________________ Date of Birth ______________

Test ______________________________ Date ______________

Scores:

Comments:

Test ______________________________ Date ______________

Scores:

Comments:

Test ______________________________ Date ______________

Scores:

Comments:

Student Checklist

M: Mastered area/skill
C: Continue instruction or use
E: Exposed to area/skill

Name ____

Teacher's Initials			
School Year	*20__ to 20__*	*20__ to 20__*	*20__ to 20__*
Information about Visual Impairment			
Vision Assessments			
Optical Aids			

Note: The categories and key used in this form can be adapted or changed for the reader's use.

(continued)

Teacher's Initials			
School Year	*20__ to 20__*	*20__ to 20__*	*20__ to 20__*
Instructional Materials (list categories)			

Student Data Card

Name ______________________ Parent(s) Name ______________________

Date of Birth __________ Address ______________________ Student I.D. # __________

Home telephone __________ Emergency telephone__________ Work telephone Mother __________ Father __________

Year	*Itinerant Teacher*	*School of Attendance*	*School of Residence*	*Gr.*	*Special Class*	*Reading Level*	*BL/ LV*	*Media Used*	*Bus*	*Other*

Gr. = Grade BL = Legally blind LV = Low vision LP = Large print BR = Braille

(continued)

Student Data Card (side 2)

RFBD # ____________ NLS ____________ Rehab. ____________ Transit I.D. ____________ SS # ____________

Hospital ____________________ Physician ____________________ Medical # ____________

Eye Condition ________________________________ Entered Program ____________

Vision Reports ____________________ | Low Vision Exam ____________________

O&M Received ____________

Acuity: ____________________

Other Handicaps ____________________

Psychological Evaluation ____________ | Comments ____________________

Passed Proficiency ____________

Graduated ____________

or Left Program ____________

RFBD = Recording for the Blind & Dyslexic NLS = National Library Service Rehab. = Department of Rehabilitation SS = Social Security O&M = Orientation & Mobility

Program Referrals

Date	*Name*	*Referred By*	*Investigating Teacher*	*School*	*Date of IEP or Closing*		*Reason for Closing*

Schedule for ______________________

Year __________

To all personnel: Please indicate the day and time you regularly use this room.

Time	*Monday*	*Tuesday*	*Wednesday*	*Thursday*	*Friday*
8:00					
9:00					
10:00					
11:00					
12:00					
1:00					
2:00					
3:00					

To ______________________________

Year ______________________________

I have listed below the days and times I will be working with you this year. Please call or e-mail my office to let me know when you are absent on one of those days.

Thank you,

- -

Dear ______________________________,

I have read your schedule of days and times to work with ______________________________.

I will help ______________________________ remember to call or e-mail you if she is absent on a day when you come to work with her.

____
Parent's signature

____
Date

Date ______________________________

To my substitute:

Please be aware that ______________________________ is in my ____ period class.

______________________________ is a student with visual impairments and reads ____________________ .

Please remember that

1. Anything you write on the board will need to be verbalized.
2. During fire drills or disaster drills, you will need to take extra care to make sure this student is safe. I have made the following special arrangements to ensure his safety:

____

____

____

3. Other: ____

____

____

____

Should you have other questions or concerns, talk with ______________________________ here at the school, or contact the teacher of students with visual impairments, ______________________________

at ____________________ or ______________________________ .

Sincerely,

____

____

Index

About the Author

Jean E. Olmstead, M.A., the author of the original edition of *Itinerant Teaching,* broke new ground in the literature and the field of educating students with visual impairments by focusing on the role and challenges of the teacher who is itinerant. In addition to her documentation of effective strategies for itinerant teachers, her nationally known advocacy efforts and other professional activities resulted in widespread attention to the needs and importance of teachers who travel to a variety of settings to deliver services to students. Retired in 2002 from the West Contra Costa Unified School District in Richmond, California, after 37 years as an itinerant teacher of students with visual impairments and orientation and mobility instructor, including work in California and Washington State public schools, Ms. Olmstead was a founding member and first chair of Division 16 for Itinerant Personnel of the Association for Education and Rehabilitation of the Blind and Visually Impaired (AER). She has written articles for the *Journal of Visual Impairment & Blindness,* the *CTEVH Journal,* and *The Driving Force* (the newsletter of AER Division 16); was associate editor of *CTEVH Journal;* and has given numerous presentations, workshops, and training sessions.

In 1998 she received an Education Award from Northern California AER to "Jean Olmstead who 'wrote the book' for itinerant teachers, persisted in the formation of Division 16, and is renowned for her dedication and humor." Currently, she is happily ensconced in the northern California redwoods near bluffs overlooking pounding ocean waves.

About the Contributors

James Carreon, M.A., is Technology Coordinator at the California School for the Blind, Fremont, and a part-time instructor at San Francisco State University, Los Angeles.

Lori Cassels, M.S., is a certified orientation and mobility specialist at Guide Dogs for the Blind, San Rafael, California. She was previously a teacher of students with visual impairments and an orientation and mobility instructor in New York. She has published in the *Journal of Visual Impairment & Blindness* and has served on the boards of the New York and Northern California State Chapters of the Association for Education and Rehabilitation of the Blind and Visually Impaired.

Frances Mary D'Andrea, M.Ed., is Director of the National Literacy Center, American Foundation for the Blind, in Atlanta, Georgia. Prior to joining AFB, she was a teacher of students with visual impairments in residential, itinerant, and other settings. She is co-editor of *Instructional Strategies for Braille Literacy* and *Looking to Learn: Promoting Literacy for Students with Low Vision;* editor of the *DOTS for Braille Literacy* newsletter; and a board member of the Braille Authority of North America. She has written and presented widely on literacy for people who are blind or visually impaired.

Faith Dunham-Sims, M.A., is a certified orientation and mobility specialist with the West Contra Costa Unified School District in Richmond, California, and with the California State Department of Rehabilitation.

Jane N. Erin, Ph.D., is Professor in the Department of Special Education, Rehabilitation, and School Psychology at the University of Arizona, Tucson. She is the author of *When You Have a Visually Impaired Student with Multiple Disabilities in Your Classroom: A Guide for Teachers* and *Visual Handicaps and Learning: A Developmental Approach* as well as co-editor of *Diversity and Visual Impairment: The Influence of Race, Gender, Religion, and Ethnicity on the Individual.* Dr. Erin is editor in chief emerita of the *Journal of Visual Impairment & Blindness* and was executive editor of *RE:view.* She has written numerous articles, book chapters, and presentations, and previously held presidencies of state or local chapters of the Association for Education and Rehabilitation of the Blind and Visually Impaired and the Council for Exceptional Children.

Cinda Wert Rapp, M.A., is Program Specialist for Early Intervention—Visually Impaired in the West Contra Costa Unified School District, El Cerrito, California. She was formerly Educational Specialist for the California Transcribers and Educators of the Visually Handicapped and has published in the *Journal of Visual Impairment & Blindness.*

Jane Stewart Redmon, M.A., a contributor to the first edition of *Itinerant Teaching,* is a teacher of children with visual impairments and a certified orientation and mobility specialist with Franklin Jefferson Special Education District in Benton, Illinois. She was previously a vision coordinator, and has worked as an itinerant teacher for almost 30 years, mostly in rural settings. She has made numerous presentations at state and national conferences.

Mary Alice Ross, M.A., is a certified orientation and mobility specialist and a teacher at the California School for the Blind, Fremont, California. She has written various articles for the *Journal of Visual Impairment & Blindness* and is the author of *Fitness for the Aging Adult with Visual Impairment: An Exercise and Resource Manual.* She won the1995 Nat Seaman Award for Dedication and Outstanding Contributions in the Field from the New York State Chapter of the Association for Education and Rehabilitation of the Blind and Visually Impaired and the 1998 Distinguished Service Award from the Physical Education Department of Manhattan College, Bronx, New York.

CPSIA information can be obtained
at www.ICGtesting.com
Printed in the USA
BVHW010915160120
569478BV00005B/295/P